D1134281

NOTES

on the book of

DEUTERONOMY

Volume II

C. H. MACKINTOSH

"Forever, O Lord, Thy Word is settled in heaven."

"Thy Word have I hid in my heart, that I might not sin against Thee."

LOIZEAUX BROTHERS

FIRST EDITION 1880

TWENTY-SIXTH PRINTING 1959

LOIZEAUX BROTHERS, INC., PUBLISHERS

*A Nonprofit Organization, Devoted to the Lord's Work
and to the Spread of His Truth*

19 WEST 21ST STREET, NEW YORK 10, N. Y.

PREFATORY NOTE

TO THE AMERICAN EDITION

A̱S several persons in America have, without any authority whatever from me, undertaken to publish my four* volumes of "Notes," I deem it my duty to inform the reader that I have given full permission to Messrs. LOIZEAUX BROTHERS to publish an edition of those books in such form as they shall consider most suitable.

C. H. MACKINTOSH.

6 West Park Terrace, Scarborough,
  May 1st, 1879.

---

* Now six.

CONTENTS

NOTES

ON

THE BOOK OF DEUTERONOMY

CHAPTER VII.

"WHEN the Lord thy God shall bring thee into the land whither thou goest to possess it, and hath cast out many nations before thee, ... seven nations greater and mightier than thou, and when the Lord thy God shall deliver them before thee, thou shalt smite them, and utterly destroy them; thou shalt make no covenant with them, nor show mercy unto them."

In reading the record of God's dealings with the nations, in connection with His people Israel, we are reminded of the opening words of Psalm ci.—"I will sing of mercy and of judgment." We see the display of mercy to His people, in pursuance of His covenant with Abraham, Isaac, and Jacob; and we see also the execution of judgment upon the nations, in consequence of their evil ways. In the former, we see divine sovereignty; in the latter, divine justice; in both, divine glory shines out. All the ways of God, whether in mercy or in judgment, speak His praise, and shall call forth the homage of

His people forever. "Great and marvelous are Thy works, Lord God Almighty; just and true are Thy ways, Thou King of nations.* Who shall not fear Thee, O Lord, and glorify Thy name? for Thou art holy; for all nations shall come and worship before Thee; for Thy judgments are made manifest." (Rev. xv. 3, 4.)

This is the true spirit in which to contemplate the ways of God in government. Some persons, allowing themselves to be influenced by a morbid feeling and false sentimentality, rather than by an enlightened judgment, find difficulty in the directions given to Israel in reference to the Canaanites, in the opening of our chapter. It seems to them inconsistent with a benevolent Being to command His people to smite their fellow-creatures, and to show them no mercy. They cannot understand how a merciful God could commission His people to slay women and children with the edge of the sword.

It is very plain that such persons could not adopt the language of Revelation xv. 3, 4. They are not prepared to say, "Just and true are Thy ways, Thou King of nations." They cannot justify God in *all* His ways; nay, they are actually sitting in judgment upon Him. They presume to measure the actings of divine government by the standard of their own shallow thoughts—to scan the infinite by the finite; in short, they measure God by themselves.

This is a fatal mistake. We are not competent to

---

*"Nations" is read by most editors: Christ is not called the "King of saints."

form a judgment upon the ways of God, and hence it is the very height of presumption for poor, ignorant, short-sighted mortals to attempt to do so. We read in the seventh chapter of Luke that "Wisdom is justified of *all* her children." Let us remember this, and hush all our sinful reasonings. "Let God be true, but every man a liar; as it is written, 'That Thou mightest be justified in Thy sayings, and mightest overcome when Thou art judged.''

Is the reader at all troubled with difficulties on this subject? If so, we should much like to quote a very fine passage which may help him. "O give thanks unto the Lord; for He is good; for His mercy endureth forever. . . . . To Him *that smote Egypt in their first-born;* for His mercy endureth forever; and brought out Israel from among them; for His mercy endureth forever; with a strong hand, and with a stretched-out arm; for His mercy endureth forever. To Him which divided the Red Sea into parts; for His mercy endureth forever; and made Israel to pass through the midst of it; for His mercy endureth forever; but *overthrew Pharaoh and his host* in the Red Sea; for His mercy endureth forever. To Him which *smote great kings;* for His mercy endureth forever; and *slew famous kings;* for His mercy endureth forever; Sihon, king of the Amorites; for His mercy endureth forever; and Og, the king of Bashan; for His mercy endureth forever; and gave their land for a heritage; for His mercy endureth forever; even a heritage unto Israel His servant; for His mercy endureth forever." (Ps. cxxxvi.)

Here we see that the smiting of Egypt's first-born and the deliverance of Israel, the passage through the Red Sea and the utter destruction of Pharaoh's host, the slaughter of the Canaanites and giving their lands to Israel—all alike illustrated the ever-lasting mercy of Jehovah.* Thus it was, thus it is, and thus it shall be. All must redound to the glory of God. Let us remember this, and fling to the winds all our silly reasonings and ignorant arguments. It is our privilege to justify God in all His ways, to bow our heads in holy worship, in view of His unsearchable judgments, and rest in the calm

---

* Very many Christians find considerable difficulty in interpreting and applying the language of a large number of the psalms which call for judgment upon the wicked. Such language would, of course, be quite unsuitable for Christians now, inasmuch as we are taught to love our enemies, to do good to them that hate us, and to pray for them that despitefully use us and persecute us.

But we must remember that what would be wholly out of place for the Church of God, a heavenly people, under grace, was, and will yet be, perfectly consistent for Israel, an earthly people, under government. No intelligent Christian could think for a moment of calling down vengeance upon his enemies or upon the wicked. It would be grossly inconsistent. We are called to be the living exponents of the grace of God to the world—to walk in the foot-steps of the meek and lowly Jesus—to suffer for righteousness—not to resist evil. God is now dealing in long-suffering mercy with the world. " He maketh His sun to rise on the evil and on the good, and sendeth rain on the just and on the unjust." This is to be our model. We are, in this, to be "perfect, even as our Father which is in heaven is perfect." For a Christian to deal with the world on the principle of righteous judgment, would be to misrepresent his heavenly Father and falsify his profession.

But by and by, when the Church shall have left the scene, God will deal with the world in righteousness; He will judge the nations for their treatment of His people Israel.

We do not attempt to quote passages, but merely call the reader's attention to the principle, in order to enable him to understand the just application of the prophetic psalms.

assurance that all God's ways are right. We do not understand them all; this would be impossible. The finite cannot grasp the infinite. This is where so many go wrong. They reason upon the actings of God's government, not considering that those actings lie as far beyond the range of human reason as the Creator is beyond the creature. What human mind can unravel the profound mysteries of divine providence? Can we account for the fact of a city full of human beings—men, women, and children, in one hour, plunged beneath a tide of burning lava? Utterly impossible; and yet this is but one fact of thousands that stand recorded on the page of human history, all lying far beyond the grasp of the most gigantic intellect. Go through the lanes, alleys, wynds, closes, and court-yards of our cities and towns; see the thousands of human beings that throng these places, living in squalid misery, poverty, wretchedness, and moral degradation. Can we account for all this? can we tell why God permits it? are we called upon to do so? Is it not perfectly plain to the reader that it is no part of our business to discuss such questions? and if we, in our ignorance and stupid folly, set about reasoning and speculating upon the inscrutable mysteries of the divine government, what can we expect but utter bewilderment, if not positive infidelity?

The foregoing line of thought will enable the reader to understand the opening lines of our chapter. The Canaanites were to receive no mercy at the hands of Israel. Their iniquities had reached the culminating point, and nothing remained but the stern execution of divine judgment. "Thou shalt smite them, and utterly destroy them; thou shalt make no covenant with them, nor show mercy unto them; neither shalt thou make marriages with them; thy daughter thou shalt not give unto his son, nor his daughter shalt thou take unto thy son. For they will turn away thy son from following Me, that they may serve other gods; so will the anger of the Lord be kindled against you, and destroy thee suddenly. But thus shall ye deal with them; ye shall destroy their altars, and break down their images, and cut down their groves, and burn their graven images with fire."

Such were the instructions given by Jehovah to His people. They were clear and explicit. No mercy for the Canaanites, no covenant with them, no union, no fellowship of any kind, unsparing judgment, intense separation.

We know, alas! how soon and how completely Israel failed to carry out these instructions. Hardly had they planted their foot upon the land of Canaan ere they made a covenant with the Gibeonites. Even Joshua himself fell into the snare. The tattered garments and mouldy bread of those wily people beguiled the princes of the congregation, and caused them to act in direct opposition to the plain commandment of God. Had they been governed by the authority of the Word, they would have been preserved from the grave error of making a league with people who ought to have been utterly destroyed; but they judged by the sight of their eyes, and had to reap the consequences.*

Implicit obedience is the grand moral safeguard against the wiles of the enemy. No doubt the story of the Gibeonites was very plausible, and their whole appearance gave a show of truth to their statements; but none of these things should have had the slightest moral weight with Joshua and the princes; nor would they, if they had but remembered the word of the Lord. But they failed in this. They reasoned on what they saw, instead of obeying what they had heard. Reason is no guide for the people of God; we must be, absolutely and completely, guided and governed by the Word of God.

This is a privilege of the very highest order, and it lies within the reach of the simplest and most unlettered child of God. The Father's word, the Father's voice, the Father's eye, can guide the youngest, feeblest child in His family. All we need is the lowly and obedient heart. It does not demand great intellectual power or cleverness; if it did, what

---

*It is at once instructive and admonitory to see that the garments, the mouldy bread, and the plausible words of the Gibeonites did what the walls of Jericho could not do. Satan's *wiles* are more to be dreaded than his *power*. "Put on the whole armor of God, that ye may be able to stand against the *wiles* of the devil." The more deeply we ponder the various parts of the whole armor of God, the more clearly we shall see that they are ranged under these two heads,—obedience and dependence. The soul that is really governed by the authority of the Word, and wholly dependent upon the power of the Spirit, is fully equipped for the conflict. It was thus the Man Christ Jesus vanquished the enemy. The devil could do nothing with a man who was perfectly obedient and perfectly dependent. May we study, in this, as in all beside, our great Exemplar.

would become of the vast majority of Christians? If it were only the educated, the deep-thinking, and the far-seeing that were capable of meeting the wiles of the adversary, then verily most of us might give up in despair.

But, thanks be to God, it is not so; indeed, on the contrary, we find, in looking through the history of the people of God in all ages, that human wisdom, human learning, human cleverness, if not kept in their right place, have proved a positive snare, and rendered their possessors only the more efficient tools in the enemy's hand. By whom have most, if not all, of the heresies been introduced which have disturbed the Church of God from age to age? Not by the simple and the unlearned, but by the educated and the intellectual. And in the passage to which we have just referred, in the book of Joshua, who was it that made a covenant with the Gibeonites? The common people? Nay; but the princes of the congregation. No doubt all were involved in the mischief, but it was the princes that led the way. The heads and leaders of the assembly fell into the snare of the devil through neglect of the plain word of God.

"Thou shalt make no covenant with them." Could aught be plainer than this? Could tattered garments, old shoes, and mouldy bread alter the meaning of the divine command, or do away with the urgent necessity for strict obedience on the part of the congregation? Assuredly not. Nothing can ever afford a warrant for lowering, the breadth of a hair, the standard of obedience to the Word of God. If there are difficulties in the way, if perplexing circumstances come before us, if things crop up for which we are not prepared, and as to which we are unable to form a judgment, what are we to do? Reason? Jump to conclusions? Act on our own or on any human judgment? Most certainly not. What then? Wait on God; wait patiently, humbly, believingly, and He will assuredly counsel and guide. "The meek will He guide in judgment; and the meek will He teach His way." Had Joshua and the princes acted thus, they never would have made a league with the Gibeonites; and if the reader acts thus, he will be delivered from every evil work and preserved unto the everlasting kingdom of our Lord and Saviour Jesus Christ.

In verse six of our chapter, Moses sets before the people the moral ground of the line of action which they were to adopt in reference to the Canaanites—the rigid separation and the unsparing judgment. "*For* thou art *a holy people unto the Lord thy God;* the Lord thy God hath chosen thee to be a special people unto Himself, above all people that are upon the face of the earth."

The principle here laid down is of the very weightiest character. Why were the people to maintain the most marked separation from the Canaanites? Why were they to refuse, with firm decision, to make any covenant, or form any matrimonial alliance with them? Why were they to demolish their altars, break their images, and cut down their groves?

Simply because they were a holy people. And who had constituted them a holy people? Jehovah. He had chosen them and set His love upon them; He had redeemed them, and separated them to Himself; and hence it was His province and prerogative to prescribe what they were to be, and how they were to act. "Be ye holy, for I am holy."

It was not by any means on the principle of "Stand by thyself, I am holier than thou." This is manifest from what follows. "The Lord did not set His love upon you, nor choose you, because ye were more in number than any people; for ye were the fewest of all people; but because the Lord loved you, and because He would keep the oath which He had sworn unto your fathers, hath the Lord brought you out with a mighty hand, and redeemed you out of the house of bondmen, from the hand of Pharaoh king of Egypt." (Ver. 7, 8.)

Seasonable words these for Israel!—most healthful and needful! They were to remember that they owed all their dignity, all their privileges, all their blessings, not to aught in themselves—their own goodness or their own greatness, but simply to the fact of Jehovah's having identified Himself with them, in His infinite goodness and sovereign grace, and in virtue of His covenant with their fathers—"a covenant ordered in all things and sure." This, while it furnished a divine antidote against self-complacency and self-confidence, formed the solid basis of their happiness and their moral security. All rested upon the eternal stability of the grace of

God, and therefore human boasting was excluded. "My soul shall make her boast in the Lord; the humble shall hear thereof and be glad."

It is the settled purpose of God that "no flesh shall glory in His presence." All human pretension must be set aside. He will hide pride from man. Israel had to be taught to remember their origin and their true condition—"bondmen in Egypt"—"fewest of all people." No room for pride or boasting. They were in no wise better than the nations around them; and therefore, if called to account for their high elevation and moral greatness, they had simply to trace it all up to the free love of God and His faithfulness to His oath. "Not unto us, O Lord, not unto us, but unto Thy name give glory, for Thy mercy and for Thy truth's sake." (Ps. cxv. 1.)

"Know therefore that the Lord thy God, He is God, the faithful God, which keepeth covenant and mercy with them that love Him and keep His commandments, to a thousand generations; and repayeth them that hate Him to their face, to destroy them: He will not be slack to him that hateth Him, He will repay him to his face." (Ver. 9, 10.)

We have two weighty facts set before us here,— one, full of rich consolation and comfort to every true lover of God; the other, fraught with deep solemnity to every hater of God. All who really love God and keep His commandments may count on His infallible faithfulness and tender mercy at all times and under all circumstances. "*All things* work *together* for good to them that love God, to

them who are the called according to His purpose.''
If, through infinite grace, we have the love of God in
our hearts, and His fear before our eyes, we may
move on with good courage and joyful confidence,
assured that all shall be well—must be well.   ''Beloved, if our heart condemn us not, then have we
confidence toward God.   And whatsoever we ask,
we receive of Him, because we keep His commandments, and do those things that are pleasing in His
sight.''

This is a grand, eternal truth—a truth for Israel,
a truth for the Church.   Dispensations make no
difference as to this.   Whether we study the seventh
of Deuteronomy or the third chapter of 1 John, we
learn the same great practical truth, that God delights in those who fear Him and love Him and keep
His commandments.

Is there aught of the legal element in this ?   Not
a tinge.   Love and legality have nothing in common ; they are as far removed as the poles.   ''This
is the love of God, that we keep His commandments ;
and His commandments are not grievous.''   The
spirit and genius, the ground and character of our
obedience all go to prove it the very reverse of
legality.   It is our deep and settled conviction that
those persons who are ever ready to cry out, ''Legal ! Legal !'' whenever obedience is pressed upon
them, are sadly and grossly mistaken.   If indeed it
were taught that we must earn by our obedience the
high position and relationship of children of God,
then verily the solemn charge of legality might justly

be urged; but to bestow such an epithet on Christian obedience, is, we repeat, a serious moral mistake. Obedience could never precede sonship, but sonship should ever be followed by obedience.

And while we are on this subject, we must call the attention of the reader to a passage or two of New-Testament scripture as to which there is a want of clearness in many minds. In the fifth chapter of Matthew, we read, "Ye have heard that it hath been said, 'Thou shalt love thy neighbor and hate thine enemy;' but *I* say unto you, Love your enemies, bless them that curse you, do good to them that hate you, and pray for them which despitefully use you and persecute you; that ye may be the sons [*vioi*] of your Father which is in heaven; for He maketh His sun to rise on the evil and on the good, and sendeth rain on the just and on the unjust. . . . Be ye therefore perfect, even as your Father which is in heaven is perfect." (Ver. 43–48.)

This passage might, in the judgment of some, seem to teach that the relationship of children can be attained by a certain line of action; but it is not so. It is a question of moral conformity or suitability to the character and ways of our Father. We sometimes hear, in every-day life, the saying, "You would not be your father's son if you were to act in such a way." It is as though our Lord had said, If you want to be the sons of your heavenly Father, you must act in grace to all; for that is what He is doing.

Again, in 2 Corinthians vi. we read, "Wherefore

come out from among them, and be ye separate,
saith the Lord, and touch not the unclean; and I
will receive you, and will be a Father unto you, and
ye shall be My sons and daughters, saith the Lord
Almighty.'' Here, it is not a question of the secret
relationship of children, formed by a divine operation, but the public acknowledgment of the position
of *sons* [υἱοὺς] as the result of our separation from
evil. *

It will be well for the reader to seize this important distinction; it is of great practical value. We
do not become children by separation from the world,
''for ye are all the children of God by faith in Christ
Jesus.'' ''As many as received Him, to them gave
He power [or authority, ἐξουσίαν] to become children [τέκνα] of God, to them that believe on His
name; which were born, not of blood, nor of the
will of the flesh, nor of the will of man, but of God.''
(Gal. iii. 26; John i. 12, 13.) ''Of His own will
begat He us by the word of truth.'' (James i. 18.)
We become children by new birth, which, thanks be
to God, is a divine operation from first to last.
What had we to do with our natural birth? Nothing.
And what have we to do with our spiritual birth?
Clearly nothing.

But then we must remember that God can only
identify Himself with, and publicly acknowledge
those who, through grace, seek to walk in a way

---

*Speaking in a general way, the word τέκνον, child, is a term
of endearment; υἱός, son, of moral dignity. παῖς is either a
child or a servant; νήπιος, a babe.

worthy of Him—a way befitting the sons and daughters of the Lord Almighty. If our ways are unlike Him, if we are mixed up with all sorts of wrong things, if we are unequally yoked together with unbelievers, how can we expect God to own us as His sons? We read, in Hebrews xi, of those who "confessed that they were strangers and pilgrims on the earth," and who "declared plainly that they sought a country;" and of them we are told that *"God was not ashamed* to be called their God." He could publicly identify Himself with them, and acknowledge them; He could own them as His.

Reader, let us seriously apply our hearts to the consideration of this great practical question. Let us look, seriously and honestly, to our ways. Let us, in truthfulness and uprightness of heart, inquire whether we are "unequally yoked together with unbelievers," on any ground, or for any object whatsoever. If so, let us give earnest heed to the words, "Come out from among them, and be ye separate, and touch not the unclean thing." It may be that the carrying out of this holy commandment will expose us to the charge of bigotry, narrowness, and intolerance; it may wear the aspect of pharisaic pride and self-complacency. We may be told, we are not to judge, or set ourselves up to be holier or better than other people.

To all this line of argument we have the one simple, conclusive answer, namely, God's plain command. He tells us to be separate, to come out, to touch not the unclean; and all this in order to His receiving us, and acknowledging us as His sons and daughters. This ought to be quite sufficient for us. Let people think or say what they will of us,—let them call us what they please; God will settle the matter with them, sooner or later; our duty is to separate ourselves from unbelievers, if we would be received and owned of God. If believers are mixed up with unbelievers, how are they to be known or distinguished as the sons and daughters of the Lord Almighty?

But we may perhaps be asked, How are we to know who are unbelievers? All profess to be Christians—all take the ground of belonging to Christ: we are not surrounded by ignorant heathen, or unbelieving Jews; how then are we to judge? It was plain enough in the early days of Christianity, when the apostle wrote his epistle to the assembly at Corinth—then the line of demarkation was as clear as a sunbeam; there were the three distinct classes—"the Jew, the Gentile, and the Church of God;" but now all is changed,—we live in a Christian land, under a Christian government, we are surrounded on all hands by Christians, and therefore 2 Corinthians vi. cannot apply to us; it was all very well when the Church was in its infancy, having just emerged from Judaism on the one hand and heathenism on the other, but to think of applying such a principle at this advanced stage of the Church's history, is wholly out of the question.

To all who take this ground, we would put a very plain question,—Is it true that the Church has

reached a stage of her history in which the New
Testament is no longer her guide and authority?
Have we got beyond the range of holy Scripture?
If so, what are we to do? whither are we to turn
for guidance? If we admit for a moment that
2 Corinthians vi. does not apply to Christians now,
what warrant have we for appropriating to ourselves
any portion of the New Testament?

The fact is, Scripture is designed for the Church
of God as a whole, and for each member of that
Church in particular; and hence, as long as the
Church is on earth, so long will the Scripture apply.
To question this is to offer a flat contradiction to the
words of the inspired apostle when he tells us that
the holy Scriptures are able to make us "*wise unto
salvation*"—that is, "wise" right onward to the day
of glory, for such is the blessed force of the word
"salvation" in 2 Timothy iii. 15.

We want no new light—no fresh revelation; we
have "*all truth*" within the covers of our precious
Bible. Thank God for it! We do not want science
or philosophy to make us wise. All true science and
all sound philosophy will leave untouched the testimony of holy Scripture; they cannot add to it, but
they will not contradict it. When infidels talk to us
about "progress," "development," "the light of
science," we fall back, in holy confidence and tranquillity, upon those precious words, "all truth,"
"wise unto salvation." It is blessedly impossible
to get beyond these. What can be added to "all
truth"? What more do we or can we want than to

be made wise right onward to the coming of our
Lord Jesus Christ?

And further, let us remember that there is no
change whatever in the relative position of the
Church and the world. It is as true to-day as it
was eighteen hundred and fifty years ago, when our
Lord uttered the words, that His people are not of
the world, even as He Himself is not of the world.
(John xvii.) The world is the world still. It may,
in some places, have changed its dress, but not its
true character, spirit, and principles. Hence, therefore, it is as wrong to-day for Christians to be "unequally yoked together with unbelievers" as it was
when Paul penned his epistle to the Church at Corinth. We cannot get over this; we cannot set aside
our responsibility in this matter. It will not, by
any means, meet the case to say, "We must not
judge." We are bound to judge. If we refuse to
judge, we refuse to obey, and what is this but positive rebellion? God says, "Come out from among
them and be ye separate;" if we reply, We cannot
judge, where are we? The fact is, we are absolutely
commanded to judge. "Do not ye judge them that
are *within?* but them that are *without* God judgeth."
(1 Cor. v. 12, 13.)

But we shall not pursue this line of argument any
further. We trust the reader is one who fully owns
the direct application to himself of the passage which
we have just quoted. It is as plain as it is pointed;
it calls upon all God's people to come out and be
separate, and touch not the unclean thing. This is

what God requires of His people, in order to His owning them as His; and surely it ought to be the deep and earnest desire of our hearts to respond to His gracious will in this matter, utterly regardless of the world's thoughts respecting us. Some of us are very much afraid of being thought narrow and bigoted; but, oh, how little it imports to a truly devoted heart what men think of us! Human thoughts perish in an hour. When we are manifested before the judgment-seat of Christ, when we stand in the full blaze of the glory, what will it matter to us whether men considered us narrow or broad, bigoted or liberal? and what should it matter to us now? Not the weight of a feather. Our one grand object should be, so to act—so to carry ourselves as to be "acceptable" to Him who has made us "accepted." May it be so with the writer and the reader, and with every member of the body of Christ?

Let us now turn, for a moment, to the weighty and very solemn truth presented to us in verse 10 of our chapter. "He will not be slack to him that hateth Him, He will repay him to his face." If the lovers of God are comforted in verse 9, and most blessedly encouraged to keep His commandments, the haters of God are called to hearken to a warning note in verse 10.

There is a time coming when God will deal personally, face to face, with His enemies. How awful the thought that any one should be *a hater of God*— a hater of that One who is said to be and who is "Light" and "Love;" the very fountain of goodness, the Author and Giver of every good and perfect gift, the Father of lights; the One whose liberal hand supplies the need of every living thing, who hears the cry of the young ravens, and quenches the thirst of the wild ass; the infinitely good, the only wise, the perfectly holy God, the Lord of all power and might, the creator of the ends of the earth, and the One who has power to destroy both soul and body in hell!

Only think, reader, of any one being a hater of such a One as God; and we know that all who are not lovers must be haters. People may not see this; very few would be disposed to own themselves to be absolute haters of God, but there is no neutral ground in this great question; we must either be for or against; and in point of fact, people are not slow in showing their colors. It often happens that the heart's deep-seated enmity to God comes out in hatred to His people, to His Word, His worship, His service. How frequently do we hear such expressions as, "I hate religious people," "I hate all cant," "I hate preachers"! The truth is, it is God Himself that is hated. "The carnal mind is enmity against God; it is not subject to the law of God, neither indeed can be;" and this enmity comes out in reference to every one and every thing connected with God. There lies deep down in every unconverted heart the most positive enmity to God. Every man in his natural state hates God.

Now, God declares, in Deuteronomy vii. 10, that "He will not be slack to him that hateth Him; He will repay him to nis face.'' This is a most solemn truth, and one which ought to be more pressed upon the attention of all whom it may concern. Men do not like to hear it; many affect and profess not to believe it. They would fain persuade themselves and persuade others also that God is too good, too kind, too merciful, too benevolent, to deal in stern judgment with His creatures. They forget that God's ways in government are as perfect as His ways in grace. They imagine that the government of God will pass over or deal lightly with evil and evil-doers.

This is a most miserable and fatal mistake, and men will find it to be so to their heavy and eternal cost. True it is, blessed be God, He can, in His rich sovereign grace and mercy, forgive us our sins, blot out our transgressions, cancel our guilt, justify us perfectly, and fill our hearts with the spirit of adoption; but this is another thing altogether. This is grace reigning through righteousness unto eternal life by Jesus Christ our Lord. It is God, in His wondrous love, providing righteousness for the poor, guilty, hell-deserving sinner who knows and feels and owns that he has no righteousness of his own, and never could have it. God, in the marvelous love of His heart, has provided a means whereby He can be just and the justifier of every poor broken-hearted, bankrupt sinner that simply believes in Jesus.

But how, we may ask, was all this done? Was it by passing over sin, as though it were nothing? was it by relaxing the claims of the divine government, lowering the standard of divine holiness, or touching, in the most remote way, the dignity, stringency, and majesty of the law? No; thanks and praise to redeeming love, it was the very reverse. Never was there or could there be a more terrible expression of God's eternal hatred of sin, or of His unflinching purpose to condemn it utterly and punish it eternally; never was there or could there be a more glorious vindication of the divine government, a more perfect maintenance of the standard of divine holiness, truth, and righteousness; never was the law more gloriously vindicated or more thoroughly established than by that most glorious scheme of redemption, planned, executed, and revealed by the Eternal Three in One,—planned by the Father, executed by the Son, and revealed by the Holy Ghost.

If we would have a just sense of the awful reality of the government of God, His wrath against sin, and the true character of His holiness, we must gaze at the cross; we must hearken to that bitter cry that issued from the heart of the Son of God and broke through the dark shadows of Calvary, "My God, My God, why hast Thou forsaken Me?" Never had such a question been asked before, never has such a question been asked since, and never shall—never can such a question be asked again. Whether we consider the One who asked it, the One of whom it was asked, or the answer, we must see that the question stands absolutely alone in the annals of eternity. The cross is the measure of God's hatred of sin, as it is the measure of His love to the sinner. It is the imperishable foundation of the throne of grace, the divinely righteous ground on which God can pardon our sins and constitute us perfectly righteous in a risen and glorified Christ.

But then if men despise all this, and persist in their hatred of God, and yet talk of His being too good and too kind to punish evil-doers, how will it be with them? "He that obeyeth not [$\dot{\alpha}\pi\epsilon\iota\theta\tilde{\omega}\nu$] the Son shall not see life, but the wrath of God abideth upon him." (John iii. 36.)* Can it be possible—can we believe for a moment that a just God should exercise judgment upon His only begotten Son, His well-beloved, His eternal delight, because He was bearing our sins in His own body on the tree, and yet allow impenitent sinners to escape? Had Jesus, the spotless, holy, perfect Man—the only perfect Man that ever trod this earth—had He to suffer for sins, the just for the unjust, and shall evil-doers, unbelievers, and haters of God be saved and blessed and taken to heaven? and all this, forsooth,

---

*John iii. 36 is a passage of immense weight and importance. It not only sets forth the great truth that all who believe in the Son of God are the privileged possessors of eternal life, but it also cuts up by the roots two leading heresies of the day, namely, universalism and annihilationism. The universalist professes to believe that, ultimately, all shall be restored and blessed. Not so, says our passage; for those who obey not the Son "shall not see life."

The annihilationist professes to believe that all who are out of Christ shall perish like the beasts. Not so, for "the wrath of God *abideth*" upon the disobedient. Abiding wrath and annihilation are wholly incompatible. It is utterly impossible to reconcile them.

It is interesting and instructive to notice the difference between the words $\dot{o}$ $\pi\iota\acute{o}\tau\epsilon\acute{v}\omega\nu$—"he that believeth"—and $\dot{o}$ $\dot{\alpha}\pi\epsilon\iota\theta\tilde{\omega}\nu$—"he that obeyeth not." They give us the two sides of the subject of faith.

because God is too kind and too good to punish sinners in hell forever! Did it cost God the giving up, the forsaking, and the bruising of His beloved Son in order to save His people *from their sins*, and shall ungodly sinners, despisers, and rebels be saved *in their sins?* Did the Lord Jesus Christ die for nothing? did Jehovah put Him to grief and hide His face from Him when there was no necessity? Why the awful horrors of Calvary? why the three hours' darkness? why that bitter cry, "My God, My God, why hast Thou forsaken Me?"—why all this if sinners can get to heaven without it? Why all this inconceivable sorrow and suffering for our blessed Lord if God is too kind and too gracious and too tender to send sinners to hell?

What egregious folly! What will not men believe, provided it be not the truth of God? The poor dark human mind will affect to believe the most monstrous absurdity in order to get a plea for rejecting the plain teaching of holy Scripture. The very thing which men would never think of attributing to a good human government they do not hesitate to attribute to the government of the only wise, the only true, the only just God. What should we think of a government that could not or would not punish evil-doers? Would we like to live under it? What should we think of the government of England if, because her majesty is so kind, so gracious, so tender-hearted, she could not allow criminals to be punished as the law directs? Who would care to live in England?

Reader, do you not see how that one verse which is now before us demolishes completely all the theories and arguments which men, in their folly and ignorance, have advanced on the subject of the divine government? "The Lord thy God, He is God, the faithful God, which . . . . repayeth them that hate Him to their face, to destroy them; He will not be slack to him that hateth Him, He will repay him to his face."

Oh that men would hearken to the Word of God! that they would be warned by its clear, emphatic, and solemn statements as to coming wrath, judgment, and eternal punishment! that, instead of seeking to persuade themselves and others that there is no hell, no deathless worm and unquenchable fire, no eternal torment, they would listen to the warning voice, and, ere it be too late, flee for refuge to the hope set before them in the gospel! Truly this would be their wisdom. God declares that He will repay those that hate Him. How awful the thought of this repayment! Who can meet it? The government of God is perfect, and because it is so, it is utterly impossible that it can allow evil to pass unjudged. Nothing can be plainer than this. All Scripture, from Genesis to Revelation, sets it forth in terms so clear and forcible as to render it the very height of folly for men to argue against it. How much better and wiser and safer to flee from the wrath to come than to deny that it is coming, and that when it does come, it will be eternal in its duration. It is utterly vain for any one to attempt

to reason in opposition to the truth of God. Every
word of God shall stand forever. We see the actings of His government in reference to His people
Israel, and in reference to Christians now. Did He
pass over evil in His people of old? Nay; on the
contrary, He visited them continually with His chastening rod, and this, too, just because they were His
people, as He said to them by His prophet Amos—
"Hear this word which the Lord hath spoken against
you, O children of Israel, against the whole family
which I brought up from the land of Egypt, saying,
'You only have I known of all the families of the
earth; therefore I will punish you for all your iniquities.'" (Amos iii. 1, 2.)

We have the same weighty principle set forth in
the first epistle of Peter, in its application to Christians now.—"For the time is come that *judgment
must begin* at the house of God; and if it first begin
at us, what shall the end be of them that obey not
the gospel of God? And if the righteous scarcely
be saved, where shall the ungodly and the sinner
appear?" (Chap. iv. 17, 18.)

God chastens His own just because they are His
own, and that they may not be condemned with the
world. (1 Cor. xi.) The children of this world are
allowed to go on their way; but their day is coming
—a dark and heavy day—a day of judgment and
unmitigated wrath. Men may question and argue
and reason, but Scripture is distinct and emphatic.
"God hath appointed a day in which He will judge
the world in righteousness, by that Man whom He

hath ordained.'' The great day of reckoning is at hand, when God will repay every man to his face.

It is truly edifying to mark the way in which Moses, that beloved and honored servant of God, led assuredly by the Spirit of God, pressed the grand and solemn realities of the divine government upon the conscience of the congregation. Hear how he pleads and exhorts: ''Thou shalt *therefore* keep the commandments, and the statutes, and the judgments, which I command thee this day, *to do them.* Wherefore it shall come to pass, if ye *hearken* to these judgments, and *keep* and *do* them, that the Lord thy God shall keep unto thee the covenant and the mercy which He sware unto thy fathers. And He will *love* thee, and *bless* thee, and *multiply* thee; He will also bless the fruit of thy womb, and the fruit of thy land, thy corn, and thy wine, and thine oil, the increase of thy kine, and the flocks of thy sheep, in the land which He sware unto thy fathers to give thee. Thou shalt be blessed above all people; there shall not be male nor female barren among you or among your cattle. And the Lord will take away from thee all sickness, and will put none of the evil diseases of Egypt, which thou knowest, upon thee; but will lay them upon all them that hate thee. And thou shalt consume all the people which the Lord thy God shall deliver thee; thine eye shall have no pity upon them; neither shalt thou serve their gods; for that will be a snare unto thee.'' (Ver. 11–16.)

What a powerful appeal! how affecting! Mark

3

the two groups of words. Israel was to "hearken," "keep," and "do." Jehovah was to "love," "bless," and "multiply." Alas! alas! Israel failed —sadly, shamefully failed, under law and under government; and hence, instead of the love and the blessing and the multiplying, there has been judgment, curse, barrenness, dispersion, desolation.

But, blessed be the God of Abraham, Isaac, and Jacob, the God and Father of our Lord Jesus Christ, if Israel has failed under *law* and *government*, He has not failed in His rich and precious sovereign *grace* and *mercy*. He will keep the covenant and the mercy which He sware unto their fathers. Not one jot or tittle of His covenant-promise shall ever fail. He will make all good by and by. He will fulfill, to the very letter, all His gracious promises. Though He cannot do this on the ground of Israel's obedience, He can and will do it through the blood of the everlasting covenant, the precious blood of Jesus, His eternal Son—all homage to His peerless name!

Yes, reader, the God of Israel cannot suffer one of His precious promises to fall to the ground. What would become of us if He could? What security, what rest, what peace could we have, if Jehovah's covenant with Abraham were to fail in any single point? True it is that Israel has forfeited all claim. If it be a question of fleshly descent, Ishmael and Esau have a prior claim: if it be a question of legal obedience, the golden calf and the broken tables tell their melancholy tale: if it be a question of government on the ground of the Moab covenant, they have not a single plea to urge.

But God will be God, spite of Israel's lamentable unfaithfulness. "The gifts and calling of God are without repentance," and hence "all Israel shall be saved." God will most assuredly make good His oath to Abraham, spite of all the wreck and ruin of Abraham's seed. We must steadfastly hold to this, in the face of every opposing thought, feeling, or opinion. Israel shall be restored and blessed and multiplied in their own beloved and holy land. They shall take down their harps from the willows and, beneath the peaceful shade of their own vines and fig-trees, chant the high praises of their loving Saviour and God, throughout that bright millennial Sabbath which lies before them. Such is the unvarying testimony of Scripture, from beginning to end, which must be maintained in its integrity, and made good in every particular, to the glory of God, and on the ground of His everlasting covenant.

But we must return to our chapter, the closing verses of which demand our special attention. It is very touching and beautiful to mark the way in which Moses seeks to encourage the heart of the people in reference to the dreaded nations of Canaan. He enters into and anticipates their very inmost thoughts and feelings.

"If thou shalt say *in thine heart*, These nations are more than I; how can I dispossess them? Thou shalt not be afraid of them; but shalt *well remember* what the Lord thy God did unto Pharaoh, and

unto all Egypt; the great temptations which thine
eyes saw, and the signs, and the wonders, and the
mighty hand, and the stretched-out arm, whereby the
Lord thy God brought thee out: *so* shall the Lord
thy God do unto all the people of whom thou art
afraid. Moreover, the Lord thy God will send the
hornet among them, until they that are left, and
hide themselves from thee, be destroyed. Thou shalt
not be affrighted at them; for *the Lord thy God is
among you, a mighty God and terrible.* And the
Lord thy God will put out those nations before thee
by little and little; thou mayest not consume them
at once, lest the beasts of the field increase upon
thee. But the Lord thy God shall deliver them unto
thee, and shall destroy them with a mighty destruction, until they be destroyed. And He shall deliver their kings into thine hand, and thou shalt
destroy their name from under heaven; there shall
no man be able to stand before thee, until thou have
destroyed them. The graven images of their gods
shall ye burn with fire; thou shalt not desire the
silver or gold that is on them, nor take it unto thee,
lest thou be snared therein; for it is an abomination
to the Lord thy God. Neither shalt thou bring *an
abomination into thine house, lest thou be a cursed
thing like it;* but thou shalt utterly detest it, and
thou shalt utterly abhor it, for it is a cursed thing."
(Ver. 17–26.)

The grand remedy for all unbelieving fears is,
simply to fix the eye upon the living God; thus
the heart is raised above the difficulties, whatever

they may be. It is of no possible use to deny that there are difficulties and opposing influences of all sorts. This will not minister comfort and encouragement to the sinking heart. Some people affect a certain style of speaking of trials and difficulties which just goes to prove, not their practical knowledge of God, but their profound ignorance of the stern realities of life. They would fain persuade us that we ought not to feel the trials, sorrows, and difficulties of the way. They might as well tell us that we ought not to have a head on our shoulders or a heart in our bosom. Such persons know not how to comfort those that are cast down. They are mere visionary theorists, wholly unfit to deal with souls passing through conflict or grappling with the actual facts of our daily history.

How did Moses seek to encourage the hearts of his brethren? "Be not affrighted," he says; but why? Was it that there were no enemies, no difficulties, no dangers? No; but "the Lord thy God is among you, a mighty God and terrible." Here is the true comfort and encouragement. The enemies were there, but God is the sure resource. Thus it was that Jehoshaphat, in his time of trial and pressure, sought to encourage himself and his brethren. "O our God, wilt Thou not judge them? For we have no might against this great company that cometh against us, neither know we what to do; but *our eyes are upon Thee.*"

Here lies the precious secret. The eyes are upon God. His power is brought in, and this settles every

thing. "If God be for us, who can be against us?"
Moses meets, by his precious ministry, the rising
fears in the heart of Israel—"These nations are
more than I." Yes, but they are not more than the
"mighty and terrible God." What nations could
stand before Him? He had a solemn controversy
with those nations because of their terrible sins;
their iniquity was full; the reckoning-time had come,
and the God of Israel was going to drive them out
before His people.

Hence, therefore, Israel had no need to fear the
power of the enemy. Jehovah would see to that.
But there was something far more to be dreaded
than the enemy's power, and that was, the insnaring
influence of their idolatry. "The graven images
of their gods shall ye burn with fire." What! the
heart might say, are we to destroy the gold and
silver that adorn these images? Might not that be
turned to some good account? Is it not a pity to
destroy what is so very valuable in itself? It is
all right to burn the images, but why not spare the
gold and silver?

Ah, it is just thus the poor heart is prone to reason; thus ofttimes we deceive ourselves when called
to judge and abandon what is evil. We persuade
ourselves of the rightness of making some reserve;
we imagine we can pick and choose and make some
distinction. We are prepared to give up some of
the evil, but not all. We are ready to burn the
wood of the idol, but spare the gold and silver.

Fatal delusion! "Thou shalt not desire the silver

or gold that is on them, nor take it unto thee, *lest thou be snared therein;* for it is an abomination to the Lord thy God." All must be given up, all destroyed. To retain an atom of the accursed thing is to fall into the snare of the devil, and link ourselves with that which, however highly esteemed among men, is an abomination in the sight of God.

And let us mark and ponder the closing verses of our chapter. To bring an abomination into the house is to become like it! How very solemn! Do we fully understand it? The man who brought an abomination into his house became a cursed thing like it!

Reader, may the Lord keep our hearts separated from all evil, and true and loyal to Himself.

CHAPTER VIII.

" ALL the commandments which I command thee this day shall ye observe to do, that ye may live, and multiply, and go in and possess the land which the Lord sware unto your fathers. And thou shalt remember *all the way* which the Lord thy God led thee these forty years in the wilderness, to humble thee, and to prove thee, to know what was in thine heart, whether thou wouldest keep His commandments or no." (Ver. 1, 2.)

It is at once refreshing, edifying, and encouraging

to look back over the whole course along which the faithful hand of our God has conducted us; to trace His wise and gracious dealings with us; to call to mind His many marvelous interpositions on our behalf; how He delivered us out of this strait and that difficulty; how, ofttimes, when we were at our wits' end, He appeared for our help, and opened the way before us, rebuking our fears and filling our hearts with songs of praise and thanksgiving.

We must not, by any means, confound this delightful exercise with the miserable habit of looking back at *our* ways, our attainments, our progress, our service, what we have been able to do, even though we are ready to admit, in a general way, that it was only by the grace of God that we were enabled to do any little work for Him. All this only ministers to self-complacency, which is destructive of all true spirituality of mind. Self-retrospection, if we may be allowed to use such a term, is quite as injurious in its moral effect as self-introspection. In short, self-occupation, in any of its multiplied phases, is most pernicious; it is, in so far as it is allowed to operate, the death-blow to fellowship. Any thing that tends to bring self before the mind must be judged and refused, with stern decision; it brings in barrenness, darkness, and feebleness. For a person to sit down to look back at his attainments or his doings, is about as wretched an occupation as any one could engage in. We may be sure it was not to any such thing as this that Moses exhorted the people when he charged them to "remember all the way by which the Lord their God had led them."

We may here recur, for a moment, to the memorable words of the apostle in Philippians iii.— "Brethren, I count not myself to have apprehended; but this one thing I do, *forgetting those things which are behind*, and reaching forth unto those things which are before, I press toward the mark for the prize of the high calling of God in Christ Jesus."

Now, the question is, what were the "things" of which the blessed apostle speaks? Did he forget the precious dealings of God with his soul throughout the whole of his wilderness-journey? Impossible!—indeed we have the very fullest and clearest evidence to the contrary. Hear his touching words before Agrippa—"Having therefore obtained help of God, I continue unto this day, witnessing both to small and great." So also, in writing to his beloved son and fellow-laborer, Timothy, he reviews the past, and speaks of the persecutions and afflictions which he had endured; "but," he adds, "out of them all the Lord delivered me." And again, "At my first answer no man stood with me, but all forsook me; I pray God that it may not be laid to their charge. Notwithstanding, the Lord stood with me, and strengthened me; that by me the preaching might be fully known, and that all the Gentiles might hear; and I was delivered out of the mouth of the lion."

To what then does the apostle refer when he speaks of "forgetting those things which are be-

hind"?   We believe he refers to all those things
which had no connection with Christ—things in
which the heart might rest, and nature might glory—
things which might act as weights and hindrances,—
all these were to be forgotten in the ardent pursuit of
those grand and glorious realities which lay before
him.   We do not believe that Paul, or any other
child of God or servant of Christ, could ever desire
to forget a single scene or circumstance in his whole
earthly career in any way illustrative of the goodness, the loving-kindness, the tender mercy, the
faithfulness of God.   On the contrary, we believe it
will ever be one of our very sweetest exercises to
dwell upon the blessed memory of all our Father's
ways with us while passing across the desert, home
to our everlasting rest.

> "There with what joy reviewing
>   Past conflicts, dangers, fears,
> Thy hand our foes subduing,
>   And drying all our tears.
> Our hearts with rapture burning,
>   The path we shall retrace,
> Where now our souls are learning
>   The riches of Thy grace."

But let us not be misunderstood.   We do not, by
any means, wish to give countenance to the habit of
dwelling merely upon our own experience.   This is
often very poor work, and resolves itself into self-
occupation.   We have to guard against this as one
of the many things which tend to lower our spiritual
tone and draw our hearts away from Christ.   But

we need never be afraid of the result of dwelling upon the record of the Lord's dealings and ways with us. This is a blessed habit, tending ever to lift us out of ourselves, and fill us with praise and thanksgiving.

Why, we may ask, were Israel charged to "remember *all* the way" by which the Lord their God had led them? Assuredly, to draw out their hearts in praise for the past, and to strengthen their confidence in God for the future. Thus it must ever be.

> "We'll praise Him for all that is past,
> And trust Him for all that's to come."

May we do so more and more. May we just move on, day by day, praising and trusting, trusting and praising. These are the two things which redound to the glory of God, and to our peace and joy in Him. When the eye rests on the "Ebenezers" which lie all along the way, the heart must give forth its sweet "halleluiahs" to Him who has helped us hitherto, and will help us right on to the end. He *hath* delivered, and He *doth* deliver, and He *will* deliver. Blessed chain! Its every link is divine deliverance.

Nor is it merely upon the signal mercies and gracious deliverances of our Father's hand that we are to dwell, with devout thankfulness, but also upon the "humblings" and the "provings" of His wise, faithful, and holy love. All these things are full of richest blessing to our souls. They are not, as people sometimes call them, "mercies in disguise," but plain, palpable, unmistakable mercies, for which we shall have to praise our God throughout the golden ages of that bright eternity which lies before us.

"Thou shalt remember *all* the way"—every stage of the journey, every scene of wilderness-life, all the dealings of God, from first to last, with the special object thereof, "to humble thee, and to prove thee, *to know what was in thine heart.*"

How wonderful to think of God's patient grace and painstaking love with His people in the wilderness! What precious instruction for us! With what intense interest and spiritual delight we can hang over the record of the divine dealings with Israel in all their desert-wanderings! How much we can learn from the marvelous history! We, too, have to be humbled and proved, and made to know what is in our hearts. It is very profitable and morally wholesome.

On our first setting out to follow the Lord, we know but little of the depths of evil and folly in our hearts. Indeed, we are superficial in every thing. It is as we get on in our practical career that we begin to prove the reality of things; we find out the depths of evil in ourselves, the utter hollowness and worthlessness of all that is in the world, and the urgent need of the most complete dependence upon the grace of God every moment. All this is very good; it makes us humble and self-distrusting; it delivers us from pride and self-sufficiency, and leads us to cling, in childlike simplicity, to the One who alone is able to keep us from falling. Thus, as we grow in self-knowledge, we get a deeper sense of grace, a more profound acquaintance with the wondrous love of the heart of God, His tenderness toward us, His marvelous patience in bearing with all our infirmities and failings, His rich mercy in having taken us up at all, His loving ministry to all our varied need, His numberless interpositions on our behalf, the exercises through which He has seen fit to lead us for our souls' deep and permanent profit.

The practical effect of all this is invaluable; it imparts depth, solidity, and mellowness to the character; it cures us of all our crude notions and vain theories; it delivers us from one-sidedness and wild extremes; it makes us tender, thoughtful, patient, and considerate toward others; it corrects our harsh judgments and gives a gracious desire to put the best possible construction upon the actions of others, and a readiness to attribute the best motives in cases which may seem to us equivocal. These are precious fruits of wilderness-experience which we may all earnestly covet.

"And He humbled thee, and suffered thee to hunger, and fed thee with manna, which thou knewest not, neither did thy fathers know, that He might make thee know that man doth not live by bread only, but by every word which proceedeth out of the mouth of the Lord doth man live." (Ver 3.)

This passage derives special interest and importance from the fact that it is the first of our Lord's quotations from the book of Deuteronomy in His conflict with the adversary in the wilderness. Let us ponder this deeply; it demands our earnest attention. Why did our Lord quote from Deuteronomy? Because that was the book which, above all others, specially applied to the condition of Israel at the moment. Israel had utterly failed, and this weighty fact is assumed in the book of Deuteronomy from beginning to end. But notwithstanding the failure of the nation, the path of obedience lay open to every faithful Israelite. It was the privilege and duty of every one who loved God to abide by His Word under all circumstances and in all places.

Now, our blessed Lord was divinely true to the position of the Israel of God. Israel after the flesh had failed and forfeited every thing; He was there, in the wilderness, as the true Israel of God, to meet the enemy by the simple authority of the Word of God. "And Jesus, being full of the Holy Ghost, returned from Jordan, and was led by the Spirit into the wilderness, being forty days tempted of the devil. And in those days He did eat nothing; and when they were ended, He afterward hungered. And the devil said unto Him, 'If Thou be the Son of God, command this stone that it be made bread.' And Jesus answered Him, saying, '*It is written*, that man shall not live by bread alone, but by every word of God.'" (Luke iv.)

Here, then, is something for us to ponder. The perfect Man, the true Israel, in the wilderness, surrounded by the wild beasts, fasting for forty days, in the presence of the great adversary of God, of man, of Israel. There was not a single feature in the scene to speak for God. It was not with the second Man as it was with the first; He was not surrounded with all the delights of Eden, but with all the dreariness and desolation of a desert—there in loneliness and hunger, but there for God!

Yes, blessed be His name, and there for man,— there to show man how to meet the enemy in all his varied temptations, there to show man how to live. We must not suppose for a moment that our adorable Lord met the adversary as God over all. True, He was God, but if it were only as such that He stood in the conflict, it could not afford any example for us. Besides, it would be needless to tell us that God was able to vanquish and put to flight a creature which His own hand had formed. But to see One who was, in every respect, a man, and in all the circumstances of humanity, sin excepted,—to see Him there in weakness, in hunger, standing amid the consequences of man's fall, and to find Him triumphing completely over the terrible foe, it is this which is so full of comfort, consolation, strength, and encouragement for us.

And how did He triumph? This is the grand and all-important question for us,—a question demanding the most profound attention of every member of the Church of God—a question the magnitude and importance of which it would be utterly impossible to overstate. How, then, did the Man Christ Jesus vanquish Satan in the wilderness? Simply by the Word of God. He overcame, not as the almighty

God, but as the humble, dependent, self-emptied, and obedient Man. We have before us the magnificent spectacle of a Man standing in the presence of the devil and utterly confounding him with no other weapon whatsoever save the Word of God. It was not by the display of divine power, for that could be no model for us; it was simply with the Word of God, in His heart and in His mouth, that the Second Man confounded the terrible enemy of God and man.

And let us carefully note that our blessed Lord does not reason with Satan. He does not appeal to any facts connected with Himself—facts with which the enemy was well acquainted. He does not say, I know I am the Son of God; the opened heavens, the descending Spirit, the Father's voice, have all borne witness to the fact of My being the Son of God. No; this would not do; it would not and could not be an example for us. *The* one special point for us to seize and learn from is, that our great Exemplar, when meeting all the temptations of the enemy, used only the weapon which we have in our possession, namely, the simple, precious, written, Word of God.

We say, "all the temptations," because in all the three instances our Lord's unvarying reply is, "*It is written.*" He does not say, "I know"—"I think"— "I feel"—"I believe" this, that, or the other; He simply appeals to the written Word of God—the book of Deuteronomy in particular,—that very book which infidels have dared to insult, but which is pre-eminently the book for every obedient man, in the face of total, universal, hopeless, wreck and ruin.

This is of unspeakable moment for us, beloved reader. It is as though our Lord Christ had said to the adversary, Whether I am the Son of God or not is not now the question, but how *man* is to live, and the answer to this question is only to be found in holy Scripture; and it is to be found there as clear as a sunbeam, quite irrespective of all questions respecting Me. Whoever I am, the Scripture is the same: "man doth not live by bread only, but by every word that proceedeth out of the mouth of the Lord."

Here we have the only true, the only safe, the only happy attitude for man, namely, hanging in earnest dependence upon "every word that proceedeth out of the mouth of the Lord." Blessed attitude! We may well say there is nothing like it in all this world. It brings the soul into direct, living, personal contact with the Lord Himself, by means of His Word. It makes the Word so absolutely essential to us, in every thing; we cannot do without it. As the natural life is sustained by bread, so the spiritual life is sustained by the Word of God. It is not merely going to the Bible to find doctrines there, or to have our opinions or views confirmed; it is very much more than this; it is going to the Bible for the staple commodity of life—the life of the new man; it is going there for food, for light, for guidance, for comfort, for authority, for strength—for all, in short, that the soul can possibly need, from first to last.

4

And let us specially note the force and value of the expression, "*every* word." How fully it shows that we cannot afford to dispense with a single word that has proceeded out of the mouth of the Lord. We want it all. We cannot tell the moment in which some exigence may present itself for which Scripture has already provided. We may not perhaps have specially noticed the scripture before, but when the difficulty arises, if we are in a right condition of soul—the true posture of heart, the Spirit of God will furnish us with the needed scripture, and we shall see a force, beauty, depth, and moral adaptation in the passage which we had never seen before. Scripture is a divine and therefore exhaustless treasury, in which God has made ample provision for all the need of His people, and for each believer in particular, right on to the end. Hence we should study it all, ponder it, dig deeply into it, and have it treasured up in our hearts, ready for use when the demand arises.

There is not a single crisis occurring in the entire history of the Church of God, not a single difficulty in the entire path of any individual believer, from beginning to end, which has not been perfectly provided for in the Bible. We have all we want in that blessed volume, and hence we should be ever seeking to make ourselves more and more acquainted with what that volume contains, so as to be "thoroughly furnished" for whatever may arise, whether it be a temptation of the devil, an allurement of the world, or a lust of the flesh; or, on the other hand, for equipment for that path of good works which God has afore prepared that we should walk in it.

And we should, further, give special attention to the expression, "*Out of the mouth of the Lord.*" This is unspeakably precious. It brings the Lord so very near to us, and gives us such a sense of the reality of feeding upon His every word—yea, of hanging upon it as something absolutely essential and indispensable. It sets forth the blessed fact that our souls can no more exist without the Word than our bodies could without food. In a word, we are taught by this passage that *man's* true position, his proper attitude, his only place of strength, safety, rest, and blessing, is to be found in habitual dependence upon the Word of God.

This is the life of faith which we are called to live —the life of dependence—the life of obedience—the life that Jesus lived perfectly. That blessed One would not move a step, utter a word, or do a single thing save by the authority of the Word of God. No doubt He could have turned stone into bread, but He had no command from God to do that; and inasmuch as He had no command, He had no motive for action. Hence Satan's temptations were perfectly powerless. He could do nothing with a man who would only act on the authority of the Word of God.

And we may also note, with very much interest and profit, that our blessed Lord does not quote Scripture for the purpose of silencing the adversary, but simply as authority for His position and conduct. Here is where we are so apt to fail; we do not sufficiently use the precious Word of God in this way; we quote it, at times, more for victory over the enemy than for power and authority for our own souls. Thus it loses its power in our hearts. We want to use the Word as a hungry man uses bread, or as a mariner uses his chart and his compass; it is that on which we live, and by which we move and act and think and speak. Such it really is, and the more fully we prove it to be all this to us, the more we shall know of its infinite preciousness. Who is it that knows most of the real value of bread? Is it a chemist? No; but a hungry man. A chemist may analyze it, and discuss its component parts, but a hungry man proves its worth. Who knows most of the real value of a chart? is it the teacher of navigation? No; but the mariner as he sails along an unknown and dangerous coast.

These are but feeble figures to illustrate what the Word of God is to the true Christian. He cannot do without it. It is absolutely indispensable, in every relationship of life and in every sphere of action. His hidden life is fed and sustained by it; his practical life is guided by it. In all the scenes and circumstances of his personal and domestic history, in the privacy of his closet, in the bosom of his family, in the management of his affairs, he is cast upon the Word of God for guidance and counsel.

And it never fails those who simply cleave to it

and confide in it. We may trust Scripture without a single shade of misgiving. Go to it when we will, we shall always find what we want. Are we in sorrow? is the poor heart bereaved, crushed, and desolate? What can soothe and comfort us like the balmy words which the Holy Spirit has penned for us? One sentence of holy Scripture can do more, in the way of comfort and consolation, than all the letters of condolence that ever were penned by human hand. Are we discouraged, faint-hearted, and cast down? The Word of God meets us with its bright and soul-stirring assurances. Are we pressed by pinching poverty? The Holy Ghost brings home to our hearts some golden promise from the page of inspiration, recalling us to Him who is "the Possessor of heaven and earth," and who, in His infinite grace, has pledged Himself to "supply all *our need* according to *His riches* in glory by Christ Jesus." Are we perplexed and harassed by the conflicting opinions of men, by the dogmas of conflicting schools of divinity, by religious and theological difficulties? A few sentences of holy Scripture will pour in a flood of divine light upon the heart and conscience, and set us at perfect rest, answering every question, solving every difficulty, removing every doubt, chasing away every cloud, giving us to know the mind of God, putting an end to conflicting opinions by the one divinely competent authority.

What a boon, therefore, is holy Scripture! What a precious treasure we possess in the Word of God!

How we should bless His holy name for having given it to us! Yes; and bless Him, too, for every thing that tends to make us more fully acquainted with the depth, fullness, and power of those words of our chapter, "Man shall not live by bread only, but by every word that proceedeth out of the mouth of the Lord doth man live."

Truly precious are these words to the heart of the believer! And hardly less so are those that follow, in which the beloved and revered lawgiver refers, with touching sweetness, to Jehovah's tender care throughout the whole of Israel's desert-wanderings. "Thy raiment," he says, "waxed not old upon thee, neither did thy foot swell, these forty years."

What marvelous grace shines out in these words! Only think, reader, of Jehovah looking after His people in such a manner, to see that their garments should not wax old or their foot swell! He not only fed them, but clothed them and cared for them in every way. He even stooped to look after their feet, that the sand of the desert might not injure them. Thus, for forty years, did He watch over them, with all the exquisite tenderness of a father's heart. What will not love undertake to do for its object? Jehovah had set His love upon His people, and this one blessed fact secured every thing for them, had they only understood it. There was not a single thing within the range of Israel's necessities, from Egypt to Canaan, which was not secured to them and included in the fact that Jehovah had undertaken to do for them. With infinite love and almighty power on their side, what could be lacking?

But then, as we know, love clothes itself in various forms. It has something more to do than to provide food and raiment for its objects. It has not only to take account of their physical but also of their moral and spiritual wants. Of this the lawgiver does not fail to remind the people. "Thou shalt also consider," he says, "*in thine heart*"—the only true and effective way to consider—"that, as a man chasteneth his son, so the Lord thy God chasteneth thee."

Now, we do not like chastening; it is not joyous, but grievous. It is all very well for a son to receive food and raiment from a father's hand, and to have all his comforts provided by a father's thoughtful love, but he does not like to see him taking down the rod. And yet that dreaded rod may be the very best thing for the son; it may do for him what no material benefits or earthly blessings could effect,—it may correct some bad habit, or deliver him from some wrong tendency, or save him from some evil influence, and thus prove a great moral and spiritual blessing for which he shall have to be forever thankful. The grand point for the son is, to see a father's love and care in the discipline and chastening just as distinctly as in the various material benefits which strew his path from day to day.

Here is precisely where we so signally fail in reference to the disciplinary dealings of our Father. We rejoice in His benefits and blessings; we are filled with praise and thankfulness as we receive.

day by day, from His liberal hand, the rich supply of all our need; we delight to dwell upon His marvelous interposition on our behalf in times of pressure and difficulty; it is a most precious exercise to look back over the path by which His good hand has led us, and mark those "Ebenezers" which tell of gracious help supplied all along the road.

All this is very good and very right and very precious, but then there is a great danger of our resting in the mercies, the blessings, and the benefits which flow, in such rich profusion, from our Father's loving heart and liberal hand. We are apt to rest in these things, and say with the Psalmist, "In *my prosperity* I said, 'I shall never be moved. Lord, by Thy favor Thou hast made *my mountain* to stand strong.'" True, it is "by Thy favor," but yet we are prone to be occupied with *our* mountain and *our* prosperity; we allow these things to come in between our hearts and the Lord, and thus they become a snare to us. Hence the need of chastening. Our Father, in His faithful love and care, is watching over us; He sees the danger and He sends trial, in one shape or another. Perhaps a telegram comes announcing the death of a beloved child, or the crash of a bank involving the loss of our earthly all; or, it may be, we are laid on a bed of pain and sickness, or called to watch by the sick bed of a beloved relative.

In a word, we are called to wade through deep waters which seem, to our poor, feeble, coward hearts, absolutely overwhelming. The enemy suggests the question. Is this love? Faith replies, without hesitation and without reserve, Yes; it is all love—perfect love; the death of the child, the loss of the property, the long, heavy, painful illness, all the sorrow, all the pressure, all the exercise, the deep waters and dark shadows—all, all is love— perfect love and unerring wisdom. I feel assured of it, even now; I do not wait to know it by and by, when I shall look back on the path from amid the full light of the glory; I know it now, and delight to own it to the praise of that infinite grace which has taken me up from the depth of my ruin, and charged itself with all that concerns me, and which deigns to occupy itself with my very failures, follies, and sins, in order to deliver me from them, and to make me a partaker of divine holiness, and conform me to the image of that blessed One who "loved Me and gave Himself for me."

Christian reader, this is the way to answer Satan, and to hush the dark reasonings which may spring up in our hearts. We must always justify God. We must look at all His disciplinary dealings in the light of His love. "Thou shalt also consider in thine heart that, *as a man chasteneth his son*, so the Lord thy God chasteneth thee." Most surely we should not like to be without the blessed pledge and proof of sonship, "*My son*, despise not thou the chastening of the Lord, nor faint when thou art rebuked of Him; for *whom the Lord loveth He chasteneth*, and scourgeth *every son* whom He receiveth. If ye endure chastening, God dealeth with you as with sons; for what son is he whom the father chasteneth not? But if ye be without chastisement, whereof all are partakers, then are ye bastards, and not sons. Furthermore, we have had fathers of our flesh which corrected us, and we gave them reverence; shall we not much rather be in subjection to the Father of spirits, and live? For they verily for a few days chastened us after their own pleasure; but He for our profit, that we might be partakers of His holiness. Now, no chastening for the present seemeth to be joyous, but grievous; nevertheless, afterward it yieldeth the peaceable fruit of righteousness unto them which are exercised thereby. Wherefore lift up the hands which hang down, and the feeble knees; and make straight paths for your feet, lest that which is lame be turned out of the way; but let it rather be healed." (Heb. xii. 5–13.)

It is at once interesting and profitable to mark the way in which Moses presses upon the congregation the varied motives of obedience arising from the past, the present, and the future. Every thing is brought to bear upon them to quicken and deepen their sense of Jehovah's claims upon them. They were to "remember" the past, they were to "consider" the present, and they were to anticipate the future; and all this was to act on their hearts, and lead them forth in holy obedience to that blessed and gracious One who had done, who was doing, and who would do such great things for them.

The thoughtful reader can hardly fail to observe in this constant presentation of moral motives a marked feature of this lovely book of Deuteronomy, and a striking proof that it is no mere attempt at a repetition of what we have in Exodus; but, on the contrary, that our book has a province, a range, a scope, and design entirely its own. To speak of mere repetition is absurd; to speak of contradiction is impious.

"Therefore thou shalt keep the commandments of the Lord thy God, to walk in His ways, and to fear Him." The word "therefore" had a retrospective and prospective force. It was designed to lead the heart back over the past dealings of Jehovah, and forward into the future. They were to think of the marvelous history of those forty years in the desert, —the teaching, the humbling, the proving, the watchful care, the gracious ministry, the full supply of all their need, the manna from heaven, the stream from the smitten rock, the care of their garments, and of their very feet, the wholesome discipline for their moral good. What powerful moral motives were here for Israel's obedience!

But this was not all: they were to look forward into the future; they were to anticipate the bright prospect which lay before them; they were to find in the future, as well as in the past and the present, the solid basis of Jehovah's claims upon their reverent and whole-hearted obedience.

"For the Lord thy God bringeth thee into a good land, a land of brooks of water, of fountains and depths that spring out of valleys and hills; a land of wheat, and barley, and vines, and fig-trees, and pomegranates, a land of oil olive, and honey; a land wherein thou shalt eat bread without scarceness, thou shalt not lack any thing in it; a land whose stones are iron, and out of whose hills thou mayest dig brass.''

How fair was the prospect! how bright the vision! How marked the contrast to the Egypt behind them and the wilderness through which they had passed! The Lord's land lay before them in all its beauty and verdure, its vine-clad hills and honeyed plains, its gushing fountains and flowing streams. How refreshing the thought of the vine, the fig-tree, the pomegranate, and the olive! How different from the leeks, onions, and garlic of Egypt! Yes, all so different! It was the Lord's own land: this was enough. It produced and contained all they could possibly want. Above its surface, rich profusion; below, untold wealth—exhaustless treasure.

What a prospect! How the faithful Israelite would long to enter upon it!—long to exchange the sand of the desert for that bright inheritance! True, the desert had its deep and blessed experiences, its holy lessons, its precious memories; there they had known Jehovah in a way they could not know Him even in Canaan;—all this was quite true, and we can fully understand it; but still the wilderness was not Canaan, and every true Israelite would long to set his foot on the land of promise, and truly we may say that Moses presents the land, in the passage just quoted, in a way eminently calculated to attract the heart. ''A land,'' he says, ''wherein thou shalt eat bread without scarceness, *thou shalt not lack any thing in it."* What more could be said? Here was the grand fact in reference to that good land into which the hand of covenant-love was about to introduce them. All their wants would be divinely met. Hunger and thirst should never be known there. Health and plenty, joy and gladness, peace and blessing, were to be the assured portion of the Israel of God in that fair inheritance upon which they were about to enter. Every enemy was to be subdued; every obstacle swept away; "the pleasant land" was to pour forth its treasures for their use; watered continually by heaven's rain, and warmed by its sunlight, it was to bring forth, in rich abundance, all that the heart could desire.

What a land! what an inheritance! what a home! Of course, we are looking at it now from a divine stand-point—looking at it according to what it was in the mind of God, and what it shall most assuredly be to Israel during that bright millennial age which lies before them. We should have but a very poor idea indeed of the Lord's land were we to think of it merely as possessed by Israel in the past, even in the very brightest days of its history, as it appeared amid the splendors of Solomon's reign. We must look onward to "the times of the restitution of all things," in order to have any thing like a true idea of what the land of Canaan will yet be to the Israel of God.

Now, Moses speaks of the land according to the divine idea of it. He presents it as given by God, and not as possessed by Israel. This makes all the difference. According to his charming description, there was neither enemy nor evil occurrent: nothing but fruitfulness and blessing from end to end. That is what it would have been, that is what it should have been, and that is what it shall be, by and by, to the seed of Abraham, in pursuance of the covenant made with their fathers—the new, the everlasting covenant, founded on the sovereign grace of God, and ratified by the blood of the cross. No power of earth or hell can hinder the purpose or the promise of God. "Hath He said, and shall He not do it?" God will make good, to the letter, every word, spite of all the enemy's opposition and the lamentable failure of His people. Though Abraham's seed have utterly failed under law and under government, yet Abraham's God will give grace and glory, for His gifts and calling are without repentance.

Moses fully understood all this. He knew how it would turn out with those who stood before him, and with their children after them, for many generations; and he looked forward into that bright future in which a covenant-God would display, in the view of all created intelligences, the triumphs of His grace in His dealings with the seed of Abraham His friend.

Meanwhile, however, the faithful servant of Jehovah, true to the object before his mind, in all those marvelous discourses in the opening of our book, proceeds to unfold to the congregation the truth as to their mode of acting in the good land on which they were about to plant their foot. As he had spoken of the past and of the present, so would he make use of the future; he would turn all to account in his holy effort to urge upon the people their obvious, bounden duty to that blessed One who had so graciously and tenderly cared for them all their journey through, and who was about to bring them in and plant them in the mountain of His inheritance. Let us hearken to his touching and powerful exhortations.

"When thou hast eaten and art full, then thou shalt bless the Lord thy God for the good land which He has given thee." How simple! how lovely! how morally suitable! Filled with the fruit of Jehovah's goodness, they were to bless and praise His holy name. He delights to surround Himself with hearts filled to overflowing with the sweet sense of His goodness, and pouring forth songs of praise and thanksgiving. He inhabits the praises of His people. He says, "Whoso offereth praise glorifieth Me." The feeblest note of praise from a grateful heart ascends as fragrant incense to the throne and to the heart of God.

Let us remember this, beloved reader. It is as true for us, most surely, as it was for Israel, that praise is comely. Our grand primary business is to praise the Lord. Our every breath should be a halleluiah. It is to this blessed and most sacred exercise the Holy Ghost exhorts us, in manifold places. "By Him therefore let us offer the sacrifice of praise to God continually, that is, the fruit of our lips giving thanks to His name." We should ever remember that nothing so gratifies the heart and

glorifies the name of our God as a thankful, worshiping spirit on the part of His people. It is well
to do good and communicate,—God is well pleased
with such sacrifices; it is our high privilege, while
we have opportunity, to do good unto all men, and
especially unto them who are of the household of
faith; we are called to be channels of blessing between the loving heart of our Father and every
form of human need that comes before us in our
daily path;—all this is most blessedly true, but we
must never forget that the very highest place is assigned to praise. It is this which shall employ our
ransomed powers throughout the golden ages of
eternity, when the sacrifices of active benevolence
shall no longer be needed.

But the faithful lawgiver knew but too well the
sad proneness of the human heart to forget all this—
to lose sight of the gracious Giver, and rest in His
gifts; hence he addresses the following admonitory
words to the congregation—wholesome words, truly,
for them and for us. May we bend our ears and
our hearts to them, in holy reverence and teachable-
ness of spirit.

"Beware that thou forget not the Lord thy God,
in not keeping His commandments, and His judgments, and His statutes, which I command thee this
day. Lest *when thou hast eaten and art full*, and
hast built goodly houses, and dwelt therein; and
when thy herds and thy flocks multiply, and thy
silver and thy gold is multiplied, and all that thou
hast is multiplied; then thine heart be lifted up, and

thou forget the Lord thy God, which brought thee
forth out of the land of Egypt, from the house of
bondage; who led thee through that great and terrible wilderness, wherein were fiery serpents, and
scorpions, and drought, where there was no water;
who brought thee forth water out of the rock of flint;
who fed thee in the wilderness with manna, which
thy fathers knew not, that He might humble thee,
and that He might prove thee, *to do thee good at thy
latter end;* and thou say in thine heart, My power
and the might of mine hand hath gotten me this
wealth. But thou shalt remember the Lord thy
God; for it is He that giveth thee power to get
wealth, that He may establish His covenant which
He sware unto thy fathers, as it is this day. And it
shall be, if thou do at all forget the Lord thy God,
and walk after other gods, and serve them, and worship them, I testify against you this day that ye
shall surely perish. As the nations which the Lord
destroyeth before your face, so shall ye perish, *because ye would not be obedient unto the voice of the
Lord your God.*" (Ver. 11-20.)

Here is something for us to ponder deeply. It
has most assuredly a voice for us, as it had for
Israel. We may perhaps feel disposed to marvel
at the frequent reiteration of the note of warning
and admonition, the constant appeals to the heart
and conscience of the people as to their bounden
duty to obey in all things the word of God, the
recurrence again and again to those grand soul-
stirring facts connected with their deliverance out

5

of Egypt and their journey through the wilderness.

But wherefore should we marvel? In the first place, do we not deeply feel and fully admit our own urgent need of warning, admonition, and exhortation? Do we not need line upon line, precept upon precept, and that continually? Are we not prone to forget the Lord our God—to rest in His gifts instead of Himself? Alas! alas! we cannot deny it. We rest in the stream, instead of getting up to the Fountain; we turn the very mercies, blessings, and benefits which strew our path in rich profusion into an occasion of self-complacency and gratulation, instead of finding in them the blessed ground of continual praise and thanksgiving.

And then, as to those great facts of which Moses so continually reminds the people, could they ever lose their moral weight, power, or preciousness? Surely not. Israel might forget and fail to appreciate those facts, but the facts remained the same. The terrible plagues of Egypt, the night of the passover, their deliverance from the land of darkness, bondage, and degradation, their marvelous passage through the Red Sea, the descent of that mysterious food from heaven morning by morning, the refreshing stream gushing forth from the flinty rock,—how could such facts as these ever lose their power over a heart possessing a spark of genuine love to God? and why should we wonder to find Moses again and again appealing to them and using them as a most powerful lever wherewith to move the hearts of the people? Moses felt the mighty moral influence of these things himself, and he would fain lead others to feel it also. To him, they were precious beyond expression, and he longed to make his brethren feel their preciousness as well as himself. It was his one object to set before them, in every possible way, the powerful claims of Jehovah upon their hearty and unreserved obedience.

This, reader, will account for what might, to an unspiritual, unintelligent, cursory reader, seem the too frequent recurrence to the scenes of the past in those wonderful discourses of Moses. We are reminded, as we read them, of the lovely words of Peter, in his second epistle,—"Wherefore I will not be negligent to put you *always in remembrance of these things*, though ye know them, and be established in the present truth. Yea, I think it meet, as long as I am in this tabernacle, *to stir you up, by putting you in remembrance;* knowing that shortly I must put off this my tabernacle, even as our Lord Jesus Christ hath showed me. Moreover, I will endeavor that ye may be able, after my decease, to have *these things always in remembrance.*" (Chap. i. 12–15.)

How striking the unity of spirit and purpose in these two beloved and venerable servants of God! Both the one and the other felt the tendency of the poor human heart to forget the things of God, of heaven, and of eternity, and they felt the supreme importance and infinite value of the things of which they spoke; hence their earnest desire to keep them continually before the hearts and abidingly in the

remembrance of the Lord's beloved people. Unbelieving, restless nature might say to Moses, or to
Peter, Have you nothing new to tell us ? Why are
you perpetually dwelling on the same old themes ?
We know all you have got to say; we have heard it
again and again. Why not strike out into some new
field of thought ? Would it not be well to try and
keep abreast of the science of the day? If we keep
perpetually moping over those antiquated themes,
we shall be left stranded on the bank, while the
stream of civilization rushes on. Pray give us
something new.

Thus might the poor unbelieving mind — the
worldly heart reason, but faith knows the answer
to all such miserable suggestions. We can well
believe that both Moses and Peter would have made
short work with all such reasonings. And so should
we. We know whence they emanate, whither they
tend, and what they are worth; and we should have,
if not on our lips, at least deep down in our hearts,
a ready answer—an answer perfectly satisfactory to
us, however contemptible it may seem to the men of
this world. Could a true Israelite ever tire of hearing of what the Lord had done for him, in Egypt, in
the Red Sea, and in the wilderness ? Never ! Such
themes would be ever fresh, ever welcome to his
heart. And just so with the Christian. Can he ever
tire of the cross and all the grand and glorious
realities that cluster around it ? can he ever tire of
Christ, His peerless glories and unsearchable riches,
His Person, His work, His offices ? Never ! No,

never, throughout the bright ages of eternity. Does he crave any thing new? Can science improve upon Christ? can human learning add aught to the great mystery of godliness, which has for its foundation God manifest in the flesh, and for its top-stone a Man glorified in heaven? can we ever get beyond this? No, reader, we could not if we would, and we would not if we could.

And even were we, for a moment, to take a lower range, and look at the works of God in creation; do we ever tire of the sun? He is not new; he has been pouring his beams upon this world for well-nigh six thousand years, and yet those beams are as fresh and as welcome to-day as they were when first created. Do we ever tire of the sea? It is not new; its tide has been ebbing and flowing for nearly six thousand years, but its waves are as fresh and as welcome on our shores as ever. True, the sun is often too dazzling to man's feeble vision, and the sea often swallows up, in a moment, man's boasted works; but yet the sun and the sea never lose their power, their freshness, their charm. Do we ever tire of the dew-drops that fall in refreshing virtue upon our gardens and fields? do we ever tire of the perfume that emanates from our hedge-rows? do we ever tire of the notes of the nightingale and the thrush? And what are all these when compared with the glories which cluster around the Person and the cross of Christ? what are they when put in contrast with the grand realities of that eternity which is before us?

Reader, let us beware how we listen to such sug-gestions, whether they come from without or spring from the depths of our own evil hearts, lest we be found, like Israel after the flesh, loathing the heav-enly Manna and despising the pleasant land; or like Demas, who forsook the blessed apostle, having loved this present age; or like those of whom we read in the sixth of John, who, offended by our Lord's close and pointed teaching, "went back, and walked no more with Him." May the Lord keep our hearts true to Himself, and fresh and fervent in His blessed cause, till He come.

CHAPTER IX.

"HEAR, O Israel: Thou art to pass over Jordan this day, to go in to possess nations greater and mightier than thyself, cities great and fenced up to heaven, a people great and tall, the children of the Anakims, whom thou knowest, and of whom thou hast heard say, 'Who can stand before the children of Anak!'" (Ver. 1, 2.)

This chapter opens with the same grand Deuter-onomic sentence, "*Hear*, O Israel." This, we may say, is the key-note of this most blessed book, and especially of those opening discourses which have been engaging our attention. But the chapter which now lies open before us presents subjects of im-mense weight and importance. In the first place,

the lawgiver sets before the congregation, in terms
of deep solemnity, that which lay before them in
their entrance upon the land. He does not hide
from them the fact that there were serious difficulties
and formidable enemies to be encountered. This he
does, we need hardly say, not to discourage their
hearts, but that they might be forewarned, fore-
armed, and prepared. What that preparation was
we shall see presently; but the faithful servant of
God felt the rightness, yea, the urgent need of putting the true state of the case before his brethren.

There are two ways of looking at difficulties; we
may look at them from a human stand-point, or from
a divine one; we may look at them in a spirit of
unbelief, or we may look at them in the calmness
and quietness of confidence in the living God. We
have an instance of the former in the report of the
unbelieving spies in Numbers xiii; we have an instance of the latter in the opening of our present
chapter.

It is not the province, nor the path, of faith to deny
that there are difficulties to be encountered by the
people of God; it would be the height of folly to do
so, inasmuch as there are difficulties, and it would be
but fool-hardiness, fanaticism, or fleshly enthusiasm
to deny it. It is always well for people to know
what they are about, and not to rush blindly into a
path for which they are not prepared. An unbelieving sluggard may say, There is a lion in the
way; a blind enthusiast may say, There is no such
thing; the true man of faith will say, Though there

were a thousand lions in the way, God can **soon** dispose of them.

But, as a great practical principle of general application, it is very important for all the Lord's people to consider, deeply and calmly, what they are about, ere they enter upon any particular path of service or line of action. If this were more attended to, we should not witness so many moral and spiritual wrecks around us. What mean those most solemn, searching, and testing words addressed by our blessed Lord to the multitudes that thronged around Him in Luke xiv?—"He turned and said to them, 'If any man *come to Me*, and hate not his father and mother, his wife and children, and brethren and sisters, yea, and his own life also, he cannot be My disciple. And whosoever doth not bear his cross, and come after Me, cannot be My disciple. For which of you, intending to build a tower, sitteth not down first, and counteth the cost, whether he have sufficient to finish it? lest haply, after he hath laid the foundation, and is not able to finish it, all that behold it begin to mock him, saying, This man began to build, and was not able to finish.'" (Ver. 26–30.)

These are solemn and seasonable words for the heart. How many unfinished buildings meet our view as we look forth over the wide field of Christian profession, giving sad occasion to the beholders for mockery! How many set out upon a path of discipleship under some sudden impulse, or under the pressure of mere human influence, without a proper understanding, or a due consideration of all that is involved; and then when difficulties arise, when trials come, when the path is found to be narrow, rough, lonely, unpopular, they give it up, thus proving that they had never really counted the cost, never taken the path in communion with God, never understood what they were doing.

Now, such cases are very sorrowful; they bring great reproach on the cause of Christ, give occasion to the adversary to blaspheme, and greatly dishearten those who care for the glory of God and the good of souls. Better far not to take the ground at all than, having taken it, to abandon it in dark unbelief and worldly-mindedness.

Hence, therefore, we can perceive the wisdom and faithfulness of the opening words of our chapter. Moses tells the people plainly what was before them; not, surely, to discourage them, but to preserve them from self-confidence, which is sure to give way in the moment of trial, and to cast them upon the living God, who never fails a trusting heart.

"Understand therefore this day, that the Lord thy God is He which goeth over before thee; as a consuming fire He shall destroy them, and He shall bring them down before thy face: so shalt thou drive them out, and destroy them quickly, as the Lord hath said unto thee."

Here, then, is the divine answer to all difficulties, be they ever so formidable. What were mighty nations, great cities, fenced walls, in the presence of Jehovah? Simply as chaff before the whirlwind.

"If God be for us, who can be against us?" The very things which scare and stumble the coward heart afford an occasion for the display of God's power, and the magnificent triumphs of faith. Faith says, Grant me but this, that God is before me and with me, and I can go any where. Thus the only thing in all this world that really glorifies God is the faith that can trust Him and use Him and praise Him; and inasmuch as faith is the only thing that glorifies God, so is it the only thing that gives man his proper place, even the place of complete dependence upon God, and this insures victory and inspires praise—unceasing praise.

But we must never forget that there is moral danger in the very moment of victory—danger arising out of what we are in ourselves. There is the danger of self-gratulation—a terrible snare to us poor mortals. In the hour of conflict we feel our weakness, our nothingness, our need. This is good and morally safe. It is well to be brought down to the very bottom of self and all that pertains to it, for there we find God, in all the fullness and blessedness of what He is, and this is sure and certain victory and consequent praise.

But our treacherous and deceitful hearts are prone to forget whence the strength and victory come; hence the moral force, value, and seasonableness of the following admonitory words addressed by the faithful minister of God to the hearts and consciences of his brethren: "Speak not thou *in thine heart*"—here is where the mischief always begins—

"after that the Lord hath cast them out from before thee, saying, For my righteousness the Lord hath brought me in to possess this land; but for the wickedness of these nations the Lord doth drive them out from before thee."

Alas! what materials there are in us! what ignorance of our own hearts! what a shallow sense of the real character of our ways! How terrible to think that we are capable of saying in our hearts such words as, "For my righteousness"! Yes, reader, we are verily capable of such egregious folly; for as Israel was capable of it, so are we, inasmuch as we are made of the very same material; and that they were capable of it is evident from the fact of their being warned against it; for, most assuredly, the Spirit of God does not warn against phantom dangers or imaginary temptations. We are verily capable of turning the actings of God on our behalf into an occasion of self-complacency; instead of seeing in those gracious actings a ground for heartfelt praise to God, we use them as a ground for self-exaltation.

Hence, therefore, we would do well to ponder the words of faithful admonition addressed by Moses to the hearts and consciences of the people; they furnish a very wholesome antidote for the self-righteousness so natural to us as well as to Israel. "Not for thy righteousness, or for the uprightness of thine heart, dost thou go to possess their land; but for the wickedness of those nations the Lord thy God doth drive them out from before thee, and that

He may perform the word which the Lord sware unto thy fathers, Abraham, Isaac, and Jacob. Understand, therefore, that the Lord giveth thee not this good land to possess it for thy righteousness; for thou art a stiff-necked people. Remember, and forget not, how thou provokedst the Lord thy God to wrath in the wilderness; from the day that thou didst depart out of the land of Egypt, until ye came unto this place, ye have been rebellious against the Lord.'' (Ver. 5–7.)

This paragraph sets forth two great principles, which, if fully laid hold of, must put the heart into a right moral attitude. In the first place, the people were reminded that their possession of the land of Canaan was simply in pursuance of God's promise to their fathers. This was placing the matter on the most solid basis—a basis which nothing could ever disturb.

As to the seven nations which were to be dispossessed, it was on the ground of their wickedness that God, in the exercise of His righteous government, was about to drive them out. Every landlord has a perfect right to eject bad tenants; and the nations of Canaan had not only failed to pay their rent, as we say, but they had injured and defiled the property to such an extent that God could no longer endure them, and therefore He was going to drive them out, irrespective altogether of the incoming tenants. Whoever was going to get possession of the property, these dreadful tenants must be evicted. The iniquity of the Amorites had reached its highest point, and nothing remained but that judgment should take its course. Men might argue and reason as to the moral fitness and consistency of a benevolent Being unroofing the houses of thousands of families and putting the occupants to the sword, but we may depend upon it the government of God will make very short work with all such arguments. God, blessed forever be His holy name, knows how to manage His own affairs, and that, too, without asking man's opinion. He had borne with the wickedness of the seven nations to such a degree that it had become absolutely insufferable; the very land itself could not bear it. Any further exercise of forbearance would have been a sanction of the most terrible abominations; and this, of course, was a moral impossibility. The glory of God absolutely demanded the expulsion of the Canaanites.

Yes; and we may add, the glory of God demanded the introduction of the seed of Abraham into possession of the property, to hold as tenants forever under the Lord God Almighty—the Most High God, Possessor of heaven and earth. Thus the matter stood for Israel, had they but seen it. Their possession of the land of promise and the maintenance of the divine glory were so bound up together that one could not be touched without touching the other. God had promised to give the land of Canaan to the seed of Abraham as an everlasting possession. Had He not a right to do so? Will infidels question God's right to do as He will with His own? Will they refuse to the Creator and

Governor of the universe a right which they claim for themselves? The land was Jehovah's, and He gave it to Abraham His friend forever; and although this was true, yet were not the Canaanites disturbed in their tenure of the property until their wickedness had become positively unbearable.

Thus we see that in the matter both of the outgoing and incoming tenants the glory of God was involved. That glory demanded that the Canaanites should be expelled, because of their ways; and that glory demanded that Israel should be put in possession, because of the promise to Abraham, Isaac, and Jacob.

But, in the second place, Israel had no ground for self-complacency, as Moses most plainly and faithfully instructs them. He rehearses in their ears, in the most touching and impressive manner, all the leading scenes of their history from Horeb to Kadesh-barnea; he refers to the golden calf, to the broken tables of the covenant, to Taberah and Massah, and Kibroth-hattaavah; and sums all up, at verse 24, with these pungent, humbling words, "Ye have been rebellious against the Lord from the day that I knew you."

This was plain dealing with heart and conscience. The solemn review of their whole career was eminently calculated to correct all false notions about themselves; every scene and circumstance in their entire history, if viewed from a proper stand-point, only brought to light the humbling fact of what they were, and how near they had been, again and again, to utter destruction. With what stunning force must the following words have fallen upon their ears!— "And the Lord said unto me, 'Arise, get thee down quickly from hence, for *thy* people which *thou* hast brought forth out of Egypt have corrupted themselves; they are quickly turned aside out of the way which I commanded them; they have made them a molten image.' Furthermore, the Lord spake unto me, saying, 'I have seen this people, and behold, it is a stiff-necked people; *let Me alone, that I may destroy* them, and blot out their name from under heaven; and I will make of thee a nation mightier and greater than they.'" (Ver. 12–14.)

How withering was all this to their natural vanity, pride, and self-righteousness! How should their hearts have been moved to their very deepest depths by those tremendous words, "Let Me alone, that I may destroy them"! How solemn to reflect upon the fact which these words revealed—their appalling nearness to national ruin and destruction! How ignorant they had been of all that passed between Jehovah and Moses on the top of Mount Horeb! They had been on the very brink of an awful precipice. Another moment might have dashed them over. The intercession of Moses had saved them, the very man whom they had accused of taking too much upon him. Alas! how they had mistaken and misjudged him! How utterly astray they had been in all their thoughts! Why, the very man whom they had accused of self-seeking and desiring to make himself altogether a prince over them, had actually refused a divinely given opportunity of becoming the head of a greater and mightier nation than they! Yes, and this same man had earnestly requested that if they were not to be forgiven and brought into the land, his name might be blotted out of the book.

How wonderful was all this! What a turning of the tables upon them! How exceedingly small they must have felt, in view of all these wonderful facts! Surely, as they reviewed all these things, they might well see the utter folly of the words, "For my righteousness the Lord hath brought me in to possess this land." How could the makers of a molten image use such language! Ought they not rather to see and feel and own themselves to be no better than the nations that were about to be driven out from before them? For what had made them to differ? The sovereign mercy and electing love of their covenant-God. And to what did they owe their deliverance out of Egypt, their sustenance in the wilderness, and their entrance into the land? Simply to the eternal stability of the covenant made with their fathers, "a covenant ordered in all things and sure," a covenant ratified and established by the blood of the Lamb, in virtue of which all Israel shall yet be saved and blessed in their own land.

But we must now quote for the reader the splendid paragraph with which our chapter closes—a paragraph eminently fitted to open Israel's eyes to the utter folly of all their thoughts respecting Moses, their thoughts respecting themselves, and their thoughts respecting that blessed One who had so marvelously borne with all their dark unbelief and daring rebellion.

"Thus I fell down before the Lord forty days and forty nights, as I fell down at the first; because the Lord had said He would destroy you. I prayed therefore unto the Lord, and said, 'O Lord God, destroy not *Thy people* and *Thine inheritance*, which Thou hast redeemed through Thy greatness, which Thou hast brought forth out of Egypt with a mighty hand. Remember thy servants, Abraham, Isaac, and Jacob; *look not unto the stubbornness of this people, nor to their wickedness, nor to their sin;* lest the land whence thou broughtest us out say, Because the Lord was not able to bring them into the land which He promised them, and because He hated them, He hath brought them out to slay them in the wilderness. *Yet they are Thy people, and Thine inheritance*, which Thou broughtest out by Thy mighty power, and by Thy stretched-out arm.'"

What marvelous words are these to be addressed by a human being to the living God! What powerful pleadings for Israel! what self-renunciation! Moses refuses the offered dignity of being the founder of a greater and mightier nation than Israel. He only desires that Jehovah should be glorified, and Israel pardoned, blessed, and brought into the promised land. He could not endure the thought of any reproach being brought upon that glorious Name so dear to his heart, neither could he bear to witness Israel's destruction. These were the two things he dreaded; and as to his own exaltation, it was just the thing about which he cared nothing at all. This beloved and honored servant cared *only* for the glory of God and the salvation of His people; and as to himself, his hopes, his interests, his all, he could rest, with perfect composure, in the assurance that his individual blessing and the divine glory were bound together by a link which could never be snapped.

And, oh, how grateful must all this have been to the heart of God! How refreshing to His spirit were those earnest, loving pleadings of His servant! How much more in harmony with His mind than the intercession of Elias against Israel hundreds of years afterward! How they remind us of the blessed ministry of our great High-Priest, who ever liveth to make intercession for His people, and whose active intervention on our behalf never ceases for a single moment!

And then how very touching and beautiful to mark the way in which Moses insists upon the fact that the people were Jehovah's inheritance, and that He had brought them up out of Egypt. The Lord had said, "*Thy* people which *thou* hast brought forth out of Egypt;" but Moses says, "They are *Thy* people, and *Thine* inheritance, which *Thou* broughtest out." This is perfectly exquisite. Indeed this whole scene is full of profound interest.

CHAPTER X

" AT that time the Lord said unto me, 'Hew thee two tables of stone like unto the first, and come up unto Me into the mount, and make thee an ark of wood; and I will write on the tables the words that were in the first tables which thou brakest, and thou shalt put them in the ark.' And I made an ark of shittim wood, and hewed two tables of stone like unto the first, and went up into the mount, having the two tables in mine hand. And He wrote on the tables, according to the first writing, the ten commandments, which the Lord spake unto you in the mount out of the midst of the fire, in the day of the assembly; and the Lord gave them unto me. And I turned myself and came down from the mount, and put the tables in the ark which I had made; and there they be, as the Lord commanded me." (Ver. 1–5.)

The beloved and revered servant of God seemed never to weary of rehearsing in the ears of the people the interesting, momentous, and significant sentences of the past. To him they were ever fresh, ever precious. His heart delighted in them. They could never lose their charm in his eyes; he found in them an exhaustless treasury for his own heart, and a mighty moral lever wherewith to move the heart of Israel.

We are constantly reminded, in these powerful

and deeply affecting addresses, of the inspired apostle's words to his beloved Philippians—"To write the same things to you, to me is not grievous, but for you it is safe." The poor, restless, fickle, vagrant heart might long for some new theme ; but the faithful apostle found his deep and unfailing delight in unfolding and dwelling upon those precious subjects which clustered, in rich luxuriance, around the Person and the cross of his adorable Lord and Saviour Jesus Christ. He had found in Christ all he needed for time and eternity. The glory of His Person had completely eclipsed all the glories of earth and of nature. He could say, "What things were *gain to me*, those I counted *loss for Christ*. Yea, doubtless, and I count all things but loss, for the excellency of the knowledge of Christ Jesus my Lord ; for whom I have suffered the loss of all things, and do count them but dung, that I may win Christ." (Phil. iii. 7, 8.)

This is the language of a true Christian, of one who had found a perfectly absorbing and commanding object in Christ. What could the world offer to such an one ? what could it do for him ? Did he want its riches, its honors, its distinctions, its pleasures ? He counted them all as dung. How was this ? Because he had found Christ ; he had seen an object in Him which so riveted his heart that to win Him and know more of Him and be found in Him was the one ruling desire of his soul. If any one had talked to Paul about something new, what would have been his answer ? If any one had sug-

gested to him the thought of getting on in the world
or of seeking to make money, what would have been
his reply? Simply this: I have found my ALL in
Christ; I want no more. I have found in Him "*unsearchable* riches"—"*durable* riches and righteousness." In Him are hid *all* the treasures of wisdom
and knowledge. What do I want of this world's
riches, its wisdom, or its learning? These things all
pass away like the vapors of the morning; and even
while they last, are wholly inadequate to satisfy the
desires and aspirations of an immortal spirit. Christ
is an eternal object, heaven's centre, the delight of
the heart of God; He shall satisfy me throughout
the countless ages of that bright eternity which is
before me; and surely, if He can satisfy me forever,
He can satisfy me now. Shall I turn to the wretched
rubbish of this world—its pursuits, its pleasures, its
amusements, its theatres, its concerts, its riches, or
its honors to supplement my portion in Christ? God
forbid! All such things would be simply an intolerable nuisance to me. Christ is my all and in all,
now and forever.

Such, we may well believe, would have been the
distinctly pronounced reply of the blessed apostle;
such was the distinct reply of his whole life; and
such, beloved Christian reader, should be ours also.
How truly deplorable, how deeply humbling, to find
a Christian turning to the world for enjoyment, rec-
reation, or pastime! It simply proves that he has
not found a satisfying portion in Christ. We may
set it down as a fixed principle that the heart which

is filled with Christ has no room for aught beside. It is not a question of the right or the wrong of things; the heart does not want them, would not have them; it has found its present and everlasting portion and rest in that blessed One that fills the heart of God, and will fill the vast universe with the beams of His glory throughout the everlasting ages.

We have been led into the foregoing line of thought in connection with the interesting fact of Moses' unwearied rehearsal of all the grand events in Israel's marvelous history from Egypt to the borders of the promised land. To him they furnished a perpetual feast; and he not only found his own deep, personal delight in dwelling upon them, but he also felt the immense importance of unfolding them before the whole congregation. To him, most surely, it was not grievous, but for them it was safe. How delightful for him, and how good and needful for them, to dwell upon the facts connected with the two sets of tables—the first set smashed to atoms, at the foot of the mountain, and the second set inclosed in the ark.

What human language could possibly unfold the deep significance and moral weight of such facts as these? Those broken tables! how impressive! how pregnant with wholesome instruction for the people! how powerfully suggestive! Will any one presume to say that we have here a mere barren repetition of the facts recorded in Exodus? Certainly no one who reverently believes in the divine inspiration of the Pentateuch.

No, reader, the tenth of Deuteronomy fills a niche and does a work entirely its own. In it the lawgiver holds up to the hearts of the people past scenes and circumstances in such a way as to rivet them upon the very tablets of the soul. He allows them to hear the conversation between Jehovah and himself; he tells them what took place during those mysterious forty days upon that cloud-capped mountain; he lets them hear Jehovah's reference to the broken tables—the apt and forcible expression of the utter worthlessness of man's covenant. For why were those tables broken? Because they had shamefully failed. Those shattered fragments told the humiliating tale of their hopeless ruin on the ground of the law. All was gone. Such was the obvious meaning of the fact. It was striking, impressive, unmistakable. Like a broken pillar over a grave, which tells at a glance that the prop and stay of the family lies mouldering beneath. There is no need of any inscription, for no human language could speak with such eloquence to the heart as that most expressive emblem. So the broken tables were calculated to convey to the heart of Israel the tremendous fact that, so far as their covenant was concerned, they were utterly ruined—hopelessly undone; they were complete bankrupts on the score of righteousness.

But then that second set of tables! What of them? Thank God, they tell a different tale altogether. They were not broken. God took care of them. "I turned myself and came down from

the mount, and put the tables in the ark which I
had made; and *there they be*, as the Lord commanded me.''

Blessed fact! "There they be." Yes, covered
up in that ark which spoke of Christ, that blessed
One who magnified the law and made it honorable,
who established every jot and tittle of it, to the glory
of God and the everlasting blessing of His people.
Thus, while the broken fragments of the first tables
told the sad and humbling tale of Israel's utter failure and ruin, the second tables, shut up intact in the
ark, set forth the glorious truth that Christ is the
end of the law for righteousness to every one that
believeth, to the Jew first, and also to the Gentile.

We do not, of course, mean to say that Israel
understood the deep meaning and far-reaching application of those wonderful facts which Moses re-
hearsed in their ears. As a nation, they certainly
did not then, though, through the sovereign mercy
of God, they will by and by. Individuals may, and
doubtless did, enter into somewhat of their significance. This is not now the question. It is for us
to see and make our own of the precious truth set
forth in those two sets of tables, namely, the failure
of every thing in the hands of man, and the eternal
stability of God's covenant of grace, ratified by the
blood of Christ, and to be displayed in all its glorious results, in the kingdom, by and by, when the
Son of David shall reign from sea to sea, and from
the river to the ends of the earth; when the seed of
Abraham shall possess, according to the divine gift,

the land of promise; and when all the nations of the earth shall rejoice under the beneficent reign of the Prince of peace.

Bright and glorious prospect for the now desolate land of Israel, and this groaning earth of ours! The King of righteousness and peace will then have it all His own way. All evil will be put down with a powerful hand. There will be no weakness in that government; no rebel tongue will be permitted to prate, in accents of insolent sedition, against the decrees and enactments thereof; no rude and sense-less demagogue will be allowed to disturb the peace of the people, or to insult the majesty of the throne. Every abuse will be put down, every disturbing ele-ment will be neutralized, every stumbling-block will be removed, and every root of bitterness eradicated. The poor and the needy shall be well looked after, yea, all shall be divinely attended to; toil, sorrow, poverty, and desolation shall be unknown; the wil-derness and the solitary place shall be glad, and the desert shall rejoice and blossom as the rose. "Be-hold a king shall reign in righteousness, and princes shall rule in judgment. And a man shall be as a hiding-place from the wind, and a covert from the tempest; as rivers of water in a dry place, as the shadow of a great rock in a weary land."

Reader, what glorious scenes are yet to be enacted in this poor sin-stricken, Satan-enslaved, sorrowful world of ours! How refreshing to think of them! What a relief to the heart amid all the mental misery, the moral degradation, and physical wretchedness

exhibited around us on every side! Thank God, the
day is rapidly approaching when the prince of this
world shall be hurled from his throne and consigned
to the bottomless pit, and the Prince of heaven, the
glorious Emmanuel shall stretch forth His blessed
sceptre over the wide universe of God, and heaven
and earth shall bask in the sunlight of His royal
countenance. Well may we cry out, O Lord, hasten
the time!

"And the children of Israel took their journey
from Beeroth of the children of Jaakan to Mosera;
there Aaron died, and there he was buried; and
Eleazar his son ministered in the priest's office in his
stead. From thence they journeyed unto Gudgodah:
and from Gudgodah to Jotbath, a land of rivers of
waters. At that time the Lord separated the tribe
of Levi, to bear the ark of the covenant of the Lord,
to stand before the Lord to minister unto Him, and
to bless in His name, unto this day. Wherefore
Levi hath no part nor inheritance with his brethren;
the Lord is His inheritance, according as the Lord
thy God promised him."

The reader must not allow his mind to be disturbed by any question of historical sequence in the
foregoing passage. It is simply a parenthesis in
which the lawgiver groups together, in a very striking and forcible manner, circumstances culled, with
holy skill, from the history of the people, illustrative
at once of the government and grace of God. The
death of Aaron exhibits the former; the election
and elevation of Levi presents the latter. Both are

placed together, not with a view to chronology, but for the grand moral end which was ever present to the mind of the lawgiver—an end which lies far away beyond the range of infidel reason, but which commends itself to the heart and understanding of the devout student of Scripture.

How utterly contemptible are the quibbles of the infidel when looked at in the brilliant light of divine inspiration! How miserable the condition of a mind which can occupy itself with chronological hair-splittings in order, if possible, to find a flaw in the divine Volume, instead of grasping the real aim and object of the inspired writer!

But why does Moses bring in, in this parenthetical and apparently abrupt manner, those two special events in Israel's history? Simply to move the heart of the people toward the one grand point of obedience. To this end he culls and groups according to the wisdom given unto him. Do we expect to find in this divinely taught servant of God the petty preciseness of a mere copyist? Infidels may affect to do so, but true Christians know better. A mere scribe could copy events in their chronological order; a true prophet will bring those events to bear, in a moral way, upon the heart and conscience. Thus, while the poor deluded infidel is groping amid the shadows of his own creation, the pious student delights himself in the moral glories of that peerless Volume which stands like a rock, against which the waves of infidel thought dash themselves with contemptible impotency.

We do not attempt to dwell upon the circumstances referred to in the above parenthesis; they have been gone into elsewhere, and therefore we only feel it needful, in this place, to point out to the reader what we may venture to call the Deuteronomic bearing of the facts—the use which the lawgiver makes of them to strengthen the foundation of his final appeal to the heart and conscience of the people, to give pungency and power to his exhortation, as he urged upon them the absolute necessity of unqualified obedience to the statutes and judgments of their covenant-God. Such was his reason for referring to the solemn fact of the death of Aaron. They were to remember that notwithstanding Aaron's high position as the high-priest of Israel, yet he was stripped of his robes and deprived of his life for disobedience to the word of Jehovah. How important, then, that they should take heed to themselves! The government of God was not to be trifled with, and the very fact of Aaron's elevation only rendered it all the more needful that his sin should be dealt with, in order that others might fear.

And then they were to remember the Lord's dealings with Levi, in which grace shines with such marvelous lustre. The fierce, cruel, self-willed Levi was taken up from the depths of his moral ruin and brought nigh to God, "to bear the ark of the covenant of the Lord, to stand before the Lord, to minister unto Him, and to bless in His name."

But why should this account of Levi be coupled with the death of Aaron? Simply to set forth the blessed consequences of obedience. If the death of Aaron displayed the awful result of disobedience, the elevation of Levi illustrates the precious fruit of obedience. Hear what the prophet Malachi says on this point.—"And ye shall know that I have sent this *commandment* unto you, that My covenant might be with Levi, saith the Lord of hosts. My covenant was with him of life and peace; and *I gave them to him for the fear wherewith he feared Me, and was afraid before My name.* The law of truth was in his mouth, and iniquity was not found in his lips; he walked with Me in peace and equity, and did turn many away from iniquity." (Chap. ii. 4–6.)

This is a very remarkable passage, and throws much light upon the subject now before us. It tells us distinctly that Jehovah gave His covenant of life and peace to Levi "for the fear wherewith he feared" Him on the terrible occasion of the golden calf which Aaron (himself a Levite of the very highest order) made. Why was Aaron judged? Because of his rebellion at the waters of Meribah. (Num. xx. 24.) Why was Levi blessed? Because of his reverent obedience at the foot of Mount Horeb. (Ex. xxxii.) Why are both grouped together in Deuteronomy x? In order to impress upon the heart and conscience of the congregation the urgent necessity of implicit obedience to the commandments of their covenant-God. How perfect is Scripture in all its parts! how beautifully it hangs together! and how plain it is to the devout reader that the lovely book of Deuteronomy has its own divine niche to fill, its own distinctive work to do, its own appointed sphere, scope, and object! How manifest it is that the fifth division of the Pentateuch is neither a contradiction nor a repetition, but a divine application of its divinely inspired predecessors! And, finally, we cannot help adding, how convincing the evidence that infidel writers know neither what they say nor whereof they affirm, when they dare to insult the oracles of God—yea, that they greatly err, not knowing the Scriptures, nor the power of God!*

At verse 10 of our chapter, Moses returns to the subject of his discourse. "And I stayed in the mount, according to the first time, forty days and forty nights; and the Lord hearkened unto me at that time also, and the Lord would not destroy thee. And the Lord said unto me, 'Arise, take thy journey before the people, that they may go in and possess the land which I sware unto their fathers to give unto them.'"

---

*We have, in human writings, numerous examples of the same thing that infidels object to in Deuteronomy x. 6-9. Suppose a man is anxious to call the attention of the English nation to some great principle of political economy, or some matter of national importance; he does not hesitate to select facts however widely separated on the page of history, and group them together in order to illustrate his subject. Do infidels object to this? No; not when found in the writings of men. It is only when it occurs in Scripture, because they hate the Word of God, and cannot bear the idea that He should give to His creatures a book-revelation of His mind. Blessed be His name, He has given it notwithstanding, and we have it in all its infinite preciousness and divine authority, for the comfort of our hearts and the guidance of our path amid all the darkness and confusion of this scene through which we are passing home to glory.

Jehovah would accomplish His promise to the fathers spite of every hindrance. He would put Israel in full possession of the land concerning which He had sworn to Abraham, Isaac, and Jacob, to give it to their seed for an everlasting inheritance.

"And now, Israel, what doth the Lord *thy* God require of thee, but to fear the Lord thy God, to walk in *all His ways*, and to love Him, and to serve the Lord *thy* God with all thy heart and with all thy soul. To keep the commandments of the Lord, and His statutes, which I command thee this day, *for thy good.*" It was all for their real good—their deep, full blessing to walk in the way of the divine commandments. The path of whole-hearted obedience is the only path of true happiness; and, blessed be God, this path can always be trodden by those who love the Lord.

This is an unspeakable comfort, at all times. God has given us His precious Word, the perfect revelation of His mind; and He has given us what Israel had not, even His Holy Spirit to dwell in us, whereby we can understand and appreciate His Word. Hence our obligations are vastly higher than were Israel's. We are bound to a life of obedience by every argument that could be brought to bear on the heart and understanding.

And surely it is for our good to be obedient. There is indeed "great reward" in keeping the commandments of our loving Father. Every thought of Him and of His gracious ways, every reference to His marvelous dealings with us—His loving

ministry, His tender care, His thoughtful love—all
should bind our hearts in affectionate devotion to
Him, and quicken our steps in treading the path of
loving obedience to Him. Wherever we turn our
eyes we are met by the most powerful evidences of
His claim upon our heart's affections and upon all
the energies of our ransomed being; and, blessed
be His name, the more fully we are enabled, by His
grace, to respond to His most precious claims, the
brighter and happier our path must be. There is
nothing in all this world more deeply blessed than
the path and portion of an obedient soul. "Great
peace have they that love Thy law, and nothing shall
offend them." The lowly disciple who finds his
meat and his drink in doing the will of his beloved
Lord and Master, possesses a peace which the
world can neither give nor take away. True, he may
be misunderstood and misinterpreted; he may be
dubbed narrow and bigoted, and such like; but
none of these things move him. One approving
smile from his Lord is more than ample recompense
for all the reproach that men can heap upon him.
He knows how to estimate at their proper worth the
thoughts of men; they are to him as the chaff which
the wind driveth away. The deep utterance of his
heart, as he moves steadily along the sacred path of
obedience, is,—

> "Let me my feebleness recline
> On that eternal love of Thine,
> And human thoughts forget;
> Childlike attend what Thou wilt say,

Go forth and serve Thee while 'tis day,
Nor leave Thy sweet retreat."

In the closing verses of our chapter, the lawgiver seems to rise higher and higher in his presentation of moral motives for obedience, and to come closer and closer to the hearts of the people. "Behold," he says, "the heaven and the heaven of heavens is the Lord's thy God, the earth also, with all that therein is. Only the Lord had a delight in thy fathers to love them, and He chose their seed after them, even you above all people, as it is this day." What a marvelous privilege to be chosen and loved by the Possessor of heaven and earth! what an honor to be called to serve and obey Him! Surely nothing in all this world could be higher or better. To be identified and associated with the Most High God, to have His name called upon them, to be His peculiar people, His special possession, the people of His choice, to be set apart from all the nations of the earth to be the servants of Jehovah and His witnesses. What, we may ask, could exceed this, except it be that to which the Church of God and the individual believer are called?

Assuredly, our privileges are higher, inasmuch as we know God in a higher, deeper, nearer, more intimate manner than the nation of Israel ever did. We know Him as the God and Father of the Lord Jesus Christ, and as our God and Father. We have the Holy Ghost dwelling in us, shedding abroad the love of God in our hearts, and leading us to cry, Abba, Father. All this is far beyond any thing that

7

God's earthly people ever knew or could know; and, inasmuch as our privileges are higher, His claims upon our hearty and unreserved obedience are also higher. Every appeal to the heart of Israel should come home with augmented force to our hearts, beloved Christian reader; every exhortation addressed to them should speak far more powerfully to us. We occupy the very highest ground on which any creature could stand. Neither the seed of Abraham on earth nor the angels of God in heaven could say what we can say or know what we know. We are linked and eternally associated with the risen and glorified Son of God. We can adopt as our own the wondrous language of 1 John iv. 17, and say, "As He is, so are we in this world." What can exceed this, as to privilege and dignity? Surely nothing, save to be, in body, soul, and spirit, conformed to His adorable image, as we shall be ere long, through the abounding grace of God.

Well then, let us ever bear in mind—yea, let us have it deep, deep down in our hearts, that according to our privileges are our obligations. Let us not refuse the wholesome word "obligation," as though it had a legal ring about it. Far from it! it would be utterly impossible to conceive any thing further removed from all thought of legality than the obligations which flow out of the Christian's position. It is a very serious mistake to be continually raising the cry of "Legal! legal!" whenever the holy responsibilities of our position are pressed upon us. We believe that every truly pious Christian will delight in all the appeals and exhortations which the Holy Ghost addresses to us as to our obligations, seeing they are all grounded upon privileges conferred upon us by the sovereign grace of God, through the precious blood of Christ, and made good to us by the mighty ministry of the Holy Ghost.

But let us hearken still further to the stirring appeals of Moses. They are truly profitable for us, with all our higher light, knowledge, and privilege.

"Circumcise therefore *the foreskin of your heart*, and be no more stiff-necked. For the Lord your God is God of gods, and Lord of lords, a great God, a mighty, and a terrible, which regardeth not persons, nor taketh reward. He doth execute the judgment of the fatherless and widow, and loveth the stranger, in giving him food and raiment."

Here, Moses speaks not merely of God's doings and dealings and ways, but of Himself, of what He is. He is high over all, the great, the mighty, and the terrible. But He has a heart for the widow and the fatherless—those helpless objects deprived of all earthly and natural props, the poor bereaved and broken-hearted widow, and the desolate orphan. God thinks of and cares for such in a very special way; they have a claim upon His loving heart and mighty hand. "A father of the fatherless, and a Judge of the widow is God in His holy habitation." "She that is a widow indeed and desolate trusteth in God, and continueth in supplications and prayers night and day." "Leave thy fatherless children, I will preserve them alive; and let thy widows trust in Me."

What a rich provision is here for widows and orphans! How wondrous God's care of such! How many widows are much better off than when they had their husbands! how many orphans are better cared and provided for than when they had their parents! God looks after them! This is enough. Thousands of husbands and thousands of parents are worse, by far, than none; but God never fails those who are cast upon Him. He is ever true to His own name, whatever relationship He takes. Let all widows and orphans remember this for their comfort and encouragement.

And then the poor stranger! He is not forgotten. "He loveth the stranger, in giving him food and raiment." How precious is this! Our God cares for all those who are bereft of earthly props, human hopes, and creature-confidences. All such have a special claim upon Him, to which He will most surely respond according to all the love of His heart. The widow, the fatherless, and the stranger are the special objects of His tender care, and all such have but to look to Him, and draw upon His exhaustless resources in all their varied need.

But then He must be known in order to be trusted. "They that know Thy name will put their trust in Thee; for Thou, Lord, hast not forsaken them that seek Thee." Those who do not know God would vastly prefer an insurance policy or a government annuity to His promise; but the true believer finds in that promise the unfailing stay of his heart, because he knows and trusts and loves the Promiser. He delights in the thought of being absolutely shut up to God—wholly dependent upon Him. He would not, for worlds, be in any other position. The very thing which would almost drive an unbeliever out of his senses is to the Christian—the man of faith, the very deepest joy of his heart. The language of such an one will ever be, "My soul, wait thou *only* upon God; for my expectation is from Him. He *only* is my rock." Blessed position! precious portion! May the reader know it as a divine reality, a living power, in his heart, by the mighty ministry of the Holy Ghost. Then will he be able to sit loose to earthly things. He will be able to tell the world that he is independent of it, having found all he wants, for time and eternity, in the living God and His Christ.

> "Thou, O Christ, art all I want;
> More than all in Thee I find."

But let us specially note the provision which God makes for the stranger. It is very simple—"food and raiment." This is enough for a true stranger, as the blessed apostle says to his son Timothy, "We brought nothing into this world, and it is certain we can carry nothing out. And having food and raiment, let us be therewith content."

Christian reader, let us ponder this. What a cure for restless ambition is here! what an antidote against covetousness! what a blessed deliverance from the feverish excitement of commercial life, the grasping spirit of the age in which our lot is cast! If we were only content with the divinely appointed provision for the stranger, what a different tale we should have to tell! how calm and even would be the current of our daily life! how simple our habits and tastes! how unworldly our spirit and style! what moral elevation above the self-indulgence and luxury so prevalent amongst professing Christians! We should simply eat and drink to the glory of God, and to keep the body in proper working order. To go beyond this, either in eating or drinking, is to indulge in "fleshly lusts, which war against the soul."

Alas! alas! how much of this there is, specially in reference to drink! It is perfectly appalling to think of the consumption of intoxicating drink amongst professing Christians. It is our thorough conviction that the devil has succeeded in ruining the testimony of hundreds, and in causing them to make shipwreck of faith and a good conscience, by the use of stimulants. Thousands ruin their fortunes, ruin their families, ruin their health, ruin their souls, through the senseless, vile, and cursed desire for stimulants.

We are not going to preach a crusade against stimulants or narcotics. The wrong is not in the things themselves, but in our inordinate and sinful use of them. It not unfrequently happens that persons who fall under the horrible dominion of drink seek to lay the blame on their medical adviser, but surely no proper medical man would ever advise his patient to *indulge* in the use of stimulants. He may prescribe the use of "a *little* wine, for the stomach's sake and frequent infirmities," and he has the very highest authority for so doing; but why should this lead any one to become a drunkard? Each one is responsible to walk in the fear of God in reference to both eating and drinking. If a doctor prescribes a little nourishing food for his patient, is he to be blamed if that patient becomes a glutton? Surely not. The evil is not in the doctor's prescription, or in the stimulant or in the nourishment, but in the wretched lust of the heart.

Here, we are persuaded, lies the root of the evil; and the remedy is found in that precious grace of God which, while it bringeth salvation unto all men, teacheth those who are saved "to live *soberly*, righteously, and godly in this present world." And be it remembered that "to live soberly" means a great deal more than temperance in eating and drinking; it means this, most surely, but it takes in also the whole range of inward self-government—the government of the thoughts, the government of the temper, the government of the tongue. The grace that saves us not only *tells* us how to live, but *teaches* how to do it, and if we follow its teachings, we shall be well content with God's provision for the stranger.

It is at once interesting and edifying to notice the way in which Moses sets the divine example before the people as their model. Jehovah "loveth the stranger, in giving him food and raiment. Love ye therefore the stranger; for ye were strangers in the land of Egypt.'' This is very touching. They were not only to keep before their eyes the divine model, but also to remember their own past history and experience, in order that their hearts might be drawn out in sympathy and compassion toward the poor homeless stranger. It was the bounden duty and high privilege of the Israel of God to place themselves in the circumstances and enter into the feelings of others. They were to be the moral representatives of that blessed One whose people they were, and whose name was called upon them. They were to imitate Him in meeting the wants and gladdening the hearts of the fatherless, the widow, and the stranger. And if God's earthly people were called to this lovely course of action, how much more are we who are ''blessed with all spiritual blessings in the heavenlies in Christ Jesus.'' May we abide more in His presence, and drink more into His spirit, that so we may more faithfully reflect His moral glories upon all with whom we come in contact.

The closing lines of our chapter give us a very fine summing up of the practical teaching which has been engaging our attention. ''Thou shalt fear the Lord thy God; Him shalt thou serve, and to Him shalt thou cleave, and swear by His name. He is thy praise, and He is thy God, that hath done for thee these great and terrible things, which thine eyes have seen. Thy fathers went down into Egypt with threescore and ten persons, and now the Lord

hath made thee as the stars of heaven for multitude."
(Ver. 20–22.)

How thoroughly bracing is all this to the moral
being! This binding of the heart to the Lord
Himself by means of all that He is, and all His
wondrous actings and gracious ways, is unspeakably
precious. It is, we may truly say, the secret spring
of all true devotedness. God grant that the writer
and the reader may abidingly realize its motive
power.

CHAPTER XI.

"THEREFORE thou shalt love the Lord thy God,
and keep His charge, and His statutes, and
His judgments, and His commandments, *alway*.
And know ye this day; for I speak not with your
children which have not known, and which have not
seen the chastisements of the Lord your God, His
greatness, His mighty hand, and His stretched-out
arm, and His miracles, and His acts, which He did
in the midst of Egypt unto Pharaoh the king of
Egypt, and unto all his land; and what He did unto
the army of Egypt, unto their horses, and to their
chariots; how He made the water of the Red Sea to
overflow them as they pursued after you, and how
the Lord hath destroyed them unto this day; and
what He did unto you in the wilderness, until ye
came into this place; and what He did unto Dathan

and Abiram, the sons of Eliab, the son of Reuben; how the earth opened her mouth, and swallowed them up, and their households, and their tents, and all the substance that was in their possession, in the midst of all Israel; but your eyes have seen all the great acts of the Lord which He did."

Moses felt it to be of the very highest importance that all the mighty acts of Jehovah should be kept prominently before the hearts of the people, and deeply engraved on the tablets of their memory. The poor human mind is vagrant, and the heart volatile, and notwithstanding all that Israel had seen of the solemn judgments of God upon Egypt and upon Pharaoh, they were in danger of forgetting them, and losing the impression which they were designed and eminently fitted to make upon them.

It may be we feel disposed to wonder how Israel could ever forget the impressive scenes of their history in Egypt from first to last—the descent of their fathers thither as a mere handful, their steady growth and progress as a people, spite of formidable difficulties and hindrances, so that from the insignificant few, they had become, by the good hand of their God upon them, as the stars of heaven for multitude.

And then those ten plagues upon the land of Egypt! How full of awful solemnity! how pre-eminently calculated to impress the heart with a sense of the mighty power of God, the utter impotency and insignificance of man, in all his boasted wisdom, strength, and glory, and the egregious folly of his attempting to set himself up against the almighty God! What was all the power of Pharaoh and of Egypt in the presence of the Lord God of Israel? In one hour all was plunged into hopeless ruin and destruction. All the chariots of Egypt, all the pomp and glory, the valor and might, of that ancient and far-famed nation—all was overwhelmed in the depths of the sea.

And why? Because they had presumed to meddle with the Israel of God; they had dared to set themselves in opposition to the eternal purpose and counsel of the Most High. They sought to crush those on whom He had set His love. He had sworn to bless the seed of Abraham, and no power of earth or hell could possibly annul His oath. Pharaoh, in his pride and hardness of heart, attempted to countervail the divine actings, but he only meddled to his own destruction. His land was shaken to its very centre, and himself and his mighty army overthrown in the Red Sea, a solemn example to all who should ever attempt to stand in the way of Jehovah's purpose to bless the seed of Abraham His friend.

Nor was it merely what Jehovah had done to Egypt and to Pharaoh that the people were called to remember, but also what He had done amongst themselves. How soul-subduing the judgment upon Dathan and Abiram and their households! How awful the thought of the earth opening her mouth and swallowing them up! And for what? For their rebellion against the divine appointment. In the history given in Numbers, Korah, the Levite, is the prominent character; but here, he is omitted,

and the two Reubenites are named—two members
of the congregation, because Moses is seeking to
act on the whole body of the people by setting before them the terrible consequence of self-will in
two of their number—two ordinary members, as we
should say, and not merely a privileged Levite.

In a word, then, whether the attention was called
to the divine actings without or within, abroad or at
home, it was all for the purpose of impressing their
hearts and minds with a deep sense of the moral
importance of obedience. This was the one grand
aim of all the rehearsals, all the comments, all the
exhortations, of the faithful servant of God who was
so soon to be removed from their midst. For this,
he ranges over their history for centuries, culling,
grouping, commenting, taking up this fact and
omitting that, as guided by the Spirit of God. The
journey down to Egypt, the sojourn there, the heavy
judgments upon the self-willed Pharaoh, the exodus,
the passage through the sea, the scenes in the
wilderness, and specially the awful fate of the two
rebellious Reubenites—all is brought to bear, with
marvelous force and clearness, upon the conscience
of the people, in order to strengthen the basis of
Jehovah's claim upon their unqualified obedience to
His holy commandments.

"Therefore shall ye *keep all the commandments*
which I command you this day, *that ye may be
strong*, and go in and possess the land, whither ye
go to possess it; and that ye may prolong your
days in the land, which the Lord **sware unto** your

fathers to give unto them and to their seed, a land that floweth with milk and honey."

Let the reader note the beautiful moral link between those two clauses—"keep *all* the commandments"—"that ye may be strong." There is great strength gained by unreserved obedience to the Word of God. It will not do to pick and choose. We are prone to this—prone to take up certain commandments and precepts which suit ourselves; but this is really self-will. What right have we to select such and such precepts from the Word, and neglect others? None whatever. To do so is, in principle, simply self-will and rebellion. What business has a servant to decide as to which of his master's commands he will obey? Surely none whatever; each commandment stands clothed with the master's authority, and therefore claims the servant's attention; and, we may add, the more implicitly the servant obeys, the more he bends his respectful attention to every one of his master's commands, be it ever so trivial, the more does he strengthen himself in his position and grow in his master's confidence and esteem. Every master loves and values an obedient, faithful, devoted servant. We all know what a comfort it is to have a servant whom we can trust—one who finds his delight in carrying out our every wish, and who does not require perpetual looking after, but knows his duty and attends to it.

Now, ought we not to seek to refresh the heart of our blessed Master, by a loving obedience to all His commandments ? Only think, reader, what a privilege it is to be allowed to give joy to the heart of that blessed One who loved us and gave Himself for us. It is something wonderful that poor creatures such as we can in any way refresh the heart of Jesus; yet so it is, blessed be His name. He delights in our keeping His commandments; and assuredly the thought of this should stir our whole moral being, and lead us to study His Word, in order to find out, more and more, what His commandments are, so that we may do them.

We are forcibly reminded, by those words of Moses which we have just quoted, of the apostle's prayer for "the saints and faithful brethren in Christ at Colosse." "For this cause we also, since the day we heard it, do not cease to pray for you, and to desire that ye might be filled with the knowledge of His will in all wisdom and spiritual understanding; that ye might walk worthy of the Lord *unto all pleasing*, being fruitful in every good work, and *increasing in the knowledge of God; strengthened with all might*, according to His glorious power, unto all patience and long-suffering with joyfulness; giving thanks unto the Father, which hath made us meet to be partakers of the inheritance of the saints in light; who hath delivered us from the power of darkness, and hath translated us into the kingdom of the Son of His love; in whom we have redemption through His blood, the forgiveness of sins." (Col. i. 9–14.)

Making allowance for the difference between the

earthly and the heavenly—between Israel and the Church, there is a striking similarity between the words of the lawgiver and the words of the apostle. Both together are eminently fitted to set forth the beauty and preciousness of a willing-hearted, loving obedience. It is precious to the Father, precious to Christ, precious to the Holy Ghost; and this surely ought to be enough to create and strengthen in our hearts the desire to be filled with the knowledge of His will, that so we might walk worthy of Him to all pleasing, being fruitful *in every good work*, and increasing in the knowledge of God. It should lead us to a more diligent study of the Word of God, so that we might be ever finding out more and more of our Lord's mind and will, learning what is well-pleasing to Him, and looking to Him for grace to do it. Thus should our hearts be kept near to Him, and we should find an ever-deepening interest in searching the Scriptures, not merely to grow in the knowledge of truth, but in the knowledge of God, the knowledge of Christ—the deep, personal, experimental knowledge of all that is treasured up in that blessed One who is the fullness of the God-head bodily. Oh, may the Spirit of God, by His most precious and powerful ministry, awaken in us a more intense desire to know and to do the will of our blessed Lord and Saviour Jesus Christ, that thus we may refresh His loving heart and be well-pleasing to Him in all things.

We must now turn, for a moment, to the lovely picture of the promised land which Moses holds up before the eyes of the people.—"For the land whither thou goest in to possess it, is not as the land of Egypt, from whence ye came out, where thou sowedst thy seed, and wateredst it with thy foot, as a garden of herbs; but the land whither ye go to possess it, is a land of hills and valleys, and drinketh water of the rain of heaven; a land which the Lord thy God careth for; the eyes of the Lord thy God are always upon it, from the beginning of the year even unto the end of the year." (Ver. 10-12.)

What a vivid contrast between Egypt and Canaan! Egypt had no rain from heaven; it was all human effort there. Not so in the Lord's land; the human foot could do nothing there, nor was there any need, for the blessed rain from heaven dropped upon it; Jehovah Himself cared for it and watered it with the early and latter rain. The land of Egypt was dependent upon its own resources; the land of Canaan was wholly dependent upon God—upon what came down from heaven. "My river is mine own," was the language of Egypt; "the river of God" was the hope of Canaan. The habit in Egypt was to water with the foot; the habit in Canaan was to look up to heaven.

We have in the sixty-fifth psalm a lovely statement of the condition of things in the Lord's land, as viewed by the eye of faith. "Thou visitest the earth, and waterest it; Thou greatly enrichest it with the river of God, which is full of water; Thou preparest them corn, when Thou hast so provided for it. Thou waterest the ridges thereof abundantly;

Thou settlest the furrows thereof; Thou makest it soft with showers; Thou blessest the springing thereof. Thou crownest the year with Thy goodness, and Thy paths drop fatness. They drop upon the pastures of the wilderness; and the little hills rejoice on every side. The pastures are clothed with flocks; the valleys also are covered over with corn; they shout for joy, they also sing." (Ver. 9–13.)

How perfectly beautiful! Only think of God watering the ridges and settling the furrows! think of His stooping down to do the work of a husbandman for His people! Yes, and delighting to do it! It was the joy of His heart to pour His sunbeams and His refreshing showers upon the "hills and valleys" of His beloved people. It was refreshing to His spirit, as it was to the praise of His name, to see the vine, the fig-tree, and the olive flourishing, the valleys covered with the golden grain, and the rich pastures covered with flocks of sheep.

Thus it should ever have been, and thus it would have been, had Israel only walked in simple obedience to the holy law of God. "It shall come to pass, if ye shall hearken diligently unto My commandments which I command you this day, *to love the Lord your God, and to serve Him with all your heart and with all your soul*, that I will give you the rain of your land in his due season, the first rain and the latter rain, that thou mayest gather in thy corn, and thy wine, and thine oil. And I will send grass in thy fields for thy cattle, that thou mayest eat and be full." (Ver. 13–15.)

8

Thus the matter stood between the God of Israel and the Israel of God. Nothing could be simpler, nothing more blessed. It was Israel's high and holy privilege to love and serve Jehovah; it was Jehovah's prerogative to bless and prosper Israel. Happiness and fruitfulness were to be the sure accompaniments of obedience. The people and their land were wholly dependent upon God. All their supplies were to come down from heaven; and hence, so long as they walked in loving obedience, the copious showers dropped upon their fields and vineyards, the heavens dropped down the dew, and the earth responded in fruitfulness and blessing.

But, on the other hand, when Israel forgot the Lord, and forsook His precious commandments, the heaven became brass and the earth iron; barrenness, desolation, famine, and misery were the melancholy accompaniments of disobedience. How could it be otherwise? "If ye be willing and obedient, ye shall eat the good of the land; but if ye refuse and rebel, ye shall be devoured with the sword; for the mouth of the Lord hath spoken it."

Now, in all this there is deep, practical instruction for the Church of God. Although we are not under law, we are called to obedience; and as we are enabled, through grace, to yield a loving, hearty obedience, we are blessed in our own spiritual state, our souls are watered, refreshed, and strengthened, and we bring forth the fruits of righteousness which are by Jesus Christ to the glory and praise of God.

The reader may refer with much profit, in connection with this great practical subject, to the opening of John xv.—a most precious scripture, and one demanding the earnest attention of every true-hearted child of God. "I am the true vine, and My Father is the Husbandman. Every branch in Me that beareth not fruit He taketh away; and every branch that beareth fruit, He purgeth it, *that it may bring forth more fruit.* Now ye are clean through the word which I have spoken unto you. Abide in Me, and I in you. As the branch cannot bear fruit of itself, except it abide in the vine; no more can ye, except ye abide in Me. I am the vine, ye are the branches: he that abideth in Me, and I in him, the same bringeth forth much fruit; for without [or apart from] Me ye can do nothing. If a man abide not in Me, he is cast forth as a branch, and is withered; and men gather them, and cast them into the fire, and they are burned. If ye abide in Me, and My words abide in you, ye shall ask what ye will, and it shall be done unto you. Herein is My Father glorified, that ye bear much fruit; so shall ye be My disciples. As the Father hath loved Me, so have I loved you; continue ye in My love. *If ye keep My commandments, ye shall abide in My love;* even as I have kept My Father's commandments, and abide in His love." (Ver. 1–10.)

This weighty passage of Scripture has suffered immensely through theological controversy and religious strife. It is as plain as it is practical, and only needs to be taken as it stands, in its own divine simplicity. If we seek to import into it what does

not belong to it, we mar its integrity and miss its
true application. In it we have Christ, the true vine,
taking the place of Israel, who had become to Jehovah the degenerate plant of a strange vine. The
scene of the parable is obviously earth, and not
heaven; we do not think of a vine and a husbandman (γεωργος) in heaven. Besides, our Lord says,
"I *am* the true vine." The figure is very distinct.
It is not the head and the members, but a tree and
its branches. Moreover, the subject of the parable
is as distinct as the parable itself; it is not eternal
life, but fruit-bearing. If this were borne in mind,
it would greatly help to an understanding of this
much-misunderstood passage of Scripture.

In a word, then, we learn from the figure of the
vine and its branches that the true secret of fruit-
bearing is, to abide in Christ, and the way to abide
in Christ is, to keep His precious commandments.
"If ye keep My commandments, ye shall abide in
My love; even as I have kept My Father's commandments, and abide in His love." This makes it
all so simple. The way to bear fruit in season is,
to abide in the love of Christ, and this abiding is
proved by our treasuring up His commandments in
our hearts and yielding a loving obedience to every
one of them. It is not running hither and thither
in the mere energy of nature; it is not the excitement of mere fleshly zeal displaying itself in spas-
modic efforts after devotedness. No; it is something
quite different from all this; it is the calm and holy
obedience of the heart—a loving obedience to our

own beloved Lord, which refreshes His heart and glorifies His name.

> "How blest are they who still abide
>   Close sheltered by Thy watchful side;
>   Who life and strength from Thee receive,
>   And with Thee move and in Thee live."

Reader, may we apply our hearts diligently to this great subject of fruit-bearing. May we better understand what it is. We are apt to make great mistakes about it. It is to be feared that much—very much of what passes for fruit would not be accredited in the divine presence. God cannot own any thing as fruit which is not the direct result of abiding in Christ. We may earn a great name among our fellows for zeal, energy, and devotedness; we may be abundant in labors, in every department of the work; we may acquit ourselves as great travelers, great preachers, earnest workers in the vineyard, great philanthropists and moral reformers; we may spend a princely fortune in promoting all the great objects of Christian benevolence, and all the while not produce a single cluster of fruit acceptable to the Father's heart.

And, on the other hand, it may be our lot to pass the time of our sojourn here in obscurity and retirement from human gaze; we may be little accounted of by the world and the professing church; we may seem to leave but little mark on the sands of time; but if only we abide in Christ, abide in His love, treasure up His precious words in our hearts, and yield ourselves up to a holy and loving obedience to

His commandments, then shall our fruit be in season, and our Father will be glorified, and we shall grow in the experimental knowledge of our Lord and Saviour Jesus Christ.

We shall now look for a moment at the remainder of our chapter, in which Moses, in words of intense earnestness, presses upon the congregation the urgent need of watchfulness and diligence in reference to all the statutes and judgments of the Lord their God. The beloved and faithful servant of God, and true lover of the people, was unwearied in his efforts to brace them up to that whole-hearted obedience which he knew to be at once the spring of their happiness and their fruitfulness; and just as our blessed Lord warns His disciples by setting before them the solemn judgment of the unfruitful branch, so does Moses warn the people as to the sure and terrible consequences of disobedience.

"Take heed to yourselves, that *your heart be not deceived*, and ye turn aside, and serve other gods, and worship them." Sad progress downward! The heart deceived. This is the beginning of all declension. "And ye turn aside." The feet are sure to follow the heart. Hence the deep need of keeping the heart with all diligence; it is the citadel of the whole moral being, and so long as it is kept for the Lord, the enemy can gain no advantage; but when once it is surrendered, all is really gone,—there is the turning aside; the secret departure of the heart is proved by the practical ways,—"other gods" are served and worshiped. The descent down along the inclined plane is terribly rapid.

"And then"—mark the sure and solemn consequences—"the Lord's wrath be kindled against you, and He *shut up the heaven*, that there be no rain, and that the land yield not her fruit; and ye perish quickly from off the good land which the Lord giveth you." What barrenness and desolation there must be when heaven is shut up! No refreshing showers coming down, no dew-drops falling, no communication between the heaven and the earth. Alas! how often had Israel tasted the awful reality of this! "He turneth rivers into a wilderness, and the water-springs into dry ground; a fruitful land into barrenness, for the wickedness of them that dwell therein."

And may we not see in the barren land and the desolate wilderness an apt and striking illustration of a soul out of communion through disobedience to the precious commandments of Christ? Such an one has no refreshing communications with heaven—no showers coming down—no unfoldings of the preciousness of Christ to the heart—no sweet ministrations of an ungrieved Spirit to the soul; the Bible seems a sealed book; all is dark, dreary, and desolate. Oh, there cannot be any thing more miserable in all this world than a soul in this condition. May the writer and the reader never experience it. May we bend our ears to the fervent exhortations addressed by Moses to the congregation of Israel. They are most seasonable, most healthful, most needful, in this day of cold indifferentism and positive willfulness. They set before us the divine antidote against the special evils to which the Church of God is exposed at this very hour—an hour critical and solemn beyond all human conception.

"Therefore shall ye lay up these *my words* in *your heart* and in *your soul*, and bind them for a sign upon your hand, that they may be as frontlets between your eyes. And ye shall teach them your children, speaking of them when thou sittest in thine house, and when thou walkest by the way, when thou liest down, and when thou risest up; and thou shalt write them upon the door-posts of thine house, and upon thy gates, that your days may be multiplied, and the days of your children, in the land which the Lord sware unto your fathers to give them, as the days of heaven upon the earth."

Blessed days! And oh, how ardently the large, loving heart of Moses longed that the people might enjoy many such days! And how simple the condition! Truly nothing could be simpler, nothing more precious. It was not a heavy yoke laid upon them, but the sweet privilege of treasuring up the precious commandments of the Lord their God in their hearts, and breathing the very atmosphere of His holy Word. All was to hinge upon this. All the blessings of the land of Canaan—that goodly, highly favored land, a land flowing with milk and honey, a land on which Jehovah's eyes ever rested in loving interest and tender care—all its precious fruits, all its rare privileges, were to be theirs in perpetuity, on the one simple condition of loving obedience to the word of their covenant-God.

"For if ye shall *diligently keep all* these commandments which I command you, to do them, *to love the Lord your God*, *to walk in all His ways*, and *to cleave unto* Him ; then will the Lord drive out all these nations from before you, and ye shall possess greater nations and mightier than yourselves." In a word, sure and certain victory was before them, a most complete overthrow of all enemies and obstacles, a triumphal march into the promised inheritance—all secured to them on the blessed ground of affectionate and reverential obedience to the most precious statutes and judgments that had ever been addressed to the human heart—statutes and judgments every one of which was but the very voice of their most gracious Deliverer.

"Every place whereon the soles of your feet shall tread shall be yours ; from the wilderness and Lebanon, from the river, the river Euphrates, even unto the uttermost sea, shall your coast be. There shall no man be able to stand before you ; for the Lord your God shall lay the fear of you and the dread of you upon all the land that ye shall tread upon, as He hath said unto you."

Here was the divine side of the question. The whole land, in its length, breadth, and fullness, lay before them ; they had but to take possession of it, as the free gift of God ; it was for them simply to plant the foot, in artless, appropriating faith, upon that fair inheritance which sovereign grace had bestowed upon them. All this we see made good in the book of Joshua, as we read in chapter xi.—"So Joshua took *the whole land*, according to all that the Lord said unto Moses; and Joshua gave it for an inheritance unto Israel, according to their divisions by their tribes. And the land rested from war." (Ver. 23.)*

But alas! there was the human side of the question as well as the divine. Canaan as promised by Jehovah and made good by the faith of Joshua was one thing, and Canaan as possessed by Israel was quite another. Hence the vast difference between Joshua and Judges. In Joshua, we see the infallible faithfulness of God to His promise; in Judges, we see Israel's miserable failure from the very outset. God pledged His immutable word that not a man should be able to stand before them, and the sword of Joshua—type of the great Captain of our salvation—made good this pledge in its every jot and tittle; but the book of Judges records the melancholy fact that Israel failed to drive out the enemy—failed to take possession of the divine grant in all its royal magnificence.

What then? Is the promise of God made of none effect? Nay, verily; but the utter failure of man is made apparent. At "Gilgal," the banner of victory floated over the twelve tribes, with their invincible captain at their head: at "Bochim," the

---

*No doubt it was in faith that Joshua took—and could take nothing less than—the whole land; but as to actual possession, chapter xiii. 1 shows there was "yet much land to be possessed."

weepers had to mourn over Israel's lamentable defeat.

Have we any difficulty in understanding the difference? None whatever. We see the two things running all through the divine Volume. Man fails to rise to the height of the divine revelation—fails to take possession of what grace bestows. This is as true in the history of the Church as it was in the history of Israel;—in the New Testament, as well as in the Old, we have Judges as well as Joshua.

Yes, reader, and in the history of each individual member of the Church we see the same thing. Where is the Christian, beneath the canopy of heaven, that lives up to the height of his spiritual privileges? where is the child of God who has not to mourn over his humiliating failure in grasping and making good practically the high and holy privileges of his calling of God? But does this make the truth of God of none effect? No; blessed forever be His holy name. His Word holds good in all its divine integrity and eternal stability. Just as in Israel's case, the land of promise lay before them in all its fair proportions and divinely given attractions; and not only so, but they could count on the faithfulness and almighty power of God to bring them in and put them in full possession; so with us, we are blessed with all spiritual blessings in the heavenlies in Christ. There is absolutely no limit to the privileges connected with our standing, and as to our actual enjoyment, it is only a question of faith taking possession of all that God's sovereign grace has made ours in Christ.

We must never forget that it is the privilege of the Christian to live at the very height of the divine revelation. There is no excuse for a shallow experience or a low walk. We have no right whatever to say that we cannot realize the fullness of our portion in Christ, that the standard is too high, the privileges are too vast, that we cannot expect to enjoy such marvelous blessings and dignities in our present imperfect state.

All this is downright unbelief, and should be so treated by every true Christian. The question is, Has the grace of God bestowed the privileges upon us? has the death of Christ made good our title to them? and has the Holy Ghost declared them to be the proper portion of the very feeblest member of the body of Christ? If so—and Scripture declares it is so—why should we not enjoy them? There is no hindrance on the divine side. It is the desire of the heart of God that we should enter into the fullness of our portion in Christ. Hear the earnest breathing of the inspired apostle on behalf of the saints at Ephesus and of all saints.—"Wherefore I also, after I heard of your faith in the Lord Jesus, and love unto all the saints, cease not to give thanks for you, making mention of you in my prayers; that the God of our Lord Jesus Christ, the Father of glory, may give unto you the spirit of wisdom and revelation in the knowledge of Him: the eyes of your understanding being enlightened; that ye may know what is the hope of His calling, and what the riches of the glory of His inheritance in the saints, and what the exceeding greatness of His power to usward who believe, according to the working of His mighty power, which He wrought in Christ, when He raised Him from the dead, and set Him at His own right hand in the heavenlies, far above all principality, and power, and might, and dominion, and every name that is named, not only in this world, but also in that which is to come: and hath put all things under His feet, and gave Him to be the head over all things to the Church, which is His body, the fullness of Him that filleth all in all." (Eph. i. 15-23.)

From this marvelous prayer we may learn how earnestly the Spirit of God desires that we should apprehend and enjoy the glorious privileges of the true Christian position. He would ever, by His precious and powerful ministry, keep our hearts up to the mark; but, alas! like Israel, we grieve Him by our sinful unbelief, and rob our own souls of incalculable blessing.

But, all praise to the God of all grace, the Father of glory, the God and Father of our Lord Jesus Christ, He will yet make good every jot and tittle of His most precious truth, both as to His earthly and heavenly people. Israel shall yet enjoy to the full all the blessings secured to them by the everlasting covenant; and the Church shall yet enter upon the perfect fruition of all that which eternal love and divine counsels have laid up for her in Christ; and not only so, but the blessed Comforter is able and willing to lead the individual believer into the present enjoyment of the hope of God's glorious calling, and the practical power of that hope, in detaching the heart from present things and separating it to God in true holiness and living devotedness.

May our hearts, beloved Christian reader, long more ardently after the full realization of all this, that thus we may live more as those who are finding their portion and their rest in a risen and glorified Christ. God, in His infinite goodness, grant it, for Jesus Christ's name and glory's sake.

The remaining verses of our chapter close the first division of the book of Deuteronomy, which, as the reader will notice, consists of a series of discourses addressed by Moses to the congregation of Israel— memorable discourses, most surely, in whatever way we view them. The closing sentences are, we need hardly say, in perfect keeping with the whole, and breathe the same deep-toned earnestness in reference to the subject of obedience—a subject which, as we have seen, formed the special burden on the heart of the beloved speaker in his affecting farewell addresses to the people.

"Behold, I set before you this day a blessing and a curse;"—How pointed and solemn is this!—"a blessing, if ye obey the commandments of the Lord your God, which I command you this day; and a curse, if ye will not obey the commandments of the Lord your God, but turn aside out of the way which I command you this day, to go after other gods, which ye have not known. And it shall come to pass, when the Lord thy God hath brought thee in unto the land whither thou goest to possess it, that thou shalt put the blessing upon Mount Gerizim, and the curse upon Mount Ebal. Are they not on the other side Jordan, by the way where the sun goeth down, in the land of the Canaanites, which dwell in the champaign over against Gilgal, beside the plains of Moreh? For ye shall pass over Jordan, to go in to possess the land which the Lord your God giveth you, and ye shall possess it, and dwell therein. AND YE SHALL OBSERVE TO DO ALL THE STATUTES AND JUDGMENTS WHICH I SET BEFORE YOU THIS DAY." (Ver. 26–32.)

Here we have the summing up of the whole matter. The blessing is linked on to obedience; the curse, to disobedience. Mount Gerizim stands over against Mount Ebal—fruitfulness and barrenness. We shall see, when we come to chapter xxvii, that Mount Gerizim and its blessings are entirely passed over. The curses of Mount Ebal fall, with awful distinctness, on Israel's ear, while terrible silence reigns on Mount Gerizim. "As many as are of the works of the law, are under the curse." The blessing of Abraham can only come on those who are on the ground of faith. But more of this by and by.

CHAPTER XII.

WE now enter upon a new section of our marvelous book. The discourses contained in the first eleven chapters having established the all-important principle of obedience, we now come to the practical application of the principle to the habits and ways of the people when settled in possession of the land. ''These are the statutes and judgments which ye shall observe to do in the land which the Lord God of thy fathers giveth thee to possess it, all the days that ye live upon the earth.''

It is of the utmost moral importance that the heart and conscience should be brought into their true attitude in reference to divine authority, irrespective altogether of any question as to details. These will find their due place when once the heart is taught to bow down, in complete and absolute submission, to the supreme authority of the Word of God.

Now, as we have seen in our studies on the first eleven chapters, the lawgiver labors, most earnestly and faithfully, to lead the heart of Israel into this all-essential condition. He felt, to speak after the manner of men, it was of no use entering upon practical details until the grand foundation-principle of all morality was fully established in the very deepest depths of the soul. The principle is this (let us Christians apply our hearts to it): It is man's bounden duty to bow implicitly to the authority of the Word of God. It matters not, in the smallest degree, what that Word may enjoin, or whether we can see the reason of this, that, or the other institution. The one grand, all-important, and conclusive point is this: Has God spoken? If He has, that is quite enough. There is no room, no need, for any further question.

Until this point is fully established, or rather until the heart is brought directly under its full moral force, we are not in a condition to enter upon details. If self-will be allowed to operate, if blind reason be permitted to speak, the heart will send up its endless questionings; as each divine institution is laid before us, some fresh difficulty will present itself as a stumbling-block in the path of simple obedience.

What! it may be said, are we not to use our reason? If not, to what end was it given? To this we have a twofold reply. In the first place, our reason is not as it was when God gave it. We have to remember that sin has come in; man is a fallen creature; his reason, his judgment, his understanding—his whole moral being is a complete wreck; and moreover, it was the neglect of the Word of God that caused all this wreck and ruin.

And then, in the second place, we must bear in mind that if reason were in a sound condition, it would prove its soundness by bowing to the Word of God. But it is not sound; it is blind, and utterly perverted; it is not to be trusted for a moment in things spiritual, divine, or heavenly.

If this simple fact were thoroughly understood, it would settle a thousand questions and remove a thousand difficulties. It is reason that makes all the infidels. The devil whispers into man's ear, "You are endowed with reason; why not use it? It was given to be used—used in every thing; you ought not to give your assent to any thing which

9

your reason cannot grasp. It is your chartered right as a man to submit every thing to the test of your reason; it is only for a fool or an idiot to receive, in blind credulity, all that is set before him.''

What is our answer to such wily and dangerous suggestions? A very simple and conclusive one; namely, this: The Word of God is above and beyond reason altogether; it is as far above reason as God is above the creature, or heaven above earth. Hence, when God speaks, all reasonings must be cast down. If it be merely man's word, man's opinion, man's judgment, then verily reason may exert its powers; or rather, to speak more correctly, we must judge what is said by the only perfect standard—the Word of God. But if reason be set to work on the Word of God, the soul must inevitably be plunged in the thick darkness of infidelity, from which the descent to the awful blackness of atheism is but too easy.

In a word, then, we have to remember—yea, to cherish in the very deepest depths of our moral being, that the only safe ground for the soul is, divinely wrought faith in the paramount authority, divine majesty, and all-sufficiency of the Word of God. This was the ground which Moses occupied in dealing with the heart and conscience of Israel. His one grand object was, to lead the people into the attitude of profound, unqualified subjection to divine authority. Without this, all was useless. If every statute, every judgment, every precept, every institution, were to be submitted to the action or human reason, then farewell to divine authority, farewell to Scripture, farewell to certainty, farewell to peace; but, on the other hand, when the soul is led by God's Spirit into the delightful attitude of absolute and unquestioning submission to the authority of God's Word, then every one of His judgments, every one of His commandments, every sentence of His blessed book, is received as coming direct from Himself, and the most simple ordinance or institution stands invested with all the importance which His authority is fitted to impart. We may not be able to understand the full meaning or exact bearing of each statute and judgment,—that is not the question; it is sufficient for us to know that it comes from God. He has spoken; this is conclusive. Till this great principle is grasped, or rather till it takes full possession of the soul, nothing is done; but when it is fully understood and submitted to, the solid foundation is laid for all true morality.

The foregoing line of thought will enable the reader to seize the connection between the chapter which now lies open before us and the preceding section of this book; and not only will it do this, but we trust it will also help him to understand the special place and bearing of the opening verses of chapter xii.

"Ye shall utterly destroy all the places wherein the nations which ye shall possess served their gods, upon the high mountains, and upon the hills, and under every green tree. And ye shall overthrow their altars, and break their pillars, and burn their groves with fire; and ye shall hew down the graven images of their gods, and destroy the names of them out of that place." (Ver. 2, 3.)

The land was Jehovah's; they were to hold as tenants under Him, and therefore their very first duty on entering upon possession was, to demolish every trace of the old idolatry. This was absolutely indispensable. It might, according to human reason, seem to be very intolerant to act in this way toward other people's religion. We reply, without any hesitation, Yes, it was intolerant; for how could the one only true and living God be otherwise than intolerant of all false gods and false worship? To suppose for a moment that He could permit the worship of idols in His land would be to suppose that He could deny Himself, which were simply blasphemy.

Let us not be misunderstood. It is not that God does not bear with the world, in His long-suffering mercy. It seems hardly needful to state this, with the history of well-nigh six thousand years of divine forbearance before our eyes. Blessed forever be His holy name, He has borne with the world most marvelously from the days of Noah, and He still bears with it, though stained with the guilt of crucifying His beloved Son.

All this is plain, but it leaves wholly untouched the great principle laid down in our chapter. Israel had to learn that they were about to take possession of the Lord's land, and that, as His tenants, their first and indispensable duty was, to obliterate every trace of idolatry. To them there was to be but "the one God." His name was called upon them. They were His people, and He could not permit them to have fellowship with demons. "Thou shalt worship the Lord thy God; and Him *only* shalt thou serve."

This might, in the judgment of the uncircumcised nations around, seem very intolerant, very narrow, very bigoted. They indeed might boast of their freedom, and glory in the broad platform of their worship which admitted "gods many and lords many." It might, according to their thinking, argue greater breadth of mind to let every one think for himself in matters of religion, and choose his own object of worship, and his own mode of worshiping also; or, still further, it might give evidence of a more advanced condition of civilization, greater polish and refinement, to erect, as in Rome, a Pantheon, in which all the gods of heathendom might find a place. "What did it matter about the form of a man's religion, or the object of his worship, provided he himself were sincere? All would be sure to come right in the end; the great point for all was, to attend to material progress, to help on national prosperity as the surest means of securing individual interests. Of course, it is all right for every man to have some religion, but as to the form of that religion, it is immaterial. The great question is, what you are yourself, not what your religion is."

All this, we can well conceive, would admirably suit the carnal mind, and be very popular amongst

the uncircumcised nations; but as for Israel, they
had to remember that one commanding sentence,
"The Lord thy God is one God;" and again,
"Thou shalt have none other gods before Me."
This was to be their religion; the platform of their
worship was to be as wide and as narrow as the one
true and living God, their Creator and Redeemer.
That, assuredly, was broad enough for every true
worshiper—every member of the circumcised assembly—all whose high and holy privilege it was to
belong to the Israel of God.   They were not to
concern themselves with the opinions or observations
of the uncircumcised nations around.   What were
they worth?   Not the weight of a feather.   What
could they know about the claims of the God of
Israel upon His circumcised people?   Just nothing.
Were they competent to decide as to the proper
breadth of Israel's platform?   Clearly not; they
were wholly ignorant of the subject.   Hence their
thoughts, reasonings, arguments, and objections
were perfectly worthless, not to be listened to for a
moment.   It was Israel's one, simple, bounden duty
to bow down to the supreme and absolute authority
of the word of God; and that word insisted upon
the complete abolition of every trace of idolatry
from that goodly land which they were privileged to
hold as tenants under Him.

But not only was it incumbent upon Israel to
abolish all the places in which the heathen had
worshiped their gods,—this they were solemnly
bound to do, most surely; but there was more than

this. The heart might readily conceive the thought of doing away with idolatry in the various places, and setting up the altar of the true God instead,— this might seem to be the right course to adopt; but God thought differently. "Ye shall not do so unto the Lord your God. But unto the place which the Lord your God shall choose out of all your tribes, to put His name there, even *unto His habitation* shall ye seek, and thither thou shalt come; and thither ye shall bring your burnt-offerings, and your sacrifices, and your tithes, and heave-offerings of your hand, and your vows, and your free-will offerings, and the firstlings of your herds and of your flocks; and *there ye shall eat before the Lord your God;* and ye shall rejoice in all that ye put your hand unto, ye and your households, wherein the Lord thy God hath blessed thee."

Here a great cardinal truth is unfolded to the congregation of Israel. They were to have one place of worship—a place chosen of God, and not of man. His habitation—the place of His presence was to be Israel's grand centre; thither they were to come with their sacrifices and their offerings, and there they were to offer their worship, and find their common joy.

Does this seem exclusive? Of course it was exclusive; how else could it be? If God was pleased to select a spot in which He would take up His abode in the midst of His redeemed people, surely they were, of necessity, shut up to that spot as their place of worship. This was divine exclusiveness, and every pious soul would delight in it. Every true lover of Jehovah would say, with all his heart, "Lord, I have loved *the habitation of Thy house*, and the place where Thine honor dwelleth;" and again, "How amiable are Thy tabernacles, O Lord of hosts! My soul longeth, yea, even fainteth for the courts of the Lord; my heart and my flesh crieth out for the living God. . . . . Blessed are they that dwell *in Thy house;* they will be still praising Thee. . . . A day *in Thy courts* is better than a thousand. I had rather be a door-keeper *in the house of My God*, than to dwell in the tents of wickedness." (Ps. xxvi, lxxxiv.)

Here was *the* one grand and all-important point. It was the dwelling-place of Jehovah which was dear to the heart of every true Israelite. Restless self-will might desire to run hither and thither, the poor vagrant heart might long for some change, but, for the heart that loved God, any change from the place of His presence, the place where He had recorded His blessed name, could only be a change for the worse. The truly devout worshiper could find satisfaction and delight, blessing and rest, only in the place of the divine presence; and this, on the double ground,—the authority of His precious Word and the powerful attractions of His presence. Such an one could never think of going any where else. Whither could he go? There was but one altar, one habitation, one God,—that was the place for every right-minded, every true-hearted Israelite. To think of any other place of worship would, in his judgment, be not only a departure from the word of Jehovah, but from His holy habitation.

This great principle is largely insisted upon throughout the whole of our chapter. Moses reminds the people that from the moment they entered Jehovah's land there was to be an end to all the irregularity and self-will that had characterized them in the plains of Moab, or in the wilderness. "Ye shall not do after all the things that we do here this day, *every man whatsoever is right in his own eyes.* For ye are not as yet come to the rest and to the inheritance, which the Lord your God giveth you. *But when ye go over Jordan,* and dwell in the land which the Lord your God giveth you to inherit, and *when He giveth you rest from all your enemies round about, so that ye dwell in safety;* then there shall be a place *which the Lord your God shall choose,* to cause His name to dwell *there; thither* shall ye bring all that I command you. . . . Take heed to thyself that thou offer not thy burnt-offerings *in every place that thou seest;* but *in the place which the Lord shall choose* in one of thy tribes, there thou shalt offer thy burnt-offerings, and there thou shalt do all that I command thee." (Ver. 4–14.)

Thus, not only in the object, but also in the place and mode of Israel's worship, they were absolutely shut up to the commandment of Jehovah. Self-pleasing—self-choosing—self-will was to have an end, in reference to the worship of God, the moment they crossed the river of death and, as a redeemed people, planted their foot on their divinely given inheritance. Once there, in the enjoyment of Jehovah's land, and the rest which the land afforded, obedience to His word was to be their reasonable, their intelligent service. Things might be allowed to pass in the wilderness which could not be tolerated in Canaan. The higher the range of privilege, the higher the responsibility and the standard of action.

Now, it may be that our broad thinkers, and those who contend for freedom of will and freedom of action, for the right of private judgment in matters of religion, for liberality of mind and catholicity of spirit, will be ready to pronounce all this which has been engaging our attention extremely narrow, and wholly unsuited to our enlightened age, and to men of intelligence and education.

What is our answer to all who adopt this form of speech? A very simple and conclusive one; it is this: Has not God a right to prescribe the mode in which His people should worship Him? Had He not a perfect right to fix the place where He would meet His people Israel? Surely we must either deny His existence, or admit His absolute and unquestionable right to set forth His will as to how, when, and where His people should approach Him. Will any one, however educated and enlightened, deny this? Is it a proof of high culture, refinement, breadth of mind, or catholicity of spirit to deny God His rights?

If then God has a right to command, is it narrowness or bigotry for His people to obey? This is just the point. It is, in our judgment, as simple as any thing can be. We are thoroughly convinced that the only true breadth of mind, largeness of heart, and catholicity of spirit is, to obey the commandments of God. Hence, when Israel were commanded to go to one place and there offer their sacrifices, it most assuredly was neither bigotry nor narrowness on their part to go thither, and to refuse, with holy decision, to go any where else. Uncircumcised Gentiles might go where they pleased; the Israel of God were to go *only* to the place of His appointment.

And oh, what an unspeakable privilege for all who loved God and loved one another to assemble themselves at the place where He recorded His name! and what touching grace shines in the fact of His desiring to gather His people around Himself from time to time! Did that fact infringe their personal rights and domestic privileges? Nay, it enhanced them immensely. God, in His infinite goodness, took care of this. It was His delight to minister to the joy and blessing of His people, privately, socially, and publicly. Hence we read, "When the Lord thy God shall enlarge thy border, as He hath promised thee, and thou shalt say, I will eat flesh, because thy soul longeth to eat flesh, thou mayest eat flesh, whatsoever thy soul lusteth after. If the place which the Lord thy God hath chosen to put His name there be too far from thee, then thou shalt kill of thy herd and of thy flock, *which the Lord hath given thee*, as I have commanded thee, and thou shalt eat in thy gates whatsoever thy soul lusteth after. Even as the roebuck and the hart is eaten, so thou shalt eat them; the unclean and the clean shall eat of them alike."

Here we have, most surely, a broad margin afforded by the goodness and tender mercy of God for the fullest range of personal and family enjoyment. The only restriction was in reference to the blood.—"Only be sure that thou eat not the blood; *for the blood is the life,* and thou mayest not eat the life with the flesh. Thou shalt not eat it; thou shalt pour it upon the earth as water. Thou shalt not eat it; that it may go well with thee, and with thy children after thee, when thou shalt do that which is right in the sight of the Lord."

This was a great cardinal principle under the law, to which reference has been made in our "Notes on Leviticus." How far Israel understood it is not the question; they were to obey, that it might go well with them and with their children after them. They were to own, in this matter, the solemn rights of God.

Having made this exception in reference to personal and family habits, the lawgiver returns to the all-important subject of their public worship.— "Only thy holy things which thou hast, and thy vows, thou shalt take, *and go unto the place which the Lord shall choose;* and thou shalt offer thy burnt-offerings, *the flesh and the blood,* upon the altar of the Lord thy God; and the blood of the sacrifices shall be poured out upon the altar of the Lord thy God, and thou shalt eat the flesh." (Ver. 26, 27.)

If reason, or self-will, were permitted to speak, it might say, Why must we all go to this one place? Can we not have an altar at home? or, at least, an altar in each principal town, or in the centre of each tribe? The conclusive answer is, God has commanded otherwise; this is enough for every true Israelite. Even though we may not be able, by reason of our ignorance, to see the why or the wherefore, simple obedience is our obvious and bounden duty. It may be, moreover, that, as we cheerfully tread the path of obedience, light will break in upon our souls as to the reason, and we shall find abundant blessing in doing that which is well-pleasing to the Lord our God.

Yes, reader; this is the proper method of answering all the reasonings and questionings of the carnal mind, which is not subject to the law of God, neither indeed can be. Light is sure to break in upon our souls as we tread, with a lowly mind, the sacred path of obedience; and not only so, but untold blessing will flow into the heart in that conscious nearness to God which is only known to those who lovingly keep His most precious commandments. Are we called upon to explain to carnal objectors and infidels our reasons for doing this or that? Most certainly not; that is no part of our business: it would be time and labor lost, inasmuch as objectors and reasoners are wholly incapable of understanding or appreciating our reasons.

For example, in the matter now under our consideration, could a carnal mind—an unbeliever—a

mere child of nature understand why Israel's twelve
tribes were commanded to worship at one altar, to
gather in one place, to cluster around one centre?
Not in the smallest degree. The grand moral reason
of such a lovely institution lies far away beyond
his ken.

But to the spiritual mind, all is as plain as it
is beautiful. Jehovah would gather His beloved
people around Himself, from time to time, that they
might rejoice together before Him, and that He
might have His own peculiar joy in them. Was
not this something most precious? Assuredly it
was, to all who really loved the Lord.

No doubt, if the heart were cold and careless toward God, it would matter little about the place of
worship,—all places would be alike; but we may
set it down as a fixed principle that every loyal,
loving heart, from Dan to Beersheba, would rejoice
to flock to the place where Jehovah had recorded
His name, and where He had appointed to meet His
people. "I was glad when they said unto me, Let
us go unto the house of the Lord. Our feet shall
stand within thy gates, O Jerusalem [God's centre
for Israel]. Jerusalem is builded as a city that is
compact together; whither the tribes go up, the tribes
of the Lord, *unto the testimony of Israel,* to give
thanks unto the name of the Lord. For *there"*—
and no where else—"are set thrones of judgment,
the thrones of the house of David. Pray for the
peace of Jerusalem: they shall prosper that love
thee. Peace be within thy walls, and prosperity

within thy palaces. *For my brethren and compan-ions' sakes*, I will now say, Peace be within thee. Because of the house of the Lord our God I will seek thy good." (Ps. cxxii.)

Here we have the lovely breathings of a heart that loved the habitation of the God of Israel—His blessed centre—the gathering-place of Israel's twelve tribes—that hallowed spot which was associated, in the mind of every true Israelite, with all that was bright and joyous in connection with the worship of Jehovah and the communion of His people.

We shall have occasion to refer to this most delightful theme again when we come to study the sixteenth chapter of our book, and shall draw this section to a close by quoting for the reader the last paragraph of the chapter before us.

"When the Lord thy God shall cut off the nations from before thee, whither thou goest to possess them, and thou succeedest them, and dwellest in their land; take heed to thyself, that thou be not snared by following them, after that they be destroyed from before thee; and that thou inquire not after their gods, saying, How did these nations serve their gods? even so will I do likewise. Thou shalt not do so unto the Lord thy God: for every abomination to the Lord, which He hateth, have they done unto their gods; for even their sons and their daughters they have burnt in the fire to their gods. *What thing soever I command you, observe to do it: thou shalt not add thereto, nor diminish from it.*" (Ver. 29–32.)

The precious Word of God was to form a sacred inclosure round about His people, within which they might enjoy His presence, and delight themselves in the abundance of His mercy and loving-kindness, and wherein they were to be entirely apart from all that was offensive to Him whose presence was to be, at once, their glory, their joy, and their grand moral safeguard from every snare and every abomination.

Alas! alas! they did not abide within that inclosure; they speedily broke down the walls thereof, and wandered away from the holy commandment of God. They did the very things they were told not to do, and they have had to reap the terrible consequences. But more of this and of their future by and by.

CHAPTER XIII.

THIS chapter abounds in most weighty principles. It consists of three distinct sections, each one of which claims our deep attention. We must not attempt to weaken the admonitory force of such a scripture, or turn aside its keen edge, by saying that it does not apply to Christians—that it is wholly Jewish in its scope and application. No doubt, primarily, it was addressed to Israel; this is so obvious as not to admit of a question. But let us not forget that it was "written for our learning," and not only so, but the more closely we study it, the more we shall see that its teaching is of universal importance.

"If there arise among you a prophet, or a dreamer of dreams, and giveth thee a sign or a wonder, and the sign or the wonder come to pass, whereof he spake unto thee, saying, Let us go after other gods, which thou hast not known, and let us serve them: thou shalt not hearken unto the words of that prophet, or that dreamer of dreams; for the Lord your God proveth you, to know whether ye love the Lord your God with all your heart and with all your soul. Ye shall walk after the Lord your God, and fear Him, and keep His commandments, and obey His voice, and ye shall serve Him, and cleave unto Him. And that prophet, or that dreamer of dreams, shall be put to death; because he hath spoken to turn you away from the Lord your God, which brought you out of the land of Egypt, and redeemed you out of the house of bondage, to thrust thee out of the way which the Lord thy God commanded thee to walk in. So shalt thou put the evil away from the midst of thee." (Ver. 1–5.)

Here we have divine provision made for all cases of false teaching and false religious influence. We all know how easily the poor human heart is led astray by any thing in the shape of a sign or a wonder, and especially when such things stand connected with religion. This is not confined to the nation of Israel; we see it every where and at all times. Any thing supernatural, any thing involving an infringement of what are called the ordinary laws of nature, is almost sure to act powerfully on the human mind. A prophet rising up in the midst of the people and confirming his teaching by miracles, signs, and wonders, would be almost sure to get a hearing and obtain an influence.

In this way, Satan has worked in all ages, and he will work yet more powerfully, at the end of this present age, in order to deceive and lead to their everlasting destruction those who will not hearken to the precious truth of the gospel. "The mystery of iniquity," which has been working in the professing church for eighteen centuries, will be headed up in the person of "*that Wicked* whom the Lord shall consume with the spirit of His mouth, and shall destroy with the brightness of His coming; even him, whose coming is after the working of Satan, with all *power* and *signs* and lying *wonders*, and with all deceivableness of unrighteousness in them that perish; because they received not *the love of the truth*, that they might be saved. And for this cause God shall send them strong delusion, that they should believe a lie; that they all might be damned *who believed not the truth*, but had pleasure in unrighteousness." (2 Thess. ii. 8–12.)

So also in the twenty-fourth chapter of Matthew, our Lord warns His disciples against the same kind of influence.—"Then if any man shall say unto you, Lo, here is Christ, or there; believe it not. For there shall arise false Christs, and false prophets, and *shall show great signs and wonders;* insomuch that, if it were possible, they shall deceive the very elect. Behold, *I have told you before.*"(Ver.23–25.)

Again, in Revelation xiii, we read of the second beast, coming up out of the earth, the great false prophet, the antichrist, doing great wonders, "so that he maketh fire come down from heaven on the earth in the sight of men, and deceiveth them that dwell on the earth by means of those miracles which he had power to do in the sight of the beast; saying to them that dwell on the earth that they should make an image to the beast, which had the wound by a sword, and did live." (Ver. 13, 14.)

Now, each of the above three passages of holy Scripture refers to scenes which shall be enacted after the Church has been taken away out of this world; but on this we do not dwell, inasmuch as our object in quoting them for the reader is, to let him see how far the devil can go in the way of signs and wonders, to lead people away from the truth; and also to set before him the one divine and therefore perfect safeguard against all the delusive power of the enemy.

The human heart has no ability whatever to resist the influence of "great signs and wonders," put forth in favor of the most deadly error. There is but the one thing which can fortify the soul, and enable it to resist the devil and his deadly delusions, and that is, the Word of God. To have the precious truth of God treasured up in the heart is the divine secret of preservation from all error, even though backed up by the most astounding miracles.

Hence, in the first of the above quotations, we see

that the reason why people will be deceived by the signs and lying wonders of "that wicked" one is, "because they received not the love of the truth, that they might be saved." It is the love of the truth that preserves from error, be it ever so persuasive, ever so fascinating, ever so strongly supported by the powerful evidence of "great signs and wonders." It is not cleverness, intellectual power, mental grasp, extensive learning—all these things are perfectly powerless in the presence of Satan's wiles and machinations. The most gigantic human intellect must fall an easy prey to the wiles of the serpent.

But, blessed be God, the craft, the subtilty, the signs and lying wonders, all the resources of Satan, all the machinery of hell, are perfectly powerless with a heart that is governed by the love of the truth. A little child who knows and believes and loves the truth is blessedly shielded, sheltered, and divinely preserved from the blinding and deceiving power of the wicked one. If ten thousand false prophets were to arise and perform the most extraordinary miracles that were ever presented to the human gaze, in order to prove that the Bible is not the inspired Word of God, or that our Lord Jesus Christ is not God over all, blessed forever, or in order to set aside the glorious truth that the blood of Jesus Christ, God's Son, cleanseth from all sin, or any other precious truth revealed in holy Scripture, it could have no effect whatever on the very simplest babe in Christ whose heart is governed by the Word of God. Yea, if an angel from heaven were to come down and preach any thing contrary to what we are taught in the Word of God, we have a divine warrant to pronounce him anathema, without any discussion or argument whatever.

This is an unspeakable mercy. It puts the simple-hearted, unlettered child of God into the most blessed position—a position, not only of moral security, but of sweetest repose. We are not called upon to analyze the false doctrine, or to weigh the evidence advanced in favor of it; we reject, with stern decision, both the one and the other, simply because we have the certainty of the truth and the love of it in our hearts. "Thou shalt not hearken unto the words of that prophet, or that dreamer of dreams;"—although the sign or the wonder had come to pass—"for the Lord your God proveth you, to know whether ye love the Lord your God with all your heart and with all your soul."

Here, beloved reader, was the all-important point for Israel, and it is the same for us. Then, now, and always, the true moral security is in having the heart fortified with the love of the truth, which is only another way of expressing the love of God. The faithful Israelite who loved Jehovah, with all his heart and with all his soul, would have a ready and conclusive answer for all the false prophets and dreamers who might arise—a thoroughly effectual method of dealing with them. "Thou shalt not hearken." If the enemy does not get the ear, he is not likely to reach the heart. The sheep follow the Shepherd; "for they know His voice. And a stranger"—even though showing signs and wonders —"will they not follow, but will *flee from him.*" Why? Is it because they are able to discuss and argue and analyze? No, thanks and praise to God; but because "they know not the voice of strangers." The simple fact of not knowing the voice is a sufficient reason for not following the speaker.

All this is full of comfort and consolation for the beloved lambs and sheep of the flock of Christ. They can hear the voice of their loving, faithful Shepherd; they can gather around Him, and find in His presence true rest and perfect safety. He makes them to lie down in green pastures, and leads them by the still waters of His love. This is enough. They may be very weak—yea, perfect weakness in themselves—but this is no hindrance to their rest and blessing; quite the contrary, it only casts them more upon His almighty power. We need never be afraid of weakness; it is fancied strength we have to dread, vain confidence in our own wisdom, our own intelligence, our scriptural knowledge, our spiritual attainments—these are the things we have to fear; but as for our weakness, the more deeply we feel it the better, for our Shepherd's strength is made perfect in weakness, and His precious grace is amply sufficient for all the need of His beloved and blood-bought flock as a whole, and for each member in particular. Only let us keep near to Him in the abiding sense of our own perfect helplessness and nothingness; let us treasure up His precious Word in our hearts; let us feed upon it, as the very sustenance of our souls, day by day, the staple article of our lives, the living bread for the strengthening of the inward man. Thus shall we be safe from every strange voice, every false prophet, every snare of the devil, every influence which might tend to draw us away from the path of obedience, and the practical confession of the name of Christ.

We must now quote for the reader the second paragraph of our chapter, in which the Lord's people are warned against another snare of the devil. Oh, how many and varied are his snares and wiles! how manifold are the dangers of the people of God! but, blessed be His holy name, there is full provision in His Word for all.

"If thy brother, *the son of thy mother*,"—nearer, dearer, and more tender than the son of the father— "or thy son, or thy daughter, or the wife of thy bosom, or thy friend which is as thine own soul, entice thee secretly, saying, Let us go and serve other gods, *which thou hast not known*, thou, nor thy fathers, namely, of the gods of the people which are round about you, nigh unto thee, or far off from thee, from the one end of the earth even unto the other end of the earth; thou shalt not consent unto him, nor hearken unto him; neither shall thine eye pity him, neither shalt thou spare, neither shalt thou conceal him; but thou shalt surely kill him; thine hand shall be first upon him to put him to death, and afterwards the hand of all the people. And thou shalt stone him with stones that he die; because he hath sought to thrust thee away from the Lord thy God, which brought thee out of the land of Egypt, from the house of bondage. And all Israel shall hear, and fear, and shall do no more any such wickedness as this is among you." (Ver. 6–11.)

Here, then, we have something quite different from the false prophet or the dreamer of dreams. Thousands might be proof against the influence of these, and yet fall before the insnaring and seductive power of natural affection. It is very hard to resist the action of this latter. It demands deep-toned devotedness, great singleness of eye, firm purpose of heart, to deal faithfully with those who live deep down in our hearts' tender affections. The trial to some of withstanding and rejecting a prophet or a dreamer with whom there was no personal relationship, no tender link of fond affection, would be as nothing compared with having to treat with stern and severe decision the wife of the bosom, the beloved brother or sister, the devoted and tenderly loved friend.

But where the claims of God, of Christ, of truth are at stake, there must be no hesitation. If any should seek to make use of the ties of affection in order to draw us aside from our allegiance to Christ, we must resist them with unqualified decision. "If any man come to Me, and hate not his father, and mother, and wife, and children, and brethren, and sisters, yea, and his own life also, he cannot be My disciple." (Luke x. 26.)

Let us see that we thoroughly understand this

aspect of the truth, and also that we give it its proper place. If poor blind reason be listened to, it will be sure to present to the mind the most hideous perversion of this great practical subject. Reason, whenever it attempts to exercise its powers in the things of God, is sure to prove itself the active and efficient agent of the devil in opposition to the truth. In things human and earthly, reason may go for what it is worth; but in things divine and heavenly, it is not only worthless, but positively mischievous.

What then, we may ask, is the true moral force of Luke xiv. 26 and Deuteronomy xiii. 8–10 ? Most assuredly, they do not mean that we are to be "without natural affection," which is one of the special marks of the apostasy of the last days. This is perfectly clear. God Himself has established our natural relationships, and each of these relationships has its characteristic affections, the exercise and display of which are in lovely harmony with the mind of God. Christianity does not interfere with our relationships in nature, but it introduces a power whereby the responsibilities which attach to those relationships can be duly fulfilled to the glory of God. And not only so, but in the various epistles, the Holy Ghost has given the most ample instructions to husbands and wives, parents and children, masters and servants, thus proving, in the very fullest and most blessed manner, the divine sanction of those relationships and the affections which belong to them.

All this is perfectly plain; but still we have to inquire how it fits in with Luke xiv. and Deuteronomy xiii. The answer is simply this: The harmony is divinely perfect. Those scriptures apply only to cases in which our natural relationships and affections interfere with the claims of God and of Christ. When they operate in this way, they must be denied and mortified. If they dare to intrude upon a domain which is wholly divine, the sentence of death must be written upon them.

In contemplating the life of the only perfect man that ever trod this earth of ours, we can see how beautifully He adjusted the various claims which, as a man and a servant, He had to meet. He could say to His mother, "Woman, what have I to do with thee?" and yet, at the fitting moment, He could, with exquisite tenderness, commend that mother to the care of the disciple whom He loved. He could say to His parents, "Wist ye not that I must be about My Father's business?" and, at the same time, go home with them and be sweetly subject to parental authority. Thus the written teachings of holy Scripture, and the perfect ways of the living Christ, do both combine to teach us how to discharge aright the claims of nature and the claims of God.

But it may be that the reader feels considerable difficulty in reference to the line of action enjoined in Deuteronomy xiii. 9, 10. He may find it hard to reconcile it with a God of love, and with the grace, gentleness, and tenderness inculcated in the New-Testament scriptures. Here again we must keep a vigilant eye upon reason. It always affects to find ample scope for its powers in the stern enactments of the divine government; but, in reality, it only displays its blindness and folly. Still, though we would make very short work with infidel reason, we earnestly desire to help any honest soul who may not be able to see his way through this question.

We have had occasion, in our studies on the earlier chapters of this book, to refer to the very weighty subject of God's governmental dealings both with Israel and the nations; but, in addition to what has already come under our notice, we have to bear in mind the very important difference between the two economies of law and grace. If this be not clearly apprehended, we shall find very considerable difficulty in such passages as Deuteronomy xiii. 9, 10. The great characteristic principle of the Jewish economy was *righteousness;* the characteristic principle of Christianity is *grace*—pure, unqualified grace.

If this fact be fully grasped, all difficulty vanishes. It was perfectly right, perfectly consistent, and in perfect harmony with the mind of God for Israel to slay their enemies. God commanded them to do so. And, in like manner, it was right and consistent for them to execute righteous judgment, even unto death, upon any member of the congregation who should seek to draw them aside after false gods, as in the passage before us. To do so was in full moral harmony with the grand ruling principles of government and law, under which they were placed, in accordance with the dispensational wisdom of God. All this is perfectly plain. It runs through the entire canon of Old-Testament scripture. God's government in Israel, and His government of the world in connection with Israel, was on the strict principle of righteousness. And as it was in the past, so shall it be in the future,—"A king shall reign in righteousness, and princes shall rule in judgment."

But in Christianity, we see something quite different. The moment we open the pages of the New Testament, and hearken to the teachings and mark the actings of the Son of God, we find ourselves on entirely new ground, and in a new atmosphere; in a word, we are in the atmosphere and on the ground of pure, unqualified grace.

Thus, as a sample of the teaching, take a passage or two from what is called The Sermon on the Mount—that marvelous and precious compendium of the principles of the kingdom of heaven.—"Ye have heard that it hath been said, 'An eye for an eye, and a tooth for a tooth'; *but I say unto you*, that ye resist not evil; but whosoever shall smite thee on the one cheek, turn to him the other also. And if any man will sue thee at the law, and take away thy coat, let him have thy cloke also. And whosoever shall compel thee to go a mile, go with him twain." Again, "Ye have heard that it hath been said, 'Thou shalt love thy neighbor and hate thine enemy'; *but I say unto you*, Love your enemies, bless them that curse you, do good to them that hate you, and pray for them which despitefully use you, and persecute you; that ye may be the *sons* [*υἱοί*] of your Father which is in heaven; *for* He maketh His sun to rise on the evil and on the good, and sendeth rain on the just and on the unjust. . . . . Be ye therefore perfect [*τέλειοι*], even as your Father which is in heaven is perfect." (Matt. v. 38–48.)

We cannot now dwell upon those blessed sentences; we merely quote them for the reader in order to let him see the immense difference between the Jewish and Christian economy. What was perfectly right and consistent for a Jew, might be quite wrong and inconsistent for a Christian.

This is so plain that a child may see it; and yet, strange to say, many of the Lord's beloved people seem to be clouded on the subject. They judge it to be perfectly right for Christians to deal in righteousness, and go to war, and to exercise worldly power. Well, then, if it be right for Christians to act thus, we would simply ask, Where is it taught in the New Testament? where have we a single sentence from the lips of our Lord Jesus Christ, or from the pen of the Holy Ghost, to warrant or sanction such a thing? As we have said, in reference to other questions that have come before us in our studies on this book, it is of no possible use for us to say, " *We think* so and so." Our thoughts are simply worth nothing. The one grand question, in all matters of Christian faith and morals, is, "What saith the New Testament?" What did our Lord and Master teach, and what did He do? He taught that His people now are not to act as His people of old acted. *Righteousness* was the principle of the old economy; *grace* is the principle of the new.

This was what Christ taught, as may be seen in numberless passages of Scripture. And how did He act? Did He deal in righteousness with people? did He assert His rights? did He exercise worldly power? did He go to law? did He vindicate Himself, or retaliate? When His poor disciples, in utter ignorance of the heavenly principles which He taught, and in total forgetfulness of His whole course of action, said to Him, on one occasion in the which a certain village of the Samaritans refused to receive Him, "Lord, wilt Thou that we command fire to come down from heaven and consume them, even as Elias did?" what was His answer? "He turned and rebuked them, and said, 'Ye know not what manner of spirit ye are of; for the Son of Man is not come to destroy men's lives, but to save.' And they went to another village." It was perfectly consistent with the spirit, principle, and genius of the dispensation of which Elias was the exponent and representative, to call down fire from heaven to consume the men sent by a godless king to arrest him; but the blessed Lord was the perfect Exponent and divine Representative of another dispensation altogether. His was a life of perfect self-surrender, from first to last. He never asserted His rights. He came to serve and to give; He came to represent God—to be the perfect expression of the Father in every way. The Father's character shone out in His every look, His every word, His every act, His every movement.

Such was the Lord Christ when He was down here among men, and such was His teaching. He did what He taught, and He taught what He did. His words expressed what He was, and His ways illustrated His words. He came to serve and to give, and His whole life was marked by those two things, from the manger to the cross. We may truly say, time would fail us to quote the passages in proof and illustration of this; nor is there any need, inasmuch as the truth of it will hardly be called in question.

Well, then, is not He our great Exemplar in all things? is it not by His teaching and ways that our course and character as Christians are to be formed? How are we to know how we ought to walk, save by hearkening to His blessed words and gazing on His perfect ways? If we as Christians are to be guided and governed by the principles and precepts of the Mosaic economy, then, assuredly, it would be right for us to go to law, to contend for our rights, to engage in war, to destroy our enemies; but then what becomes of the teaching and example of our adorable Lord and Saviour? what of the teachings of the Holy Ghost? what of the New Testament? Is it not as plain as a sunbeam to the reader that for a Christian to do these things is to act in flagrant opposition to the teaching and example of his Lord?

Here, however, we may be met by the old and oft-repeated inquiry, "What would become of the world, what would become of its institutions, what would become of society, if such principles were to be universally dominant?" The infidel historian, in speaking of the early Christians, and their refusal to join the Roman army, sneeringly inquires, "What would have become of the empire, surrounded as it was on all sides by barbarians, if every one had indulged in such pusillanimous ideas as these?"

We reply at once, If those spiritual and heavenly principles were universally dominant, there would be no wars—no fighting, and hence there would be no need of soldiers, no need of standing armies or navies, no need of constabulary or police; there would be no wrong-doings, no strife about property, and hence no need of courts of law, judges, or magistrates; in short, the world as it now is would have an end; the kingdoms of this world would have become the kingdoms of our Lord and of His Christ.

But the plain fact is, those heavenly principles of which we speak are not intended for the world at all, inasmuch as the world could not adopt them, or act upon them for a single hour; to do so would involve the immediate and complete break-up of the present system of things, the dissolution of the entire framework of society as at present constituted.

Hence, the objection of the infidel crumbles into dust beneath our feet, like all other infidel objections, and the questions and the difficulties which are based upon them. They are deprived of every atom of moral force. Heavenly principles are not designed for "this present evil world" at all; they are de-signed for the Church, which is not of the world, even as Jesus is not of the world. "If," said our Lord to Pilate, "My kingdom were of this world, then would My servants fight, that I should not be delivered to the Jews; but *now* is My kingdom not from hence."

Mark the word "now." By and by, the kingdoms of this world will become the kingdom of our Lord; but now, He is rejected, and all who belong to Him —His Church—His people—are called to share His rejection, to follow Him into the outside place, and walk as pilgrims and strangers here below, waiting for the moment when He shall come to receive them to Himself, that where He is, there they may be also.

Now, it is the attempt to mix the world and the Church together that produces such terrible confu-sion. It is one of Satan's special wiles, and it has done more to mar the testimony of the Church of God and hinder its progress than most of us are aware. It involves a complete turning of things upside down, a confounding of things that differ essentially, an utter denial of the Church's true character, her position, her walk, and her hope. We sometimes hear the expression, "Christian world:" what does it mean? It is simply an at-tempt to combine two things which in their source, nature, and character are as diverse as light and darkness. It is an effort to tack a new piece upon an old garment, which, as our Lord tells us, only makes the rent worse.

11

It is not God's object to Christianize the world, but to call His people out of the world, to be a heavenly people, governed by heavenly principles, formed by a heavenly object, and cheered by a heavenly hope. If this be not clearly seen; if the truth as to the Church's true calling and course be not realized as a living power in the soul, we shall be sure to make the most grievous mistakes in our work, walk, and service. We shall make an entirely wrong use of the Old-Testament scriptures, not only on prophetic subjects, but in reference to the whole range of practical life; indeed, it would be utterly impossible to calculate the loss which must result from not seeing the distinctive calling, position, and hope of the Church of God, her association and identification—her living union with a rejected, risen, and glorified Christ.

We cannot attempt to enlarge upon this most precious and interesting theme; but we should just like to point out to the reader an instance or two illustrative of the Spirit's method of quoting and applying Old-Testament scripture. Take, for example, the following passage from that lovely thirty-fourth psalm,—"The face of the Lord is against them that do evil, to cut off the remembrance of them from the earth." Now, mark the way in which the Holy Spirit quotes this passage in the first epistle of Peter.—"The face of the Lord is against them that do evil." (Chap. iii. 12.) Not a word about cutting off. Why is this? Because the Lord is not now acting upon the principle of cutting off.

He acted upon it under the law, and He will act upon it in the kingdom by and by; but just now, He is acting in grace and long-suffering mercy. His face is quite as much and quite as decidedly against all evil-doers as ever it was or ever it will be, but not now to cut off the remembrance of them from the earth. The most striking illustration of this marvelous grace and forbearance, and of the difference between the two principles on which we have been dwelling, is seen in the fact that the very men who with wicked hands crucified His only begotten and well-beloved Son—evil-doers, surely, of the most pronounced type,—instead of being cut off from the earth, were the very first to hear the message of full and free pardon through the blood of the cross.

Now, it may appear to some that we are making too much of the mere omission of a single clause of Old-Testament scripture. Let not the reader think so. Even had we but this one instance, it would be a serious mistake to treat it with any thing like indifference. But the fact is, there are scores of passages of the same character as the one just quoted, all illustrative of the contrast between the Jewish and Christian economies, and also between Christianity and the coming kingdom.

God is now dealing in grace with the world, and so should His people, if they want to be like Him, and such they are called to be. "Be ye therefore perfect, even as your Father which is in heaven is perfect." And again, "Be ye therefore imitators of God, as dear children; and walk in love, as Christ also hath loved us, and hath given Himself for us, an offering and a sacrifice to God for a sweet-smelling savor." (Eph. v. 1.)

This is our model. We are called to copy our Father's example—to imitate Him. He is not going to law with the world; He is not enforcing His rights with the strong hand of power. By and by He will; but just now, in this day of grace, He showers His blessings and benefits in rich profusion upon those whose life is one of enmity and rebellion against Him.

All this is perfectly marvelous, but thus it is; and we, as Christians, are called to act on this morally glorious principle. It may be said by some, How could we ever get on in the world—how could we conduct our business on such a principle as this? We should be robbed and ruined; designing people would take advantage of us if they knew that we would not go to law with them; they would take our goods, or borrow our money, or occupy our houses, and refuse to pay us. In short, we could never get on in a world like this if we did not assert our rights and establish our claims by the strong hand of power. What is the law for but to make people behave themselves? Are not the powers that be ordained of God for the very purpose of maintaining peace and good order in our midst? What would become of society if we had not soldiers, policemen, magistrates, and judges? And if God has ordained that such things should be, why should not His people avail themselves of them? and not only so, but who so fit to occupy places of authority and power, or to wield the sword of justice, as the people of God?

There is, no doubt, very great apparent force in all this line of argument. The powers that be are ordained of God. The king, the governor, the judge, the magistrate, are, each in his place, the expression of the power of God. It is God who invests each with the power which he wields; it is He who has put the sword into his hand, for the punishment of evil-doers, and the praise of them that do well. We bless God with all our hearts for the constituted authorities of the country. Day and night, in private and in public, we pray for them. It is our bounden duty to obey and submit ourselves to them in all things, provided always that they do not call upon us to disobey God, or do violence to conscience. If they do this, we must— what? Resist? Nay, but suffer.

All this is perfectly plain. The world as it now is could not go on for a single day if men were not kept in order by the strong hand of power. We could not live, or at least life would be perfectly intolerable, were it not that evil-doers are kept in terror of the glittering sword of justice. Even as it is, through lack of moral power on the part of those who bear the sword, lawless demagogues are allowed to stir up the evil passions of men to resist the law of the land and disturb the peace and threaten the lives and property of well-disposed and harmless subjects of the government.

But admitting all this, in the fullest possible manner, as every intelligent Christian, every one taught by Scripture, most assuredly will, it leaves wholly untouched the question of the Christian's path in this world. Christianity fully recognizes all the governmental institutions of the country. It forms no part of the Christian's business to interfere, in any one way, with such institutions. Wherever he is, whatever be the principle or character of the government of the country in which his lot is cast, it is his duty to recognize its municipal and political arrangements, to pay taxes, pray for the government, honor governors in their official capacity, wish well to the legislature and the executive, pray for the peace of the country, live in peace with all, so far as in him lies.

We see all this in the blessed Master Himself in perfection, blessed be His holy name for evermore! In His memorable reply to the crafty Herodians, He recognizes the principle of subjection to the powers that be—"Render to Cæsar the things that be Cæsar's, and to God the things that be God's." And not only so, but we find Him also paying tribute, athough personally free. They had no right to demand it of Him, as He plainly shows to Peter; and it might be said, Why did He not appeal? Appeal! Nay; He shows us something quite different. Hear His exquisite reply to His mistaken apostle—"Notwithstanding, *lest we should offend them*, go thou to the sea, and cast a hook, and take up the fish that first cometh up; and when thou hast opened his mouth, thou shalt find a piece of money; that take and give unto them *for Me and thee.*"* (Matt. xvii.)

And here we get back, with increased moral force, to our thesis, namely, the Christian's path in this world. What is it? He is to follow his Master—to imitate Him in all things. Did He assert His rights? did He go to law? did He try to regulate the world? did He meddle with municipal or political matters? was He a politician? did He wield the sword? did He consent to be a judge or a divider, even when appealed to, as we say, to arbitrate about property? was not His whole life one of complete self-surrender, from first to last? was He not continually giving up, until, at the cross, He gave up His precious life as a ransom for many?

We shall leave these questions to find their answer deep down in the heart of the Christian reader, and to produce their practical effect in his life. We trust that the foregoing line of truth will enable him to interpret aright such passages as Deuteronomy xiii. 9, 10. Our opposition to idolatry and our separation from evil, in every shape and form, while not less intense and decided, most surely, than that of Israel of old, is not to be displayed in the same way. The Church is imperatively called upon to put away evil and evil-doers, but not after the same fashion as Israel. It is no part of her duty to stone idolaters and blasphemers, or burn witches. The church

---

*The fact that the tribute-money may have been for the temple does not touch the principle set forth in the text.

of Rome has acted upon this principle, and even Protestants (to the shame of Protestantism) have followed her example.* The Church is not called— nay, she is positively and peremptorily forbidden to use the temporal sword. It is a flat denial of her calling, character, and mission to do so. When Peter, in ignorant zeal and carnal haste, drew the sword in defense of his blessed Master, he was at once corrected by his Master's faithful word, and instructed by his Master's gracious act,—"Put up thy sword into the sheath; for all they that take the sword shall perish by the sword." And having thus reproved the act of His mistaken though well-meaning servant, He undid the mischief by His gracious touch. "The weapons of our warfare," says the inspired apostle, "are not carnal, but mighty through God to the pulling down of strongholds, casting down imaginations, and every high thing that exalteth itself against the knowledge of God, and bringing into captivity every thought to the obedience of Christ." (2 Cor. x. 4, 5.)

The professing church has gone all astray as to this great and most important question. She has joined herself with the world, and sought to further

---

*The burning of Servetus, in 1553, for his theological opinions, is a frightful blot upon the Reformation, and upon the man who sanctioned such an unchristian proceeding. True, the opinions of Servetus were fatally and fundamentally false,—he held the Arian heresy, which is simply blasphemy against the Son of God; but to burn him, or any one else, for false doctrine, was a flagrant sin against the spirit, genius, and principle of the gospel, the deplorable fruit of ignorance as to the essential difference between Judaism and Christianity.

the cause of Christ by carnal and worldly agency. She had ignorantly attempted to maintain the Christian faith by the most shameful denial of Christian practice. The burning of heretics stands as a most fearful moral blot upon the page of the church's history. We can form no adequate idea of the terrible consequences resulting from the notion that the Church was called to take Israel's place and act on Israel's principles.* It completely falsified her testimony, robbed her of her entirely spiritual and heavenly character, and led her upon a path which ends in Revelation xvii. and xviii. Let him that readeth understand.

But we must not pursue this line of things further here. We trust that what has passed before us will lead all whom it may concern to consider the whole subject in the light of the New Testament, and thus be the means, through the infinite goodness of God, of leading them to see the path of entire separation which we as Christians are called to tread; *in* the world, but not *of* it, even as our Lord Christ is not of it. This will solve a thousand difficulties, and furnish a grand general principle which can be practically applied to a thousand details.

We shall now conclude our study of Deuteronomy xiii. by a glance at its closing paragraph.

"If thou shalt hear say in one of thy cities, which

---

*It is one thing for the Church to learn from the history of Israel, and another thing altogether to take Israel's place, act on Israel's principles, and appropriate Israel's promises. The former is the Church's duty and privilege; the latter has been the Church's fatal mistake.

the Lord thy God hath given thee to dwell there, saying, Certain men, the children of Belial, are gone out from among you, and have withdrawn the inhabitants of their city, saying, Let us go and serve other gods, which ye have not known; *then shalt thou inquire, and make search, and ask diligently;* and, behold, *if it be truth, and the thing certain*, that such abomination is *wrought among you*, thou shalt surely smite the inhabitants of that city with the edge of the sword, destroying it utterly, and all that is therein, and the cattle thereof, with the edge of the sword. And thou shalt gather all the spoil of it into the midst of the street thereof, and shalt burn with fire the city, and all the spoil thereof every whit, *for the Lord thy God;* and it shall be a heap forever; it shall not be built again. And there shall cleave naught of the cursed thing to thine hand; that the Lord may turn from the fierceness of His anger, and show thee mercy, and have compassion upon thee, and multiply thee, as He hath sworn unto thy fathers; when thou shalt hearken to the voice of the Lord thy God, to keep all His commandments which I command thee this day, to do that which is right in the eyes of the Lord thy God.'' (Ver. 12–18.)

Here we have instruction of the most solemn and weighty character. But the reader must bear in mind that, solemn and weighty as it most surely is, it is based upon a truth of unspeakable value, and that is, Israel's national unity. If we do not see this, we shall miss the real force and meaning of the foregoing quotation. A case is supposed of grave error in some one of the cities of Israel, and the question might naturally arise, Are all the cities involved in the evil of one?*

Assuredly, inasmuch as the nation was one. The cities and tribes were not independent; they were bound up together by a sacred bond of national unity—a unity which had its centre in the place of the divine presence. Israel's twelve tribes were indissolubly bound together. The twelve loaves on the golden table in the sanctuary formed the beauteous type of this unity, and every true Israelite owned and rejoiced in this unity. The twelve stones in Jordan's bed, the twelve stones on Jordan's bank, Elijah's twelve stones on Mount Carmel—all set forth the same grand truth—the indissoluble unity of Israel's twelve tribes. The good king Hezekiah recognized this truth when he commanded that the burnt-offering and the sin-offering should be made for *all Israel.* (2 Chron. xxix. 24.) The faithful Josiah owned it and acted upon it when he carried his reformatory operations into all the countries that pertained to the children of Israel. (2 Chron xxxiv. 33.) Paul, in his magnificent address before king Agrippa, bears witness to the same truth when he says, "Unto which promise *our twelve tribes*, instantly serving God day and night, hope to come."† (Acts

---

*It is, of course, needful to bear in mind that the evil referred to in the text was of the very gravest character. It was an attempt to draw the people away from the one living and true God. It touched the very foundation of Israel's national existence. It was not merely a local or municipal question, but a national one.

†It may interest the reader to know that the word rendered,

xxvi. 7.) And when we look forward into the bright future, the same glorious truth shines, with heavenly lustre, in the seventh chapter of Revelation, where we see the twelve tribes sealed and secured for blessing, rest, and glory, in connection with a countless multitude of the Gentiles. And finally, in Revelation xxi. we see the names of the twelve tribes engraved on the gates of the holy Jerusalem, the seat and centre of the glory of God and the Lamb.

Thus, from the golden table in the sanctuary to the golden city descending out of heaven from God, we have a marvelous chain of evidence in proof of the grand truth of the indissoluble unity of Israel's twelve tribes.

And then, if the question be asked, Where is this unity to be seen? or how did Elijah or Hezekiah or Josiah or Paul see it? The answer is a very simple one—They saw it by faith; they looked within the sanctuary of God, and there, on the golden table, they beheld the twelve loaves, setting forth the perfect distinctness and yet the perfect oneness of the twelve tribes. Nothing can be more beautiful. The truth of God must stand forever. Israel's unity was seen in the past, and it will be seen in the future; and though, like the higher unity of the Church, it is unseen in the present, faith believes it all the same, holds it and confesses it in the face of ten thousand hostile influences.

---

in the above passage, "twelve tribes," is singular—τὸ δῶδε-κάφυλον. It certainly gives very full and vivid expression to the grand idea of indissoluble unity which is so precious to God, and therefore so precious to faith.

And now let us look for a moment at the practical application of this most glorious truth, as presented in the closing paragraph of Deuteronomy xiii. A report reaches a city in the far north of the land of Israel of serious error taught in a certain city in the extreme south—deadly error, tending to draw the inhabitants away from the true God.

What is to be done? The law is as plain as possible; the path of duty is laid down with such distinctness that it only needs a single eye to see it, and a devoted heart to tread it. "Then shalt thou inquire, and make search, and ask diligently." This surely is simple enough.

But some of the citizens might say, "What have we in the north to do with error taught in the south? Thank God, there is no error taught amongst us; it is entirely a local question; each city is responsible for the maintenance of the truth within its own walls. How could we be expected to examine into every case of error which may spring up here and there all over the land? our whole time would be taken up, so that we could not attend to our fields, our vineyards, our oliveyards, our flocks, and our herds. It is quite as much as we can do to keep our own borders all right. We certainly condemn the error, and if any one holding or teaching it were to come here, and that we knew of it, we should most decidedly shut our gates against him. Beyond this, we do not feel ourselves responsible to go.

Now, what, we may ask, would be the reply of the faithful Israelite to all this line of argument which, in the judgment of mere nature, seems so exceedingly plausible? A very simple and very conclusive one, we may be sure. He would say it was simply a denial of Israel's unity. If every city and every tribe were to take independent ground, then verily the high-priest might take the twelve loaves off the golden table before the Lord and scatter them here and there and every where; our unity is gone; we are all broken up into independent atoms, having no national ground of action.

Besides, the commandment is most distinct and explicit—"Thou shalt inquire, and make search, and ask diligently." We are bound, therefore, on the double ground of the nation's unity and the plain command of our covenant-God. It is of no possible use to say there is no error taught amongst *us*, unless we want to separate ourselves from the nation; if we belong to Israel, then verily the error is taught amongst us, as the Word says, "Such abomination is wrought *among you.*" How far does the "you" extend? As far as the national boundaries. Error taught at Dan affects those dwelling at Beersheba. How is this? Because Israel is one.

And then the Word is so plain, so distinct, so emphatic. We are bound to search into it. We cannot fold our arms and sit down in cold indifference and culpable neutrality, else we shall be involved in the awful consequences of this evil; yea, we *are* involved until we clear ourselves of it by judging it, with unflinching decision and unsparing severity.

Such, beloved reader, would be the language of

every loyal Israelite, and such his mode of acting in reference to error and evil wherever found. To speak or act otherwise would simply be indifference as to the truth and glory of God, and independency as regards Israel. For any to say that they were not responsible to act according to the instructions given in Deuteronomy xiii. 12–18, would be a complete surrender of the truth of God and of Israel's unity. All were bound to act, or else be involved in the judgment of the guilty city.

And surely if all this was true in Israel of old, it is not less true in the Church of God now. We may rest assured that any thing like indifference where Christ is concerned is most hateful to God. It is the eternal purpose and counsel of God to glorify His Son; that every knee should bow to Him, and every tongue confess that He is Lord to the glory of God the Father; "that all should honor the Son even as they honor the Father."

Hence, if Christ be dishonored,—if doctrines be taught derogatory to the glory of His Person, the efficacy of His work, or the virtue of His offices, we are bound, by every motive which could possibly act on our hearts, to reject, with stern decision, such doctrines. Indifference or neutrality where the Son of God is concerned is high treason in the judgment of the high court of Heaven. We would not be indifferent if it were a question of our own reputation, our personal character, or our personal or family property; we should be thoroughly alive to any thing affecting ourselves or those dear to us.

How much more deeply ought we to feel in reference to what concerns the glory and honor, the name and cause, of the One to whom we owe our present and everlasting all—the One who laid aside His glory, came down into this wretched world, and died a shameful death upon the cross, in order to save us from the everlasting flames of hell. Could we be indifferent to Him? neutral where He is concerned? God, in His great mercy, forbid!

No, reader; it must not be. The honor and glory of Christ must be more to us than all beside. Reputation, property, family, friends—all must stand aside if the claims of Christ are involved. Does not the Christian reader own this, with all the energy of his ransomed soul? We feel persuaded he does, even now; and oh, how shall we feel when we see Him face to face, and stand in the full light of His moral glory? with what feelings shall we then contemplate the idea of indifference or neutrality with respect to Him!

And are we not justified in declaring that next to the glory of the Head stands the great truth of the unity of His body—the Church? Unquestionably. If the nation of Israel was one, how much more is the body of Christ one! and if independency was wrong in Israel, how much more wrong in the Church of God! The plain fact is this: the idea of independency cannot be maintained for a moment in the light of the New Testament. As well might we say that the hand is independent of the foot, or the eye of the ear, as assert that the members of the body of Christ are independent one of another. "For as the body is one, and hath many members, and all the members of that one body, being many, are one body; *so also is Christ*"—a very remarkable statement, setting forth the intimate union of Christ and the Church.—"*For by one Spirit are we all baptized into one body*, whether we be Jews or Gentiles, whether bond or free; and have been all made to drink into one Spirit. For the body is not one member, but many. If the foot shall say, Because I am not the hand, I am not of the body; is it therefore not of the body? And if the ear shall say, Because I am not the eye, I am not of the body; is it therefore not of the body? If the whole body were an eye, where were the hearing? If the whole were hearing, where were the smelling? But now hath God set the members every one of them in the body, as 'it hath pleased Him. And if they were all one member, where were the body? But now are they many members, yet but one body. And the eye cannot say unto the hand, I have no need of thee; nor again, the head to the feet, I have no need of you. Nay, much more, those members of the body which seem to be more feeble, are necessary; and those members of the body which we think to be less honorable, upon these we bestow more abundant honor; and our uncomely parts have more abundant comeliness; for our comely parts have no need; but God hath tempered the body together, having given more abundant honor to that part which lacked: *that there should be no schism in the body;* but that the members should have the same care one for another. And whether one member suffer, all the members suffer with it; or one member be honored, all the members rejoice with it. Now YE ARE THE BODY OF CHRIST, AND MEMBERS IN PARTICULAR." (1 Cor. xii. 12–27.)

We do not attempt to dwell upon this truly marvelous scripture; but we earnestly desire to call the attention of the Christian reader to the special truth which it so forcibly sets before us—a truth which intimately concerns every true believer on the face of the earth, namely, *that he is a member of the body of Christ.* This is a great practical truth, involving, at once, the very highest privileges and the very weightiest responsibilities. It is not merely a true doctrine, a sound principle, or an orthodox opinion; it is a living fact, designed to be a divine power in the soul. The Christian can no longer view himself as an independent person, having no association, no vital link, with others. He is livingly bound up with all the children of God—all true believers—all the members of Christ's body upon the face of the earth.

"By one Spirit are we all baptized into one body." The Church of God is not a mere club, or a society, an association, or a brotherhood; it is a body united by the Holy Ghost to the Head in heaven; and all its members on earth are indissolubly bound together. This being so, it follows, of necessity, that all the members of the body are affected by the state and walk of each. "If one member suffer, all the members suffer with it,"—that is, all the members of the body. If there is any thing wrong with the foot, the hand feels it. How? Through the head. So in the Church of God, if any thing goes wrong with an individual member, all feel it through the Head with whom all are livingly connected by the Holy Ghost.

Some find it very hard to grasp this great truth; but there it stands plainly revealed on the inspired page, not to be reasoned about, or submitted in any way to the human judgment, but simply to be believed. It is a divine revelation. No human mind could ever have conceived such a thought; but God reveals it, faith believes it, and walks in the blessed power of it.

It may be the reader feels disposed to ask, How is it possible for the state of one believer to affect those who know nothing about it? The answer is, "If one member suffer, all the members suffer with it." All the members of what? Is it of any mere local assembly or company who may happen to know or be locally connected with the person concerned? Nay, but the members of the body wherever they are. Even in the case of Israel, where it was only a national unity, we have seen that if there was evil in any one of their cities, all were concerned, all involved, all affected. Hence, when Achan sinned, although there were myriads of people totally ignorant of the fact, the Lord said, "*Israel* hath sinned," and the whole assembly suffered a humiliating defeat.

Can reason grasp this weighty truth? No; but

faith can. If we listen to reason, we shall believe
nothing; but, by the grace of God, we shall not
listen to reason, but believe what God says because
He says it.

And oh, beloved Christian reader, what an immense truth is this unity of the body! What practical consequences flow out of it! How eminently
calculated it is to minister to holiness of walk and
life! How watchful it would make us over ourselves
—our habits, our ways, our whole moral condition!
How careful it would make us not to dishonor the
Head *to* whom we are united, or grieve the Spirit *by*
whom we are united, or injure the members *with*
whom we are united!

But we must close this chapter, much as we should
like to linger over one of the very grandest, most
profound, and most powerful formative truths that
can possibly engage our attention. May the Spirit of
God make it a living power in the soul of every true
believer on the face of the earth.

CHAPTER XIV.

"YE are the children of the Lord your God; ye
shall not cut yourselves, nor make any baldness between your eyes for the dead; for thou art
a holy people unto the Lord thy God, and the Lord
hath chosen thee to be a peculiar people unto Himself, above all the nations that are upon the earth."
(Ver. 1. 2.)

The opening clause of this chapter sets before us the basis of all the privileges and responsibilities of the Israel of God. It is a familiar thought amongst us that we must be in a relationship before we can know the affections or discharge the duties which belong to it. This is a plain and undeniable truth. If a man were not a father, no amount of argument or explanation could make him understand the feelings or affections of a father's heart; but the very moment he enters upon the relationship, he knows all about them.

Thus it is as to every relationship and position, and thus it is in the things of God. We cannot understand the affections or the duties of a child of God until we are on the ground. We must be Christians before we can perform Christian duties. Even when we are Christians, it is only by the gracious aid of the Holy Ghost that we can walk as such; but clearly, if we are not on Christian ground, we can know nothing of Christian affections or Christian duties. This is so obvious that argument is needless.

Now, most evidently, it is God's prerogative to declare how His children ought to conduct themselves, and it is their high privilege and holy responsibility to seek, in all things, to meet His gracious approval. "Ye *are* the children of the Lord your God: ye shall not cut yourselves." They were not their own; they belonged to Him, and therefore they had no right to cut themselves or disfigure their faces for the dead. Nature, in its pride and self-will, might say, Why may we not do like other people? What harm can there be in cutting ourselves, or making a baldness between our eyes? It is only an expression of grief, an affectionate tribute to our loved departed ones. Surely there can be nothing morally wrong in such a suited expression of sorrow.

To all this there was one simple but conclusive answer—"Ye are the children of the Lord your God." This fact altered every thing. The poor ignorant and uncircumcised Gentiles around them might cut and disfigure themselves, inasmuch as they knew not God, and were not in relationship to Him; but as for Israel, they were on the high and holy ground of nearness to God, and this one fact was to give tone and character to all their habits. They were not called upon to adopt or refrain from any particular habit or custom *in order to be* the children of God. This would be, as we say, beginning at the wrong end; but *being* His children, they were to act as such.

"Thou *art* a holy people unto the Lord thy God." He does not say, Ye *ought to be* a holy people. How could they ever make themselves a holy people, or a peculiar people, unto Jehovah? Utterly impossible. If they were not His people, no efforts of theirs could ever make them such. But God, in His sovereign grace, in pursuance of His covenant with their fathers, had *made* them His children, *made* them a peculiar people above all the nations that were upon the earth. Here was the solid foundation of Israel's moral edifice. All their habits and customs, all their doings and ways, their food and their clothing, what they did and what they did not do—all was to flow out of the one grand fact, with which they had no more to do than with their natural birth, namely, that they actually were the children of God, the people of His choice, the people of His own special possession.

Now, we cannot but acknowledge it to be a privilege of the very highest order to have the Lord so near to us, and so interested in all our habits and ways. To mere nature, no doubt—to one who does not know the Lord—is not in relationship to Him, the very idea of His holy presence, or of nearness to Him, would be simply intolerable: but to every true believer—every one who really loves God, it is a most delightful thought to have Him near us, and to know that He interests Himself in all the most minute details of our personal history and most private life; that He takes cognizance of what we eat and what we wear; that He looks after us by day and by night, sleeping and waking, at home and abroad; in short, that His interest in and care for us go far beyond those of the most tender, loving mother for her babe.

All this is perfectly wonderful; and surely, if we only realized it more fully, we should live a very different sort of life, and have a very different tale to tell. What a holy privilege—what a precious reality, to know that our loving Lord is about our path by day, and about our bed by night; that His eye rests upon us when we are dressing in the morning, when we sit down to our meals, when we go about our business, and in all our intercourse from morning till night! May the sense of this be a living and abiding power in the heart of every child of God on the face of the earth.

From verse 3 to 20, we have the law as to clean and unclean beasts, fishes, and fowls. The leading principles as to all these have already come under our notice in the eleventh chapter of Leviticus;* but there is a very important difference between the two scriptures. The instructions in Leviticus are given primarily to Moses and Aaron; in Deuteronomy, they are given directly to the people. This is perfectly characteristic of the two books. Leviticus may be specially termed, The priest's guide-book. In Deuteronomy, the priests are almost entirely in the back-ground, and the people are prominent. This is strikingly apparent all through the book, so that there is not the slightest foundation for the idea that Deuteronomy merely repeats Leviticus. Nothing can be further from the truth. Each book has its own peculiar province, its own design, its own work. The devout student sees and owns this with deep delight. Infidels are willfully blind, and can see nothing.

In verse 21 of our chapter, the marked distinction between the Israel of God and the stranger

---

*As we have given in our "Notes on the Book of Leviticus," chapter xi., what we believe to be the scriptural import of verses 4-20 of our chapter, we must refer the reader to what is there advanced.

is strikingly presented.—"Ye shall not eat of any thing that dieth of itself; *thou shalt give it unto the stranger* that is in thy gates, that *he may eat it;* or thou mayest sell it unto an alien; for thou art a holy people unto the Lord thy God." The grand fact of Israel's relationship to Jehovah marked them off from all the nations under the sun. It was not that they were, in themselves, a whit better or holier than others; but Jehovah was holy, and they were His people. "Be ye holy, for I am holy."

Worldly people often think that Christians are very pharisaic in separating themselves from other people, and refusing to take part in the pleasures and amusements of the world; but they do not really understand the question. The fact is, for a Christian to participate in the vanities and follies of a sinful world would be, to use a typical phrase, like an Israelite eating that which had died of itself. The Christian, thank God, has gotten something better to feed upon than the poor dead things of this world. He has the Living Bread that came down from heaven—the true Manna; and not only so, but he eats of "the old corn of the land of Canaan," type of the risen and glorified Man in the heavens. Of these most precious things the poor unconverted worldling knows absolutely nothing, and hence he must feed upon what the world has to offer him. It is not a question of the right or the wrong of things looked at in themselves. No one could possibly have known aught about the wrong of eating of any thing that had died of itself if God's word had not settled it.

This is the all-important point for us. We cannot expect the world to see or feel with us as to matters of right and wrong. It is our business to look at things from a divine stand-point. Many things may be quite consistent for a worldly man to do which a Christian could not touch at all, simply because he is a Christian. The question which the true believer has to ask as to every thing which comes before him is simply, Can I do this to the glory of God ? can I connect the name of Christ with it ? If not, he must not touch it.

In a word, the Christian's standard and test for every thing is Christ. This makes it all so simple. Instead of asking, Is such a thing consistent with *our* profession, *our* principles, *our* character, or *our* reputation ? we have to ask, Is it consistent with Christ ? This makes all the difference. Whatever is unworthy of Christ is unworthy of a Christian. If this be thoroughly understood and laid hold of, it will furnish a great practical rule which may be applied to a thousand details. If the heart be true to Christ,—if we walk according to the instincts of the divine nature, as strengthened by the ministry of the Holy Ghost, and guided by the authority of holy Scripture, we shall not be much troubled with questions of right or wrong in our daily life.

Before proceeding to quote for the reader the lovely paragraph which closes our chapter, we would very briefly call his attention to the last clause of verse 21.—"Thou shalt not seethe a kid in his mother's milk." The fact that this commandment is given three times, in various connections, is sufficient to mark it as one of special interest and practical importance. The question is, What does it mean ? what are we to learn from it ? We believe it teaches very plainly that the Lord's people must carefully avoid every thing contrary to nature. Now, it was manifestly contrary to nature that what was intended for a creature's nourishment should be used to seethe it.

We find, all through the Word of God, great prominence given to what is according to nature— what is comely. "Does not even nature itself teach you ?" says the inspired apostle to the assembly at Corinth. There are certain feelings and instincts implanted in nature by the Creator which must never be outraged. We may set it down as a fixed principle, an axiom in Christian ethics, that no action can possibly be of God that offers violence to the sensibilities proper to nature. The Spirit of God may, and often does, lead us beyond and above nature, but never against it.

We shall now turn to the closing verses of our chapter, in which we shall find some uncommonly fine practical instruction. "Thou shalt truly tithe all the increase of thy seed, that the field bringeth forth year by year. And thou shalt eat before the Lord thy God, in the place which He shall choose to place His name there, the tithe of thy corn, of thy wine, and of thine oil, and the firstlings of thy herds and of thy flocks; that thou mayest learn to fear the Lord thy God always. And if the way be too long for thee, so that thou art not able to carry it; or if the place be too far from thee, which the Lord thy God shall choose to set His name there, when the Lord thy God hath blessed thee; then shalt thou turn it into money, and bind up the money in thine hand, and shalt go unto the place which the Lord thy God shall choose; and thou shalt bestow that money for whatsoever thy soul lusteth after—for oxen, or for sheep, or for wine, or for strong drink, or for whatsoever thy soul desireth; and thou shalt eat there before the Lord thy God, and thou shalt rejoice, thou, and thine household, and the Levite that is within thy gates; thou shalt not forsake him, for he hath no part nor inheritance with thee. At the end of three years thou shalt bring forth all the tithe of thine increase the same year, and shalt lay it up within thy gates. And the Levite (because he hath no part nor inheritance with thee), and the stranger, and the fatherless, and the widow, which are within thy gates, shall come, and shall eat and be satisfied, that the Lord thy God may bless thee in all the work of thine hand which thou doest." (Ver. 22–29.)

This is a deeply interesting and most important passage, setting before us, with special simplicity, the *basis*, the *centre*, and *practical features* of Israel's national and domestic religion. The grand foundation of Israel's worship was laid in the fact that both they themselves and their land belonged to Jehovah.

The land was His, and they held as tenants under Him. To this precious truth they were called, periodically, to bear testimony by faithfully tithing their land "Thou shalt *truly* tithe all the increase of thy seed that thy field bringeth forth year by year." They were to own, in this practical way, the proprietorship of Jehovah, and never lose sight of it: they were to own no other landlord but the Lord their God. All they were and all they had belonged to Him. This was the solid ground-work of their national worship—their national religion.

And then as to the centre, it is set forth with equal clearness. They were to gather to the place where Jehovah recorded His name. Precious privilege for all who truly loved that glorious name! We see in this passage, as also in many other portions of the Word of God, what importance He attached to the periodical gatherings of His people around Himself. Blessed be His name, He delighted to see His beloved people assembled in His presence, happy in Him and in one another; rejoicing together in their common portion, and feeding in sweet and loving fellowship on the fruit of Jehovah's land. "Thou shalt eat before the Lord thy God, *in the place which He shall choose*, to place His name there, the tithe of thy corn, ... *that thou mayest learn to fear the Lord thy God always.*"

There was, there could be, no other place like that, in the judgment of every faithful Israelite, every true lover of Jehovah. All such would delight to flock to the hallowed spot where that beloved and

revered name was recorded. It might seem strange
and unaccountable to those who knew not the God
of Israel, and cared nothing about Him, to see the
people traveling—many of them—a long distance
from their homes, and carrying their tithes to one
particular spot. They might feel disposed to call in
question the needs-be for such a custom. Why not
eat at home? they might say. But the simple fact
is, such persons knew nothing whatever about the
matter, and were wholly incapable of entering into
the preciousness of it. To the Israel of God, there
was the one grand moral reason for journeying to
the appointed place, and that reason was found in
the glorious motto, *Jehovah Shammah*—"The Lord
is there." If an Israelite had willfully determined
to stay at home, or to go to some place of his own
choosing, he would neither have met Jehovah there
nor his brethren, and hence he would have eaten
alone. Such a course would have incurred the judgment of God; it would have been an abomination.
There was but one centre, and that was not of man's
choosing, but of God's. The godless Jeroboam, for
his own selfish, political ends, presumed to interfere
with the divine order, and set up his calves at Bethel
and Dan; but the worship offered there was offered
to demons and not to God. It was a daring act of
wickedness, which brought down upon him and upon
his house the righteous judgment of God; and we
see, in Israel's after history, that "Jeroboam the son
of Nebat" is used as the terrible model of iniquity
for all the wicked kings.

But all the faithful in Israel were sure to be found at the one divine centre, and no where else. You would not find such making all sorts of excuses for staying at home; neither would you find them running hither and thither to places of their own or other people's choosing; no, you would find them gathered to Jehovah Shammah, and there alone. Was this narrowness and bigotry? Nay; it was the fear and love of God. If Jehovah had appointed a place where He would meet His people, assuredly His people should meet Him there.

And not only had He appointed a place, but, in His abounding goodness, He devised a means of making that place as convenient as possible for His worshiping people. Thus we read, "And if the way be too long for thee, so that thou art not able to carry it; or if *the place* be too far from thee *which the Lord thy God shall choose to set His name there*, when the Lord thy God hath blessed thee; then thou shalt turn it into money, and bind up the money in thine hand, and shalt go unto the place which the Lord thy God shall choose: . . . and *thou shalt eat there before the Lord thy God*, and thou shalt rejoice, thou and thy household."

This is perfectly beautiful. The Lord, in His tender care and considerate love, took account of every thing. He would not leave a single difficulty in the way of His beloved people, in the matter of their assembling around Himself. He had His own special joy in seeing His redeemed people happy in his presence, and all who loved His name would delight to meet the loving desire of His heart by being found at the divinely appointed centre.

If any Israelite were found neglecting the blessed occasion of assembling with his brethren at the divinely chosen place and time, it would have simply proved that he had no heart for God or for His people, or, what was worse, that he was willfully absent. He might reason as he pleased about his being happy at home, happy elsewhere; it was a false happiness, inasmuch as it was happiness found in the path of disobedience, the path of willful neglect of the divine appointment.

All this is full of most valuable instruction for the Church of God now. It is the will of God now, no less than of old, that His people should assemble in His presence, on divinely appointed ground, and to a divinely appointed centre. This, we presume, will hardly be called in question by any one having a spark of divine light in his soul. The instincts of the divine nature, the leadings of the Holy Ghost, and the teachings of holy Scripture do all most unquestionably lead the Lord's people to assemble themselves together for worship, communion, and edification. However dispensations may differ, there are certain great principles and leading characteristics which always hold good, and the assembling of ourselves together is most assuredly one of these. Whether under the old economy or under the new, the assembling of the Lord's people is a divine institution.

Now, this being so, it is not a question of *our*

happiness, one way or the other; though we may be perfectly sure that all true Christians will be happy in being found in their divinely appointed place. There is ever deep joy and blessing in the assembly of God's people. It is impossible for us to find ourselves together in the Lord's presence and not be truly happy. It is simply heaven upon earth for the Lord's dear people—those who love His name, love His person, love one another, to be together around His table, around Himself. What can exceed the blessedness of being allowed to break bread together in remembrance of our beloved and adorable Lord, to show forth His death until He come; to raise, in holy concert, our anthems of praise to God and the Lamb; to edify, exhort, and comfort one another, according to the gift and grace bestowed upon us by the risen and glorified Head of the Church; to pour out our hearts, in sweet fellowship, in prayer, supplication, intercession, and giving of thanks for all men, for kings and all in authority, for the whole household of faith—the Church of God—the body of Christ, for the Lord's work and workmen all over the earth?

Where, we would ask with all possible confidence, is there a true Christian, in a right state of soul, who would not delight in all this, and say, from the very depths of his heart, that there is nothing this side the glory to be compared with it?

But, we repeat, our happiness is not the question; it is less than secondary. We are to be ruled, in this as in all beside, by the will of God as revealed

13

in His holy Word. The question for us is simply this: Is it according to the mind of God that His people should assemble themselves together for worship and mutual edification ? If this be so, woe be to all who willfully refuse, or indolently neglect to do so, on any ground whatsoever; they not only suffer serious loss in their own souls, but they are offering dishonor to God, grieving His Spirit, and doing injury to the assembly of His people.

These are very weighty consequences, and they demand the serious attention of all the Lord's people. It must be obvious to the reader that it is according to the revealed will of God that His people should assemble themselves together, in His presence. The inspired apostle exhorts us, in the tenth chapter of his epistle to the Hebrews, not to forsake the assembling of ourselves together. There is special value, interest, and importance attaching to the assembly. The truth as to this begins to dawn upon us in the opening pages of the New Testament. Thus, in Matthew xviii. 20, we read the words of our blessed Lord—"Where *two or three are gathered together* in My name, *there am* I in the midst of them." Here we have the divine centre. "*My name.*" This answers to "The place which the Lord thy God shall choose to place His name there," so constantly named and so strongly insisted upon in the book of Deuteronomy. It was absolutely essential that Israel should gather at that one place. It was not a matter as to which people might choose for themselves. Human choice was absolutely and

rigidly excluded.   It was "*The* place which the
Lord thy God shall choose," and no other.   This
we have seen distinctly.   It is so plain that we have
only to say, "How readest thou ?"

Nor is it otherwise with the Church of God.   It is
not human choice, or human judgment, or human
opinion, or human reason, or human any thing.   It
is absolutely and entirely divine.   The *ground* of our
gathering is divine, for it is accomplished redemption ; the *centre* around which we are gathered is
divine, for it is the Name of Jesus ; the *power* by
which we are gathered is divine, for it is the Holy
Ghost ; and the *authority* for our gathering is divine,
for it is the Word of God.

All this is as clear as it is precious, and all we
need is the simplicity of faith to take it in and act
upon it.   If we begin to reason about it, we shall
be sure to get into darkness ; and if we listen to
human opinions, we shall be plunged in hopeless
perplexity between the conflicting claims of christendom's sects and parties.   Our only refuge, our only
resource, our only strength, our only comfort, our
only authority, is the precious Word of God.   Take
away that, and we have absolutely nothing ; give us
that, and we want no more.

This is what makes it all so real and so solid for
our souls.   Yes, reader ; and so consolatory and
tranquilizing too.   The truth as to our assembly
is as clear and as simple and as unquestionable as
the truth in reference to our salvation.   It is the
privilege of all Christians to be as sure that they

are gathered on God's ground, around God's centre, by God's power, and on God's authority, as that they are within the blessed circle of God's salvation.

And then, if we be asked, How can we be certain of being around God's centre? we reply, Simply by the Word of God. How could Israel of old be sure as to God's chosen place for their assembly? By His express commandment. Were they at any loss for guidance? Surely not. His word was as clear and as distinct as to their place of worship as it was in reference to every thing else. It left not the slightest ground for uncertainty. It was so plainly set before them that for any one to raise a question could only be regarded as willful ignorance or positive disobedience.

Now, the question is, Are Christians worse off than Israel in reference to the great subject of their place of worship, the centre and ground of their assembly? Are they left in doubt and uncertainty? Is it an open question? Is it a matter as to which every man is left to do what is right in his own eyes? Has God given us no positive, definite instruction on a question so intensely interesting and so vitally important? Could we imagine for a moment that the One who graciously condescended to instruct His people of old in matters which we, in our fancied wisdom, would deem unworthy of notice, would leave His Church now without any definite guidance as to the ground, centre, and characteristic features of our worship? Utterly impossible! Every spirítual mind must reject, with decision and energy, any such idea.

No, beloved Christian reader; you know it would not be like our gracious God to deal thus with His heavenly people. True, there is no such thing now as a particular place to which all Christians are to betake themselves periodically for worship. There *was* such a place for God's earthly people, and there *will be* such a place for restored Israel and for all nations by and by. "It shall come to pass in the last days, that the mountain of the Lord's house shall be established in the top of the mountains, and shall be exalted above the hills; and *all nations* shall flow unto it. And many people shall go and say, Come ye, and let us go up to the mountain of the Lord, to the house of the God of Jacob; and He will teach us of His ways, and we will walk in His paths; for *out of Zion* shall go forth the law, and the word of the Lord from Jerusalem." (Is. ii.) And again, "It shall come to pass, that every one that is left of all the nations which came against Jerusalem shall even go up from year to year to worship the King, the Lord of Hosts, and to keep the feast of tabernacles. And it shall be that whoso will not come up of *all the families of the earth unto Jerusalem* to worship the King, the Lord of Hosts, even upon them shall be no rain." (Zech. xiv. 16, 17.)

Here are two passages culled, one from the first, and the other from the last but one of the divinely inspired prophets, both pointing forward to the glorious time when Jerusalem shall be God's centre

for Israel and for all nations. And we may assert,
with all possible confidence, that the reader will find
all the prophets, with one consent, in full harmony
with Isaiah and Zechariah on this profoundly interesting subject. To apply such passages to the
Church, or to heaven, is to do violence to the
clearest and grandest utterances that ever fell on
human ears; it is to confound things heavenly and
earthly, and to give a flat contradiction to the
divinely harmonious voices of prophets and apostles.

It is needless to multiply quotations. All Scripture goes to prove that Jerusalem was, and will yet
be, God's earthly centre for His people,·and for all
nations; but *just now*—that is to say, from the day
of Pentecost, when God the Holy Ghost came down
to form the Church of God, the body of Christ,
until the moment when our Lord Jesus Christ shall
come to take His people away out of this world—
there is no place, no city, no sacred locality, no
earthly centre, for the Lord's people. To talk to
Christians about holy places, or consecrated ground,
is as thoroughly foreign to them (at least, it ought
to be) as it would have been to talk to a Jew about
having his place of worship in heaven. The idea is
wholly out of place, wholly out of character.

If the reader will turn for a moment to the fourth
chapter of John, he will find, in our Lord's marvelous discourse with the woman of Sychar, the most
blessed teaching on this subject. "The woman
saith unto Him, 'Sir, I perceive that Thou art a
prophet. Our fathers worshiped in this mountain,

and ye say that in Jerusalem is the place where men ought to worship.' Jesus saith unto her, 'Woman, believe Me ; the hour cometh, when ye shall neither in this mountain nor yet at Jerusalem worship the Father. Ye worship ye know not what; we know what we worship, for salvation is of the Jews. But the hour cometh, and now is, when the true worshipers shall worship the Father in spirit and in truth, for the Father *seeketh* such to worship Him. God is a spirit, and they that worship Him *must* worship Him in spirit and in truth.' '' (Ver. 19–24.)

This passage entirely sets aside the thought of any special place of worship now. There really is no such thing. '' *The Most High dwelleth not in temples made with hands;* as saith the prophet, 'Heaven is My throne, and earth is My footstool: what house will ye build Me?' saith the Lord, 'or what is the place of My rest ? Hath not My hand made all these things ?' '' (Acts vii. 48–50.) And again, ''God that made the world, and all things therein, seeing that He is Lord of heaven and earth, *dwelleth not in temples made with hands; neither is worshiped with men's hands*, as though He needed any thing, seeing He giveth to all life and breath and all things.'' (Acts xvii. 24, 25.)

The teaching of the New Testament, from beginning to end, is clear and decided as to the subject of worship ; and the Christian reader is solemnly bound to give heed to that teaching, and to seek to understand, and submit his whole moral being to its authority. There has ever been, from the very earliest ages of the Church's history, a strong and fatal tendency to return to Judaism, not only on the subject of righteousness, but also on that of worship. Christians have not only been put under the law for life and righteousness, but also under the Levitical ritual for the order and character of their worship. We have dealt with the former of these in chapters iv. and v. of these "Notes," but the latter is hardly less serious in its effect upon the whole tone and character of Christian life and conduct.

We have to bear in mind that Satan's great object is, to cast the Church of God down from her excellency, in reference to her standing, her walk, and her worship. No sooner was the Church set up on the day of Pentecost than he commenced his corrupting and undermining process, and for eighteen long centuries he has carried it on with diabolical persistency. In the face of these plain passages quoted above, in reference to the character of worship which the Father is now seeking, and as to the fact that God does not dwell in temples made with hands, we have seen, in all ages, the strong tendency to return to the condition of things under the Mosaic economy. Hence the desire for great buildings, imposing rituals, sacerdotal orders, choral services, all of which are in direct opposition to the mind of Christ and to the plainest teachings of the New Testament. The professing church has entirely departed from the spirit and authority of the Lord in all these things; and yet, strange and sad to say, these very things are continually appealed to as

proofs of the wonderful progress of Christianity.
We are told by some of our public teachers and
guides that the blessed apostle Paul had little idea
of the grandeur to which the Church was to attain;
but if he could only see one of our venerable cathe-
drals, with its lofty aisles and painted windows, and
listen to the peals of the organ and the voices of the
choristers, he would see what an advance had been
made upon the upper room at Jerusalem!

Ah! reader, be assured, it is all a most thorough
delusion. It is true indeed, the Church has made
progress, but it is in the wrong direction; it is not
upward, but downward. It is away from Christ,
away from the Father, away from the Spirit, away
from the Word.

We should like to ask the reader this one question: If the apostle Paul were to come to London
for next Lord's day, where could he find what he
found in Troas eighteen hundred years ago, as
recorded in Acts xx. 7? Where could he find a
company of disciples gathered simply by the Holy
Ghost, to the Name of Jesus, to break bread in
remembrance of Him, and to show forth His death
till He come? Such was the divine order then, and
such must be the divine order now. We cannot for
a moment believe that the apostle would accept any
thing else. He would look for the divine thing; he
would have that or nothing. Now, where could he
find it? where could he go and find the table of his
Lord, as appointed by Himself the same night in
which He was betrayed?

Mark, reader, we are bound to believe that the apostle Paul would insist upon having the table and the supper of his Lord as he had received them direct from Himself in the glory, and given them by the Spirit in the tenth and eleventh chapters of his epistle to the Corinthians—an epistle addressed to "all that in every place call on the name of our Lord Jesus Christ, both theirs and ours." We cannot believe that he would teach God's order in the first century and accept man's disorder in the nineteenth. Man has no right to tamper with a divine institution. He has no more authority to alter a single jot or tittle connected with the Lord's supper than Israel had to interfere with the order of the passover.

Now, we repeat the question, and earnestly entreat the reader to ponder and answer it in the divine presence and in the light of Scripture,— Where could the apostle find this in London, or any where else in christendom, on next Lord's day? Where could he go and take his seat at the table of his Lord, in the midst of a company of disciples gathered simply on the *ground* of the one body, to the one *centre*—the Name of Jesus, by the *power* of the Holy Ghost, and on the *authority* of the Word of God ? Where could he find a sphere in which he could exercise his gifts without human authority, appointment, or ordination ? We ask these questions in order to exercise the heart and conscience of the reader. We are fully convinced that there are places here and there where Paul could find these things carried out, though in weakness and failure, and we believe the Christian reader is solemnly responsible to find them out. Alas! alas! they are few and far between, compared with the mass of Christians meeting otherwise.

We may perhaps be told that if people knew that it was the apostle Paul, they would willingly allow him to minister. But then he would neither seek nor accept their permission, inasmuch as he tells us plainly, in the first chapter of Galatians, that his ministry was "not of men, neither by man, but by Jesus Christ, and God the Father, who raised Him from the dead."

And not only so, but we may rest assured that the blessed apostle would insist upon having the Lord's table spread upon the divine ground of the one body, and he could only consent to eat the Lord's supper according to its divine order as laid down in the New Testament. He could not accept for a moment any thing but the divine reality. He would say, Either that or nothing. He could not admit any human interference with a divine institution; neither could he accept any new ground of gathering, or any new principle of organization. He would repeat his own inspired statements—"There is *one body* and one Spirit," and, "We being many, are one bread—*one body,* for we are all partakers of that one bread." These words apply to "all that in every place call on the name of Jesus Christ our Lord," and they hold good in all ages of the Church's existence on earth.

The reader must be very clear and distinct as to

this. God's principle of gathering and unity must on no account be surrendered. The moment men begin to organize—to form societies, churches, or associations, they act in direct opposition to the Word of God, the mind of Christ, and the present action of the Holy Ghost. Man might as well set about to form a world as to form a church. It is entirely a divine work. The Holy Ghost came down on the day of Pentecost to form *the* Church of God —*the* body of Christ, and this is the only Church— the only body that Scripture recognizes; all else is contrary to God, even though it may be sanctioned and defended by thousands of true Christians.

Let not the reader misunderstand us. We are not speaking of salvation, of eternal life, or of divine righteousness, but of the true ground of gathering, the divine principle on which the Lord's table should be spread and the Lord's supper cele- brated. Thousands of the Lord's beloved people have lived and died in the communion of the church of Rome; but the church of Rome is not the Church of God, but a horrible apostasy; and the sacrifice of the mass is not the Lord's supper, but a marred, mutilated, and miserable invention of the devil. If the question in the mind of the reader be merely what amount of error he can sanction without for- feiting his soul's salvation, it is useless to proceed with the grand and important subject before us.

But where is the heart that loves Christ that could be content to take such miserably low ground as this? What would have been thought of an Israelite

of old who could content himself with being a child
of Abraham, and could enjoy his vine and his fig-
tree, his flocks and his herds, but never think of
going to worship at the place where Jehovah had
recorded His name? Where was the faithful Jew
who did not love that sacred spot? "Lord, I have
loved the habitation of Thine house, and the place
where Thine honor dwelleth."

And when, by reason of Israel's sin, the national
polity was broken up, and the people were in captivity, we hear the true-hearted exiles amongst them
pouring forth their lament in the following touching
and eloquent strain, "By the rivers of Babylon,
there we sat down; yea, *we wept when we remembered Zion.* We hanged our harps upon the willows
in the midst thereof. For there they that carried us
away captive required of us a song, and they that
wasted us required of us mirth, saying, 'Sing us one
of the songs of Zion.' How shall we sing the Lord's
song in a strange land? If I forget thee, O Jerusalem [God's centre for His earthly people], let my
right hand forget her cunning. If I do not remember thee, let my tongue cleave to the roof of my
mouth; if I prefer not Jerusalem above my chief
joy." (Ps. cxxxvii.)

And again, in the sixth chapter of Daniel, we find
that beloved exile opening his window three times a
day, and praying toward Jerusalem, although he
knew that the lions' den was the penalty. But why
insist upon praying toward Jerusalem? Was it a
piece of Jewish superstition? Nay, it was a mag-

nificent display of divine principle; it was an un-
furling of the divine standard amid the depressing
and humiliating consequences of Israel's folly and
sin. True, Jerusalem was in ruins; but God's
thoughts respecting Jerusalem were not in ruins.
It was His centre for His earthly people. "Jerusalem is builded as a city that is compact together,
whither the tribes go up, the tribes of the Lord,
unto the testimony of Israel, to give thanks unto
the name of the Lord. For there are set thrones of
judgment, the thrones of the house of David. Pray
for the peace of Jerusalem; they shall prosper that
love thee. Peace be within thy walls, and prosperity
within thy palaces. *For my brethren and compan-
ions' sakes*, I will now say, Peace be within thee.
Because of the house of the Lord our God I will seek
thy good." (Ps. cxxii.)

Jerusalem was the centre for Israel's twelve tribes
in days gone by, and it will be so in the future. To
apply the above and similar passages to the Church
of God here or hereafter—on earth or in heaven, is
simply turning things upside down, confounding
things essentially different, and thus doing an incalculable amount of damage both to Scripture and the
souls of men. We must not allow ourselves to take
such unwarrantable liberties with the Word of God.

Jerusalem was and will be God's earthly centre;
but now, the Church of God should own no centre
but the glorious and infinitely precious Name of
Jesus. "Where two or three are gathered together
in My name, there am I in the midst of them."

Precious centre ! To this alone the New Testament points, to this alone the Holy Ghost gathers. It matters not where we are gathered—in Jerusalem or Rome, London, Paris, or Canton. It is not *where*, but *how*.

But be it remembered, it must be a divinely real thing. It is of no possible use to profess to be gathered in, or to, the blessed Name of Jesus, if we are not really so. The apostle's word as to faith may apply with equal force to the question of our centre of gathering.—"What doth it profit, my brethren, though a man *say*" he is gathered to the Name of Jesus ? God deals in moral realities ; and while it is perfectly clear that a man who desires to be true to Christ cannot possibly consent to own any other centre or any other ground of gathering but His Name, yet it is quite possible—alas ! alas ! how very possible—for people to profess to be on that blessed and holy ground, while their spirit and conduct, their habits and ways, their whole course and character, go to prove that they are not in the power of their profession.

The apostle said to the Corinthians that he would "know, not the speech, but the power." A weighty word, most surely, and much needed at all times, but specially needed in reference to the important subject now before us. We would lovingly, yet most solemnly, press upon the conscience of the Christian reader his responsibility to consider this matter in the holy retirement of the Lord's presence, and in the light of the New Testament. Let him

not set it aside on the plea of its not being essential.
It is in the very highest degree essential, inasmuch
as it concerns the Lord's glory and the maintenance
of His truth.   This is the only standard by which
to decide what is essential and what is not.   Was it
essential for Israel to gather at the divinely appointed
centre ? Was it left an open question ? Might every
man choose a centre for himself ? Let the answer
be weighed in the light of Deuteronomy xiv. It was
absolutely essential that the Israel of God should
assemble around the centre of the God of Israel.
This is unquestionable.   Woe be to the man who
presumed to turn his back on the place where Jehovah had set His Name.   He would very speedily
have been taught his mistake.   And if this was true
for God's earthly people, is it not equally true for
the Church and the individual Christian? Assuredly
it is.   We are bound, by the very highest and most
sacred obligations, to refuse every *ground* of gathering but the one body, every *centre* of gathering but
the Name of Jesus, every *power* of gathering but
the Holy Ghost, every *authority* of gathering but
the Word of God.   May all the Lord's beloved
people every where be led to consider these things,
in the fear and love of His holy name.

We shall now close this section by quoting the
last paragraph of our chapter, in which we shall find
some valuable practical teaching.

" At the end of three years, thou shalt bring forth
all the tithe of thine increase the same year, and
shalt lay it up within thy gates ; and the Levite,

(because he hath no part nor inheritance with thee,) and the stranger, and the fatherless, and the widow, which are within thy gates, *shall come*, and *shall eat* and *be satisfied;* that the Lord thy God may bless thee in all the work of thine hand which thou doest.''

Here we have a lovely home-scene, a most touching display of the divine character, a beautiful outshining of the grace and kindness of the God of Israel. It does the heart good to breathe the fragrant air of such a passage as this. It stands in vivid and striking contrast with the cold selfishness of the scene around us. God would teach His people to think of and care for all who were in need. The tithe belonged to Him, but He would give them the rare and exquisite privilege of devoting it to the blessed object of making hearts glad.

There is peculiar sweetness in the words, ''shall come''—''shall eat''—''and be satisfied.'' So like our own ever-gracious God! He delights to meet the need of all. He opens His hand, and satisfies the desire of every living thing. And not only so, but it is His joy to make His people the channel through which the grace, the kindness, and the sympathy of His heart may flow forth to all. How precious is this! What a privilege to be God's almoners—the dispensers of His bounty—the exponents of His goodness! Would that we entered more fully into the deep blessedness of all this! May we breathe more the atmosphere of the divine presence, and then we shall more faithfully reflect the divine character.

As the deeply interesting and practical subject presented in verses 28 and 29 will come before us in another connection in our study of chapter xxvi, we shall not dwell further upon it here.

CHAPTER XV.

" A T the end of every seven years thou shalt make a release. And this is the manner of the release: Every creditor that lendeth aught unto his neighbor shall release it; he shall not exact it of his neighbor, or of his brother, *because it is called the Lord's release.* Of a foreigner thou mayest exact it again; but that which is thine with thy brother thine hand shall release, save when there shall be no poor among you; for the Lord shall greatly bless thee in the land which the Lord thy God giveth thee for an inheritance to possess it; only if thou carefully hearken unto the voice of the Lord thy God, to observe to do all these commandments which I command thee this day. For the Lord thy God blesseth thee, as He promised thee; and thou shalt lend unto many nations, but thou shalt not borrow; and thou shalt reign over many nations, but they shall not reign over thee." (Ver. 1–6.)

It is truly edifying to mark the way in which the God of Israel was ever seeking to draw the hearts of His people to Himself by means of the various sacrifices, solemnities, and institutions of the Levitical ceremonial. There was the morning and evening lamb every *day*, there was the holy Sabbath every *week*, there was the new moon every *month*, there was the passover every *year*, there was the tithing every *three years*, there was the release every *seven years*, and there was the jubilee every *fifty years*.

All this is full of deepest interest. It tells its own sweet tale, and teaches its own precious lesson to the heart. The morning and evening lamb, as we know, pointed ever to "the Lamb of God, which taketh away the sin of the world;" the Sabbath was the lovely type of the rest that remaineth to the people of God; the new moon beautifully prefigured the time when restored Israel shall reflect back the beams of the Sun of Righteousness upon the nations; the passover was the standing memorial of the nation's deliverance from Egyptian bondage; the year of tithing set forth the fact of Jehovah's proprietorship of the land, as also the lovely way in which His rents were to be expended in meeting the need of His workmen and of His poor; the sabbatic year gave promise of a bright time when all debts would be canceled, all loans disposed of, all burdens removed; and finally, the jubilee was the magnificent type of the times of the restitution of all things, when the captive shall be set free, when the exile shall return to his long-lost home and inheritance, and when the land of Israel and the whole earth shall rejoice beneath the beneficent government of the Son of David.

Now, in all these lovely institutions we notice two prominent characteristic features, namely, glory to

God, and blessing to man. These two things are
linked together by a divine and everlasting bond.
God has so ordained that His full glory and the
creature's full blessing should be indissolubly bound
up together. This is deep joy to the heart, and it
helps us to understand more fully the force and
beauty of that familiar sentence—"We rejoice in
hope of the glory of God." When that glory shines
forth in its full lustre, then, assuredly, human blessedness, rest, and felicity shall reach their full and
eternal consummation.

We see a lovely pledge and foreshadowing of all
this in the seventh year. It was "the Lord's release," and therefore its blessed influence was to be
felt by every poor debtor from Dan to Beersheba.
Jehovah would grant unto His people the high and
holy privilege of having fellowship with Him in
causing the debtor's heart to sing for joy. He would
teach them, if they would only learn, the deep blessedness of frankly forgiving all. This is what He
Himself delights in, blessed forever be His great
and glorious name.

But, alas! the poor human heart is not up to this
lovely mark. It is not fully prepared to tread this
heavenly road. It is sadly cramped and hindered,
by a low and miserable selfishness, in grasping and
carrying out the divine principle of grace. It is not
quite at home in this heavenly atmosphere; it is but
ill-prepared for being the vessel and channel of that
royal grace which shines so brightly in all the ways
of God. This will only too fully account for the

cautionary clauses of the following passage. "If there be among you a poor man of one of thy brethren within any of thy gates, in thy land, which the Lord thy God giveth thee, *thou shalt not harden thine heart, nor shut thine hand* from thy poor brother; but thou shalt *open thine hand wide* unto him, and surely lend him sufficient for his need, in that which he wanteth. Beware that there be not a thought *in thy wicked heart*, saying, The seventh year, the year of release, is at hand; and *thine eye be evil* against thy poor brother, and thou *givest* him naught; and he cry unto the Lord against thee, and it be sin unto thee. *Thou shalt surely give him,* and thine heart shall not be grieved when thou givest unto him; because that for this thing the Lord thy God shall bless thee in all thy works, and in all that thou puttest thine hand unto. For the poor shall never cease out of thy land; therefore I command thee, saying, *Thou shalt open thine hand wide* unto thy brother, to thy poor, and to thy needy, in thy land." (Ver. 7–11.)

Here the deep springs of the poor selfish heart are discovered and judged. There is nothing like grace for making manifest the hidden roots of evil in human nature. Man must be renewed in the very deepest springs of his moral being ere he can be the vehicle of divine love; and even those who are thus through grace renewed, have to watch continually against the hideous forms of selfishness in which our fallen nature clothes itself. Nothing but grace can keep the heart open wide to every form of human

need.   We must abide hard by the fountain of
heavenly love if we would be channels of blessing in
the midst of a scene of misery and desolation like
that in which our lot is cast.

How lovely are those words, "Thou shalt open
thine hand wide"!   They breathe the very air of
heaven.   An open heart and a wide hand are like
God.   "The Lord loveth a cheerful giver," because
that is precisely what He is Himself.   "He giveth to
all liberally, and upbraideth not."   And He would
grant unto us the rare and most exquisite privilege
of being imitators of Him.   Marvelous grace! The
very thought of it fills the heart with wonder, love,
and praise.   We are not only saved by grace, but
we stand in grace, live under the blessed reign of
grace, breathe the very atmosphere of grace, and
are called to be the living exponents of grace, not
only to our brethren, but to the whole human family.
"As we therefore have opportunity, let us do good
unto all, especially unto them which are of the
household of faith."

Christian reader, let us diligently apply our hearts
to all this divine instruction.   It is most precious ;
but its real preciousness can only be tasted in the
practical carrying out of it.   We are surrounded by
ten thousand forms of human misery, human sorrow,
human need.   There are broken hearts, crushed
spirits, desolate homes, around us on every side.
The widow, the orphan, and the stranger meet us
daily in our walks.   How do we carry ourselves in
reference to all these? Are we hardening our hearts

and closing our hands against them? or are we seeking to act in the lovely spirit of "the Lord's release"? We must bear in mind that we are called to be reflectors of the divine nature and character— to be direct channels of communication between our Father's loving heart and every form of human need. We are not to live for ourselves; to do so is a most miserable denial of every feature and principle of that morally glorious Christianity which we profess. It is our high and holy privilege, yea, it is our special mission, to shed around us the blessed light of that heaven to which we belong. Wherever we are—in the family, in the field, in the mart or the manufactory, in the shop or in the counting-house, all who come in contact with us should see the grace of Jesus shining out in our ways, our words, our very looks. And then, if any object of need come before us, if we can do nothing more, we should drop a soothing word into the ear, or shed a tear or heave a sigh of genuine, heart-felt sympathy.

Reader, is it thus with us? Are we so living near the fountain of divine love, and so breathing the very air of heaven, that the blessed fragrance of these things shall be diffused around us? or are we displaying the odious selfishness of nature, the unholy tempers and dispositions of our fallen and corrupt humanity? What an unsightly object is a selfish Christian! He is a standing contradiction, a living, moving lie. The Christianity which he professes throws into dark and terrible relief the unholy selfishness which governs his heart and comes out in his life.

The Lord grant that all who profess and call themselves Christians may so carry themselves, in daily
life, as to be an unblotted epistle of Christ, known
and read of all men. In this way, infidelity will, at
least, be deprived of one of its weightiest arguments,
its gravest objections. Nothing affords a stronger
plea to the infidel than the inconsistent lives of professing Christians.

Not that such a plea will stand for a moment, or
even be urged, before the judgment-seat of Christ,
inasmuch as each one who has within his reach a
copy of the holy Scriptures will be judged by the
light of those Scriptures, even though there were not
a single consistent Christian on the face of the earth.
Nevertheless, Christians are solemnly responsible to
let their light so shine before men that they may see
their good works and glorify our Father in heaven.
We are solemnly bound to exhibit and illustrate in
daily life the heavenly principles unfolded in the
Word of God. We should leave the infidel without
a shred of a plea or an argument; we are responsible so to do.

May we lay these things to heart, and then we
shall have occasion to bless God for our meditation
on the delightful institution of "the Lord's release."

We shall now quote for the reader the touching
and beautiful institution in reference to the Hebrew
servant. We increasingly feel the importance of
giving the veritable language of the Holy Ghost;
for albeit it may be said that the reader has his Bible
to refer to, yet we know, as a fact, that when pas-

sages of Scripture are referred to, there is, in many
cases, a reluctance to lay down the volume which we
hold in our hand in order to read the reference.
And beside, there is nothing like the Word of God;
and as to any remarks which we may offer, their
object is simply to help the beloved Christian reader
to understand and appreciate the scriptures which
we quote.

"If thy brother, a Hebrew man, or a Hebrew
woman, be sold unto thee, and serve thee six years,
then in the seventh year thou shalt let him go free
from thee. And when thou sendest him out free
from thee, thou shalt not let him go away empty;
thou shalt furnish him liberally out of thy flock, and
out of thy floor, and out of thy wine-press; of that
wherewith the Lord thy God hath blessed thee thou
shalt give unto him."

How perfectly beautiful! how like our own ever-
gracious God is all this! He would not have the
brother go away empty. Liberty and poverty would
not be in moral harmony. The brother was to be
sent on his way free and full, emancipated and endowed, not only with his liberty, but with a liberal
fortune to start with.

Truly, this is divine. We do not want to be told
the school where such exquisite ethics are taught.
They have the very ring of heaven about them; they
emit the fragrant odor of the very paradise of God.
Is it not in this way that our God has dealt with us?
All praise to His glorious name! He has not only
given us life and liberty, but He has furnished us

liberally with all we can possibly want for time and eternity. He has opened the exhaustless treasury of heaven for us; yea, He has given the Son of His bosom for us and to us—*for* us, to *save;* *to* us, to *satisfy.* He has given us all things that pertain to life and godliness; all that pertains to the life that now is, and to that which is to come, is fully and perfectly secured by our Father's liberal hand.

And is it not deeply affecting to mark how the heart of God expresses itself in the style in which the Hebrew servant was to be treated? "Thou shalt furnish him *liberally*." Not grudgingly, or of necessity. It was to be done in a manner worthy of God. The actings of His people are to be the reflection of Himself. We are called to the high and holy dignity of being His moral representatives. It is marvelous; but thus it is, through His infinite grace. He has not only delivered us from the flames of an everlasting hell, but He calls us to act for Him, and to be like Him, in the midst of a world that crucified His Son. And not only has He conferred this lofty dignity upon us, but He has endowed us with a princely fortune to support it. The inexhaustible resources of heaven are at our disposal. "All things are ours," through His infinite grace. Oh that we may more fully realize our privileges, and thus more faithfully discharge our holy responsibilities!

At verse 15 of our chapter, we have a very touching motive presented to the heart of the people, one eminently calculated to stir their affections and sympathies. "And thou shalt remember that thou wast a bondman in the land of Egypt, and the Lord thy God redeemed thee; *therefore* I command thee this thing to-day." The remembrance of Jehovah's grace in redeeming them out of Egypt was to be the ever-abiding and all-powerful motive-spring of their actings toward the poor brother. This is a never-failing principle, and nothing lower than this will ever stand. If we look for our motive-springs any where but in God Himself, and in His dealings with us, we shall soon break down in our practical career. It is only as we keep before our hearts the marvelous grace of God displayed toward us in the redemption which is in Christ Jesus that we shall be able to pursue a course of true, active benevolence, whether toward our brethren or those outside. Mere kindly feelings, bubbling up in our own hearts, or drawn out by the sorrows and distresses and necessities of others, will prove evanescent. It is only in the living God Himself we can find perennial springs.

At verse 16, a case is contemplated in which a servant might prefer remaining with his master. "And it shall be, if he say unto thee, I will not go away from thee, because he loveth thee and thine house, because he is well with thee, then thou shalt take an awl, and thrust it through his ear unto the door, and he shall be thy servant forever."

In comparing this passage with Exodus xxi. 1–6, we observe a marked difference arising, as we might expect, from the distinctive character of each book. In Exodus, the *typical* feature is prominent; in Deuteronomy, the *moral*. Hence, in the latter, the inspired writer omits all about the wife and the children, as foreign to his purpose here, though so essential to the beauty and perfectness of the type in Exodus xxi. We merely notice this as one of the many striking proofs that Deuteronomy is very far indeed from being a barren repetition of its predecessors. There is neither repetition on the one hand, nor contradiction on the other, but lovely variety in perfect accordance with the divine object and scope of each book. So much for the contemptible shallowness and ignorance of those infidel writers who have had the impious temerity to level their shafts at this magnificent portion of the oracles of God.

In our chapter, then, we have the moral aspect of this interesting institution. The servant loved his master, and was happy with him. He preferred perpetual slavery and the mark thereof with a master whom he loved, to liberty and a liberal portion away from him. This, of course, would argue well for both parties. It is ever a good sign for both master and servant when the connection is of long standing. Perpetual changing may, as a general rule, be taken as a proof of moral wrong somewhere. No doubt there are exceptions; and not only so, but in the relation of master and servant, as in every thing else, there are two sides to be considered. For instance, we have to consider whether the master is perpetually changing his servants, or the servant perpetually changing his masters. In the former case, appearances would tell against the master; in the latter, against the servant.

The fact is, we have all to judge ourselves in this matter. Those of us who are masters have to consider how far we really seek the comfort, happiness, and solid profit of our servants. We should bear in mind that we have very much more to think of, in reference to our servants, than the amount of work we can get out of them. Even upon the low-level principle of "live and let live," we are bound to seek, in every possible way, to make our servants happy and comfortable; to make them feel that they have a home under our roof; that we are not content merely with the labor of their hands, but that we want the love of their hearts. We remember once asking the head of a very large establishment, "How many *hearts* do you employ?" He shook his head, and owned, with real sorrow, how little heart there is in the relation of master and servant. Hence the common, heartless phrase of "employing *hands*."

But the Christian master is called to stand upon a higher level altogether; he is privileged to be an imitator of his Master—Christ. The remembrance of this will regulate all his actings toward the servant; it will lead him to study, with ever-deepening interest and solid profit, his divine model, in order to reproduce Him in all the practical details of daily life.

So also in reference to the Christian servant, in his position and line of action. He, as well as the master, has to study the great example set before him in the path and ministry of the only true Servant that ever trod this earth. He is called to walk in His blessed footsteps, to drink into His spirit, to study His Word. It is not a little remarkable that the Holy Ghost has devoted more attention to the instruction of servants than to all the other relationships put together. This the reader can see at a glance, in the epistles to the Ephesians, Colossians, and Titus. The Christian servant can adorn the doctrine of God our Saviour by not purloining and not answering again. He can serve the Lord Christ in the most common-place duties of domestic life just as effectually as the man who is called to address thousands on the grand realities of eternity.

Thus, when both master and servant are mutually governed by heavenly principles, both seeking to serve and glorify the one Lord, they will get on happily together. The master will not be severe, arbitrary, and exacting; and the servant will not be self-seeking, heady, and high-minded: each will contribute, by the faithful discharge of their relative duties, to the comfort and happiness of the other, and to the peace and happiness of the whole domestic circle. Would that it were more after this heavenly fashion in every Christian household on the face of the earth! Then indeed would the truth of God be vindicated, His Word honored, and His name glorified in our domestic relations and practical ways.

In verse 18, we have an admonitory word which reveals to us, very faithfully, but with great delicacy, a moral root in the poor human heart. "It shall not seem hard unto thee when thou sendest him away free from thee, for he has been worth a double

hired servant to thee in serving thee six years, and
the Lord thy God shall bless thee in all that thou
doest."

This is very affecting. Only think of the most
high God condescending to stand before the human
heart—the heart of a master, to plead the cause of a
poor servant, and set forth his claims! It is as if He
were asking a favor for Himself. He leaves nothing
unsaid in order to strengthen the case; He reminds
the master of the value of six years' service, and
encourages him by the promise of enlarged blessing
as a reward for his generous acting. It is perfectly
beautiful. The Lord would not only have the
generous thing done, but done in such a way as to
gladden the heart of the one to whom it was done;
He thinks not only of the *substance* of an action, but
also of the *style*. We may, at times, brace ourselves
up to the business of doing a kindness; we do it as
a matter of duty, and all the while it may "*seem*
hard" that we should have to do it; thus the act will
be robbed of all its charms. It is the generous heart
that adorns the generous act. We should so do a
kindness as to assure the recipient that our own heart
is made glad by the act. This is the divine way:
"When they had nothing to pay, he *frankly* forgave
them both."—"It is meet that *we* should make merry,
and be glad."—"There is joy in heaven over one
sinner that repenteth." Oh, to be a brighter reflection of the precious grace of our Father's heart!

Ere closing our remarks on this deeply interesting
chapter, we shall quote for the reader its last para-

graph. "All the firstling males that come of thy herd and of thy flock thou shalt sanctify unto the Lord thy God; thou shalt do no work with the firstling of thy bullock, nor shear the firstling of thy sheep; thou shalt eat it before the Lord thy God year by year *in the place which the Lord shall choose*, thou and thy household. And if there be any blemish therein, as if it be lame, or blind, or have any ill blemish, thou shalt not sacrifice it unto the Lord thy God. Thou shalt eat it within thy gates, the unclean and the clean person shall eat it alike, as the roebuck, and as the hart. Only thou shalt not eat the blood thereof; thou shalt pour it upon the ground as water." (Ver. 19–23.)

Only that which was perfect was to be offered to God. The first-born, unblemished male, the apt figure of the spotless Lamb of God, offered upon the cross for us, the imperishable foundation of our peace, and the precious food of our souls, in the presence of God. This was the divine thing,—the assembly gathered together around the divine centre, feasting in the presence of God on that which was the appointed type of Christ, who is at once our sacrifice, our centre, and our feast. Eternal and universal homage to His most precious and glorious Name!

CHAPTER XVI

WE now approach one of the most profound and comprehensive sections of the book of Deuteronomy, in which the inspired writer presents to our view what we may call the three great cardinal feasts of the Jewish year, namely, the passover, Pentecost, and tabernacles; or, redemption, the Holy Ghost, and the glory. We have here a more condensed view of those lovely institutions than that given in Leviticus xxiii, where we have, if we count the Sabbath, eight feasts; but if we view the Sabbath as distinct, and having its own special place as the type of God's own eternal rest, then there are seven feasts, namely, the passover, the feast of unleavened bread, the feast of first-fruits, Pentecost, trumpets, the day of atonement, and tabernacles.

Such is the order of feasts in the book of Leviticus, which, as we have ventured to remark in our studies on that most marvelous book, may be called " *The priest's* guide-book." But in Deuteronomy, which is pre-eminently *the people's* book, we have less of ceremonial detail, and the lawgiver confines himself to those great moral and national landmarks which, in the very simplest manner, as adapted to the people, present the past, the present, and the future.

"Observe the month of Abib, and keep the passover unto the Lord thy God; for in the month of Abib the Lord thy God brought thee forth out of

Egypt by night. Thou shalt therefore sacrifice the passover unto the Lord thy God, of the flock and the herd, *in the place which the Lord shall choose to place His name there.* Thou shalt eat no leavened bread with it; seven days shalt thou eat unleavened bread therewith, even *the bread of affliction;* for thou camest forth out of the land of Egypt in haste: that thou mayest remember the day when thou camest forth out of the land of Egypt all the days of thy life. And there shall be no leavened bread seen with thee in all thy coasts seven days; neither shall there any thing of the flesh, which thou sacrificedst the first day at even, remain all night until the morning. Thou mayest not sacrifice the passover within any of thy gates which the Lord thy God giveth thee"—as if it were a matter of no importance where, provided the feast were kept—"*but at the place which the Lord thy God shall choose to place His name in, there* [and no where else.] thou shalt sacrifice the passover at even, at the going down of the sun, at the season that thou camest forth out of Egypt. And thou shalt roast and eat it *in the place which the Lord thy God shall choose;* and thou shalt turn in the morning, and go unto thy tents. Six days thou shalt eat unleavened bread; and on the seventh day shall be a solemn assembly to the Lord thy God; thou shalt do no work therein."(Ver. 1–8.)

Having, in our "Notes on Exodus," gone somewhat fully into the great leading principles of this foundation-feast, we must refer the reader to that volume if he desires to study the subject. But there are certain features peculiar to Deuteronomy to which we feel it our duty to call his special attention; and, in the first place, we have to notice the remarkable emphasis laid upon "the place" where the feast was to be kept. This is full of interest and practical moment. The people were not to choose for themselves. It might, according to human thinking, appear a very small matter how or where the feast was kept, provided it was kept at all. But, be it carefully noted and deeply pondered by the reader, human thinking had nothing whatever to do in the matter; it was divine thinking and divine authority altogether. God had a right to prescribe and definitively settle where He would meet His people; and this He does in the most distinct and emphatic manner, in the above passage, where, three times over, He inserts the weighty clause, "In the place which the Lord thy God shall choose."

Is this vain repetition? Let no one dare to think, much less to assert it. It is most necessary emphasis. Why most necessary? Because of our ignorance, our indifference, and our willfulness. God, in His infinite goodness, takes special pains to impress upon the heart, the conscience, and the understanding of His people that He would have one place in particular where the memorable and most significant feast of the passover was to be kept.

And be it remarked that it is only in Deuteronomy that the *place* of celebration is insisted upon. We have nothing about it in Exodus, because there it

was kept *in Egypt;* we have nothing about it in
Numbers, because there it was kept *in the wilder-*
ness; but in Deuteronomy it is anthoritatively and
definitively settled, because there we have the instructions for *the land.* Another striking proof
that Deuteronomy is very far indeed from being a
barren repetition of its predecessors.

The all-important point in reference to "the
place," so prominently and so peremptorily insisted
upon in all the three great solemnities recorded in
our chapter, is this: God would gather His beloved
people around Himself, that they might feast together in His presence, that He might rejoice in
them and they in Him and in one another. All this
could only be in the one special place of divine
appointment. All who desired to meet Jehovah and
to meet His people—all who desired worship and
communion according to God, would thankfully
betake themselves to the divinely appointed centre.
Self-will might say, Can we not keep the feast in the
bosom of our families? What need is there of a
long journey? Surely if the heart is right, it cannot
matter much as to the place. To all this we reply
that the clearest, finest, and best proof of the heart
being right would be found in the simple, earnest
desire to do the will of God. It was quite sufficient
for every one who loved and feared God that He
had appointed a place where He would meet His
people; there they would be found, and no where
else. His presence it was that could alone impart
joy, comfort, strength, and blessing to all their great

national reunions. It was not the mere fact of a
large number of people gathering together, three
times a year, to feast and rejoice together; this
might minister to human pride, self-complacency,
and excitement. But to flock together to meet Jehovah, to assemble in His blessed presence, to own
the place where He had recorded His Name, this
would be the deep joy of every truly loyal heart
throughout the twelve tribes of Israel. For any one
willfully to abide at home, or to go any where else
than to the one divinely appointed place, would not
only be to neglect and insult Jehovah, but actually
to rebel against His supreme authority.

And now, having briefly spoken of the *place*, we
may, for a moment, glance at the *mode* of celebration. This, too, is, as we might expect, quite
characteristic of our book. The leading feature
here is "the unleavened bread." But the reader
will specially note the interesting fact that this
bread is styled "*The bread of affliction.*" Now,
what is the meaning of this? We all understand
that unleavened bread is the type of that holiness
of heart and life so absolutely essential to the enjoyment of true communion with God. We are not
saved *by* personal holiness, but, thank God, we are
saved *to* it. It is not the ground of our salvation,
but it is an essential element in our communion.
*Allowed leaven is the death-blow to communion and
worship.*

We must never, for one moment, lose sight of this
great cardinal principle in that life of personal holi-

ness and practical godliness which, as redeemed by the blood of the Lamb, we are called, bound, and privileged to live from day to day, in the midst of the scenes and circumstances through which we are journeying home to our eternal rest in the heavens. To speak of communion and worship while living in known sin is the melancholy proof that we know nothing of either the one or the other. In order to enjoy communion with God or the communion of saints, and in order to worship God in spirit and in truth, we must be living a life of personal holiness, a life of separation from all known evil. To take our place in the assembly of God's people, and appear to take part in the holy fellowship and worship pertaining thereto, while living in secret sin, or allowing evil in others, is to defile the assembly, grieve the Holy Ghost, sin against Christ, and bring down upon us the judgment of God, who is *now* judging His house and chastening His children in order that they may not ultimately be condemned with the world.

All this is most solemn, and calls for the earnest attention of all who really desire to walk with God and serve Him with reverence and godly fear. It is one thing to have the doctrine of the type in the region of our understanding, and another thing altogether to have its great moral lesson engraved on the heart and worked out in the life. May all who profess to have the blood of the Lamb sprinkled on their conscience seek to keep the feast of un-leavened bread. "Know ye not that a little leaven leaveneth the whole lump? Purge out therefore the old leaven, that ye may be a new lump, as ye are unleavened. For even Christ our passover is sacrificed for us; therefore let us keep the feast, not with old leaven, neither with the leaven of malice and wickedness, but with the unleavened bread of sincerity and truth." (1 Cor. v. 6–8.)

But what are we to understand by "the bread of affliction"? Should we not rather look for joy, praise, and triumph in connection with a feast in memory of deliverance from Egyptian bondage and misery? No doubt there is very deep and real joy, thankfulness, and praise in realizing the blessed truth of our full deliverance from our former condition, with all its accompaniments and all its consequences; but it is very plain that these were not the prominent features of the paschal feast—indeed, they are not even named. We have "the bread of affliction," but not a word about joy, praise, or triumph.

Now, why is this? what great moral lesson is conveyed to our hearts by the bread of affliction? We believe it sets before us those deep exercises of heart which the Holy Ghost produces by bringing powerfully before us what it cost our adorable Lord and Saviour to deliver us from our sins and from the judgment which those sins deserved. Those exercises are also typified by the "bitter herbs" of Exodus xii, and they are illustrated again and again in the history of God's people of old, who were led, under the powerful action of the Word and Spirit of

God, to chasten themselves and "afflict their souls" in the divine presence.

And be it remembered that there is not a tinge of the legal element or of unbelief in these holy exercises—far from it. When an Israelite partook of the bread of affliction, with the roasted flesh of the passover, did it express a doubt or a fear as to his full deliverance? Impossible! How could it? He was in the land; he was gathered to God's own centre—His own very presence. How could he, then, doubt his full and final deliverance from the land of Egypt? The thought is simply absurd.

But although he had no doubts or fears as to his deliverance, yet had he to eat the bread of affliction ; it was an essential element in his paschal feast, "For thou camest forth out of the land of Egypt *in haste*, that thou mayest remember the day when thou camest forth out of the land of Egypt *all the days of thy life.*"

This was very deep and real work. They were never to forget their exodus out of Egypt, but to keep up the remembrance of it, in the promised land, throughout all generations. They were to commemorate their deliverance by a feast emblematical of those holy exercises which ever characterize true, practical, Christian piety.

We would very earnestly commend to the serious attention of the Christian reader the whole line of truth indicated by "the bread of affliction." We believe it is much needed by those who profess great familiarity with what are called the doctrines of grace. There is very great danger, especially to young professors, while seeking to avoid legality and bondage, of running into the opposite extreme of levity—a most terrible snare. Aged and experienced Christians are not so liable to fall into this sad evil; it is the young amongst us who so need to be most solemnly warned against it. They hear, it may be, a great deal about salvation by grace, justification by faith, deliverance from the law, and all the peculiar privileges of the Christian position.

Now, we need hardly say that all these are of cardinal importance; and it would be utterly impossible for any one to hear too much about them. Would they were more spoken about, written about, and preached about! Thousands of the Lord's beloved people spend all their days in darkness, doubt, and legal bondage, through ignorance of those great foundation-truths.

But while all this is perfectly true, there are, on the other hand, many—alas! too many—who have a merely intellectual familiarity with the principles of grace, but (if we are to judge from their habits and manners, their style and deportment—the only way we have of judging) who know but little of the sanctifying power of those great principles—their power in the heart and in the life.

Now, to speak according to the teaching of the paschal feast, it would not have been according to the mind of God for any one to attempt to keep that feast without the unleavened bread, even the bread of affliction. Such a thing would not have been tolerated in Israel of old. It was an absolutely essential ingredient. And so, we may rest assured, it is an integral part of that feast which we, as Christians, are exhorted to keep, to cultivate personal holiness and that condition of soul which is so aptly expressed by the "bitter herbs" of Exodus xii. or the Deuteronomic ingredient—"the bread of affliction," which latter would seem to be the permanent figure for the land.

In a word, then, we believe there is a deep and urgent need amongst us of those spiritual feelings and affections, those profound exercises of soul, which the Holy Ghost would produce by unfolding to our hearts the sufferings of Christ—what it cost Him to put our sins away—what He endured for us when passing under the billows and waves of God's righteous wrath against our sins. We are sadly lacking —if one may be permitted to speak for others—in that deep contrition of heart which flows from spiritual occupation with the sufferings and death of our precious Saviour. It is one thing to have the blood of Christ sprinkled on the conscience, and another thing to have the death of Christ brought home, in a spiritual way, to the heart, and the cross of Christ applied, in a practical way, to our whole course and character.

How is it that we can so lightly commit sin, in thought, word, and deed? how is it that there is so much levity, so much unsubduedness, so much self-indulgence, so much carnal ease, so much that is merely frothy and superficial? Is it not because that ingredient typified by "the bread of affliction" is lacking in our feast? We cannot doubt it. We fear there is a very deplorable lack of depth and serious-ness in our Christianity. There is too much flippant discussion of the profound mysteries of the Christian faith, too much head-knowledge without the inward power.

All this demands the serious attention of the reader. We cannot shake off the impression that not a little of this melancholy condition of things is but too justly traceable to a certain style of preaching the gospel, adopted, no doubt, with the very best intentions, but none the less pernicious in its moral effects. It is all right to preach a simple gospel. It cannot, by any possibility, be put more simply than God the Holy Ghost has given it to us in Scripture.

All this is fully admitted; but, at the same time, we are persuaded there is a very serious defect in the preaching of which we speak. There is a want of spiritual depth, a lack of holy seriousness. In the effort to counteract legality, there is that which tends to levity. Now, while legality is a great evil, levity is much greater. We must guard against both. We believe grace is the remedy for the former, truth for the latter; but spiritual wisdom is needed to enable us rightly to adjust and apply these two. If we find a soul deeply exercised under the powerful action of truth, thoroughly plowed up by the mighty ministry of the Holy Ghost, we should pour in the deep con-solation of the pure and precious grace of God, as set forth in the divinely efficacious sacrifice of Christ. This is the divine remedy for a broken heart, a contrite spirit, a convicted conscience. When the deep furrow has been made by the spiritual plowshare, we have only to cast in the incorruptible seed of the gospel of God, in the assurance that it will take root, and bring forth fruit in due season.

But, on the other hand, if we find a person going on in a light, airy, unbroken condition, using very high-flown language about grace, talking loudly against legality, and seeking, in a merely human way, to set forth an easy way of being saved, we consider this to be a case calling for a very solemn application of *truth* to the heart and conscience.

Now, we greatly fear there is a vast amount of this last named element abroad in the professing church. To speak according to the language of our type, there is a tendency to separate the passover from the feast of unleavened bread—to rest in the fact of being delivered from judgment and forget the *roasted* lamb, the bread of *holiness*, and the bread of *affliction*. In reality, they never can be separated, inasmuch as God has bound them together; and hence we do not believe that any soul can be really in the enjoyment of the precious truth that "Christ our passover is sacrificed for us," who is not seeking to "keep the feast." When the Holy Spirit unfolds to our hearts something of the deep blessedness, preciousness, and efficacy of the death of our Lord Jesus Christ, He leads us to meditate upon the soul-subduing mystery of His sufferings—to ponder in our hearts all that He passed through for us, all that it cost Him to save us from the eternal consequences of that which we, alas! so often lightly commit.

Now, this is very deep and holy work, and leads the soul into those exercises which correspond with "the bread of affliction" in the feast of unleavened bread. There is a wide difference between the feelings produced by dwelling upon our sins and those which flow from dwelling upon the sufferings of Christ to put those sins away.

True, we can never forget our sins, never forget the hole of the pit from whence we were digged; but it is one thing to dwell upon the pit, and another and a deeper thing altogether to dwell upon the grace that digged us out of it, and what it cost our precious Saviour to do it. It is this latter we so much need to keep continually in the remembrance of the thoughts of our hearts. We are so terribly volatile, so ready to forget.

We need to look very earnestly to God to enable us to enter more deeply and practically into the sufferings of Christ, and into the application of the cross to all that in us which is contrary to Him. This will impart depth of tone, tenderness of spirit, an intense breathing after holiness of heart and life, practical separation from the world, in its every phase, a holy subduedness, jealous watchfulness over ourselves, our thoughts, our words, our ways, our whole deportment in daily life. In a word, it would lead to a totally different type of Christianity from what we see around us, and what, alas! we exhibit in our own personal history. May the Spirit of God graciously unfold to our hearts, by His own direct and powerful ministry, more and more of what is meant by "the *roasted* lamb," the "*unleavened* bread," and "the bread of *affliction*." *

---

* For further remarks on the passover and the feast of unleavened bread, the reader is referred to Exodus xii. and Numbers ix. Specially in the latter—the connection between the passover and the Lord's supper. This is a point of deepest interest and immense practical importance. The passover looked forward to the death of Christ; the Lord's supper looks back to it. What the former was to a faithful Israelite, the latter is to the Church. If this were more fully seen, it would greatly tend to meet the prevailing laxity, indifference, and error as to the table and supper of the Lord.

To any one who lives habitually in the holy atmosphere of Scripture, it must seem strange indeed to mark the confusion of thought and the diversity of practice in reference to a subject so very important, and one so simply and clearly presented in the Word of God.

It can hardly be called in question, by any one who bows to Scripture, that the apostles and the early Church assembled on the first day of the week to break bread. There is not a shadow of warrant in the New Testament for confining that most precious ordinance to once a month, once a quarter, or once in six months. This can only be viewed as a human interference with a divine institution. We are aware that much is sought to be made of the words, "As oft as ye do it;" but we do not see how any argument based on this clause can stand for a moment in the face of apostolic precedent in Acts xx. 7. The first day of the week is unquestionably the day for the Church to celebrate the Lord's supper.

Does the Christian reader admit this? If so, does he act upon it? It is a serious thing to neglect a special ordinance of Christ, and one appointed by Him the same night in which He was betrayed, under circumstances so deeply affecting. Surely, all who love the Lord Jesus Christ in sincerity would desire to remember Him in this special way, according to His own word—"This do in remembrance of Me." Can we understand any true lover of Christ living in the habitual neglect of this precious memorial? If an Israelite of old neglected the passover, he would have been "cut off." But this was law, and we are under grace. True; but is that a reason for neglecting our Lord's commandment?

We would commend this subject to the reader's careful attention. There is much more involved in it than most of us are aware. We

We shall now briefly consider the **feast of Pentecost**, which stands next in order to the passover. "Seven weeks shalt thou number unto thee; begin to number the seven weeks from such time as thou beginnest to put the sickle to the corn. And thou shalt keep the feast of weeks unto the Lord thy God with a tribute of a free-will offering of thine hand, which thou shalt give unto the Lord thy God, according as the Lord thy God hath blessed thee; and thou shalt rejoice before the Lord thy God, thou, and thy son, and thy daughter, and thy man-servant, and thy maid-servant, and the Levite that is within thy gates, and the stranger, and the father-less, and the widow, that are among you, *in the place which the Lord thy God hath chosen to place His name there.* And thou shalt remember that thou wast a bondman in Egypt; and thou shalt observe and do these statutes." (Ver. 9–12.)

Here we have the well-known and beautiful type of the day of Pentecost. The passover sets forth the death of Christ; the sheaf of first-fruits is the

believe the entire history of the Lord's supper for the last eighteen centuries is full of interest and instruction. We may see in the way in which the Lord's table has been treated a striking moral index of the Church's real condition. In proportion as the Church departed from Christ and His Word did she neglect and pervert the precious institution of the Lord's supper; and on the other hand, just as the Spirit of God wrought, at any time, with special power in the Church, the Lord's supper has found its true place in the hearts of His people.

But we cannot pursue this subject further in a foot-note; we have ventured to suggest it to the reader, and we trust he may be led to follow it up for himself. We believe he will find it a most profitable and suggestive study.

striking figure of a risen Christ; and in the feast of
weeks, we have prefigured before us the descent of
the Holy Ghost, fifty days after the resurrection.

We speak, of course, of what these feasts convey
to us, according to the mind of God, irrespective
altogether of the question of Israel's apprehension
of their meaning. It is our privilege to look at all
these typical institutions in the light of the New
Testament; and when we so view them, we are filled
with wonder and delight at the divine perfectness,
beauty, and order of all those marvelous types.

And not only so, but—what is of immense value
to us—we see how the scriptures of the New Testament dovetail, as it were, into those of the Old; we
see the lovely unity of the divine Volume, and how
manifestly it is one Spirit that breathes through the
whole, from beginning to end. In this way we are
inwardly strengthened in our apprehension of the
precious truth of the divine inspiration of the holy
Scriptures, and our hearts are fortified against all the
blasphemous attacks of infidel writers. Our souls
are conducted to the top of the mountain where the
moral glories of the Volume shine upon us in all
their heavenly lustre, and from whence we can look
down and see the clouds and chilling mists of infidel
thought rolling beneath us. These clouds and mists
cannot affect us, inasmuch as they are far away
below the level on which, through infinite grace, we
stand. Infidel writers know absolutely nothing of
the moral glories of Scripture; but one thing is
awfully certain, namely, that one moment in eternity

will completely revolutionize the thoughts of all the
infidels and atheists that have ever raved or written
against the Bible and its Author.

Now, in looking at the deeply interesting feast of
weeks, or Pentecost, we are at once struck with the
difference between it and the feast of unleavened
bread. In the first place, we read of "a free-will
offering." Here we have a figure of the Church,
formed by the Holy Ghost and presented to God as
"a kind of first-fruits of His creatures."

We have dwelt upon this feature of the type in
the "Notes on Leviticus," chapter xxiii, and shall
not therefore enter upon it here, but confine ourselves to what is purely Deuteronomic. The people
were to present a tribute of a free-will offering of
their hand, according as the Lord their God had
blessed them. There was nothing like this at the
passover, because that sets forth Christ offering
Himself for us, as a sacrifice, and not our offering
any thing. We remember our deliverance from sin
and Satan, and what that deliverance cost; we
meditate upon the deep and varied sufferings of our
precious Saviour as prefigured by the roasted lamb;
we remember that it was our sins that were laid
upon Him. He was bruised for our iniquities—
judged in our stead, and this leads to deep and
hearty contrition, or, what we may call true Christian repentance. For we must never forget that
repentance is not a mere transient emotion of a
sinner when his eyes are first opened, but an abiding moral condition of the Christian, in view of the

16

cross and passion of our Lord Jesus Christ. If this
were better understood and more fully entered into,
it would impart a depth and solidity to the Christian
life and character in which the great majority of us
are lamentably deficient.

But in the feast of Pentecost, we have before us
the power of the Holy Ghost, and the varied effects
of His blessed presence in us and with us. He enables us to present our bodies and all that we have
as a free-will offering unto our God, according as
He hath blessed us. This, we need hardly say, can
only be done by the power of the Holy Ghost; and
hence the striking type of it is presented, not in the
passover, which prefigures the death of Christ; not
in the feast of unleavened bread, which sets forth
the moral effect of that death upon us, in repentance, self-judgment, and practical holiness; but in
Pentecost, which is the acknowledged type of the
precious gift of the Holy Ghost.

Now, it is the Spirit who enables us to enter into
the claims of God upon us—claims which are to be
measured only by the extent of the divine blessing.
He gives us to see and understand that all we are
and all we have belong to God. He gives us to
delight in consecrating ourselves—spirit, soul, and
body—to God. It is truly "a free-will offering."
It is not of constraint, but willingly. There is not
an atom of bondage, for "where the Spirit of the
Lord is, there is liberty."

In short, we have here the lovely spirit and moral
character of the entire Christian life and service. A

soul under law cannot understand the force and beauty of this. Souls under the law never received the Spirit. The two things are wholly incompatible. Thus the apostle says to the poor misguided assemblies of Galatia, "This only would I learn of you, Received ye the Spirit by works of law, or by the hearing of faith? . . . He therefore that ministereth to you the Spirit, and worketh miracles among you, doeth He it by works of law, or by the hearing of faith?" The precious gift of the Spirit is consequent upon the death, resurrection, ascension, and glorification of our adorable Lord and Saviour Jesus Christ, and consequently can have nothing whatever to do with "works of law" in any shape or form. The presence of the Holy Ghost on earth, His dwelling with and in all true believers, is a grand characteristic truth of Christianity. It was not, and could not be, known in Old-Testament times. It was not even known by the disciples in our Lord's lifetime. He Himself said to them, on the eve of His departure, "Nevertheless, I tell you the truth; it is expedient [or profitable—$\sigma v \mu \varphi \acute{\epsilon} \rho \epsilon \iota$] for you that I go away; for if I go not away, the Comforter will not come unto you; but if I depart, I will send Him unto you." (John xvi. 7.)

This proves, in the most conclusive manner, that even the very men who enjoyed the high and precious privilege of personal companionship with the Lord Himself were to be put in an advanced position by His going away and the coming of the Comforter. Again, we read, "If ye love Me, keep My commandments; and I will pray the Father, and He shall give you another Comforter, that He may abide with you forever; even the Spirit of truth; whom the world cannot receive, because it seeth Him not, neither knoweth Him; but ye know Him, for He dwelleth with you and shall be in you."

We cannot, however, attempt to go elaborately into this immense subject here; our space does not admit of it, much as we should delight in it. We must confine ourselves to one or two points suggested by the feast of weeks, as presented in our chapter.

We have referred to the very interesting fact that the Spirit of God is the living spring and power of the life of personal devotedness and consecration beautifully prefigured by "the tribute of a free-will offering." The sacrifice of Christ is the ground, the presence of the Holy Ghost is the power, of the Christian's dedication of himself—spirit, soul, and body—to God. "I beseech you therefore, brethren, by the mercies of God, that ye present your bodies a living sacrifice, holy, acceptable unto God, which is your reasonable service." (Rom. xii. 1.)

But there is another point of deepest interest presented in verse 11 of our chapter,—"And thou shalt *rejoice* before the Lord thy God." We have no such word in the paschal feast, or in the feast of unleavened bread. It would not be in moral keeping with either of these solemnities. True it is, the passover lies at the very foundation of all the joy we can or ever shall realize here or hereafter; but we must ever think of the death of Christ, His sufferings, His sorrows—all that He passed through when the waves and billows of God's righteous wrath passed over His soul. It is upon these profound mysteries that our hearts are, or ought to be, mainly fixed when we surround the Lord's table and keep that feast by which we show the Lord's death until He come.

Now, it is plain to the spiritual and thoughtful reader that the feelings proper to such a holy and solemn institution are not of a jubilant character. We certainly can and do rejoice that the sorrows and sufferings of our blessed Lord are over, and over forever—that those terrible hours are passed, never to return; but what we recall in the feast is not simply their being over, but their being gone through, and that for us. "Ye do show the Lord's death;" and we know that whatever may accrue to us from that precious death, yet when we are called to meditate upon it, our joy is chastened by those profound exercises of soul which the Holy Spirit produces by unfolding to us the sorrows, the sufferings, the cross, and passion of our blessed Saviour. Our Lord's words are, "This do in remembrance of *Me;*" but what we especially *remember* in the supper is, Christ suffering and dying for us; what we *show*, is His death; and with these solemn realities before our souls, in the power of the Holy Ghost, there will, there must be, holy subduedness and seriousness.

We speak, of course, of what becomes the imme-

diate occasion of the celebration of the supper—the
suited feelings and affections of such a moment.
But these must be produced by the powerful ministry of the Holy Ghost. It can be of no possible
use to seek, by any pious efforts of our own, to
work ourselves up to a suitable state of mind. This
would be ascending by steps to the altar, a thing
most offensive to God. It is only by the Holy
Spirit's ministry that we can worthily celebrate the
holy supper of the Lord. He alone can enable us
to put away all levity, all formality, all mere routine,
all wandering thoughts, and to discern the body and
blood of the Lord in those memorials which, by His
own appointment, are laid on His table.

But in the feast of Pentecost, rejoicing was a
prominent feature. We hear nothing of "bitter
herbs" or "bread of affliction" on this occasion,
because it is the type of the coming of the other
Comforter—the descent of the Holy Ghost, proceeding from the Father, and sent down by the
risen, ascended, and glorified Head in the heavens,
to fill the hearts of His people with praise, thanksgiving, and triumphant joy—yea, to lead them into
full and blessed fellowship with their glorified Head,
in His triumph over sin, death, hell, Satan, and all
the powers of darkness. The Spirit's presence is
connected with liberty, light, power, and joy. Thus
we read, "The disciples were filled with joy and
with the Holy Ghost." Doubts, fears, and legal
bondage flee away before the precious ministry of
the Holy Ghost.

But we must distinguish between His work and His indwelling—His quickening and His sealing. The very first dawn of conviction in the soul is the fruit of the Spirit's work. It is His blessed operation that leads to all true repentance, and this is not joyful work. It is very good, very needful, absolutely essential; but it is not joy—nay, it is deep sorrow. But when, through grace, we are enabled to believe in a risen and glorified Saviour, then the Holy Ghost comes and takes up His abode in us, as the seal of our acceptance and the earnest of our inheritance.

Now, this fills us with joy unspeakable and full of glory; and being thus filled ourselves, we become channels of blessing to others. "He that believeth on Me, as the Scripture hath said, out of his belly shall flow rivers of living water. But this spake He of the Spirit, which they that believe on Him should receive; for the Holy Ghost was not yet, because that Jesus was not yet glorified." The Spirit is the spring of power and joy in the heart of the believer. He fits, fills, and uses us as His vessels in ministering to poor thirsty, needy souls around us. He links us with the Man in the glory, maintains us in living communion with Him, and enables us to be, in our feeble measure, the expression of what He is. Every movement of the Christian should be redolent with the fragrance of Christ. For one who professes to be a Christian to exhibit unholy tempers, selfish ways, a grasping, covetous, worldly spirit, envy and jealousy, pride and ambition, is to belie his profession, dishonor the holy name of Christ, and

bring reproach upon that glorious Christianity which
he professes, and of which we have the lovely type
in the feast of weeks—a feast pre-eminently characterized by a joy which had its source in the goodness of God, and which flowed out far and wide,
and embraced in its hallowed circle every object of
need. "Thou shalt rejoice before the Lord thy God,
thou, and thy son, and thy daughter, and thy man-
servant, and thy maid-servant, and *the Levite* that is
within thy gates, and *the stranger*, and *the fatherless*,
and *the widow*, that are among you."

How lovely! how perfectly beautiful! Oh that
its antitype were more faithfully exhibited amongst
us! Where are those streams of refreshing which
ought to flow from the Church of God? where those
unblotted epistles of Christ known and read of all
men? where can we see a practical exhibition of
Christ in the ways of His people—something to
which we could point and say, There is true Christianity? Oh, may the Spirit of God stir up our
hearts to a more intense desire after conformity to
the image of Christ, in all things! May He clothe
with His own mighty power the Word of God, which
we have in our hands and in our homes, that it may
speak to our hearts and consciences, and lead us to
judge ourselves, our ways, and our associations by
its heavenly light, so that there may be a thoroughly
devoted band of witnesses gathered out to His name,
to wait for His appearing. Will the reader join us
in asking for this?

We shall now turn for a moment to the lovely

institution of the feast of tabernacles, which gives such remarkable completeness to the range of truth presented in our chapter.

"Thou shalt observe the feast of tabernacles seven days, after that thou hast gathered in thy corn and thy wine; and thou shalt rejoice in thy feast, thou, and thy son, and thy daughter, and thy man-servant, and thy maid-servant, and the Levite, the stranger, and the fatherless, and the widow, that are within thy gates. Seven days shalt thou keep a solemn feast unto the Lord thy God *in the place which the Lord* shall choose; because the Lord thy God shall bless thee in all thine increase, and in all the works of thine hands, therefore thou shalt surely rejoice. Three times in a year shall all thy males appear before the Lord thy God *in the place which He shall choose;* in the feast of unleavened bread, and in the feast of weeks, and in the feast of tabernacles; and they shall not appear before the Lord empty; every man shall give as he is able, according to the blessing of the Lord thy God which He hath given thee." (Ver. 13–17.)

Here, then, we have the striking and beautiful type of Israel's future. The feast of tabernacles has not yet had its antitype. The passover and Pentecost have had their fulfillment in the precious death of Christ and the descent of the Holy Ghost, but the third great solemnity points forward to the times of the restitution of all things, which God has spoken of by the mouth of all His holy prophets which have been since the world began.

And let the reader note particularly the time of the celebration of this feast. It was to be "after thou hast gathered in thy corn and thy wine;" in other words, it was after the harvest and the vintage. Now, there is a very marked distinction between these two things. The one speaks of grace, the other of judgment. At the end of the age, God will gather His wheat into His garner, and then will come the treading of the wine-press, in awful judgment.

We have in the fourteenth chapter of the book of Revelation a very solemn passage bearing upon the subject now before us. "And I looked, and behold a white cloud, and upon the cloud one sat like unto the Son of Man, having on his head a golden crown, and in his hand a sharp sickle. And another angel came out of the temple, crying with a loud voice to him that sat on the cloud, 'Thrust in thy sickle, and reap; for the time is come for thee to reap; for the harvest of the earth is ripe.' And he that sat on the cloud thrust in his sickle on the earth, and the earth was reaped."

Here we have the harvest; and then "another angel came out of the temple which is in heaven, he also having a sharp sickle. And another angel came out from the altar, which had power over fire"—the emblem of judgment—"and cried with a loud cry to him that had the sharp sickle, saying, 'Thrust in thy sharp sickle, and gather the clusters of the vine of the earth, for her grapes are fully ripe.' And the angel thrust in his sickle into the earth, and gathered the vine of the earth, and cast it into the great wine-press of the wrath of God. And the wine-press was trodden without the city, and blood came out of the wine-press, even unto the horse-bridles, by the space of a thousand and six hundred furlongs"—equal to the whole length of the land of Palestine!

Now, these apocalyptic figures set before us, in their own characteristic way, scenes which must be enacted previous to the celebration of the feast of tabernacles. Christ will gather His wheat into His heavenly garner, and after that He will come in crushing judgment upon christendom. Thus, every section of the volume of inspiration—Moses, the Psalms, the Prophets, the Gospels (or the acts of Christ), the Acts of the Holy Ghost, the Epistles, and Apocalypse—all go to establish, unanswerably, the fact that the world will not be converted by the gospel, that things are not improving, and will not improve, but grow worse and worse. That glorious time prefigured by the feast of tabernacles *must* be preceeded by the vintage, the treading of the wine-press of the wrath of almighty God.

Why, then, we may well ask, in the face of such an overwhelming body of divine evidence, furnished by every section of the inspired canon, will men persist in cherishing the delusive hope of a world converted by the gospel? What mean "gathered wheat and a trodden wine-press"? Assuredly, they do not and cannot mean a converted world.

We shall perhaps be told that we cannot build

any thing upon Mosaic types and apocalyptic symbols. Perhaps not, if we had but types and symbols; but when the accumulated rays of Inspiration's heavenly lamp converge upon these types and symbols and unfold their deep meaning to our souls, we find them in perfect harmony with the voices of prophets and apostles, and the living teachings of our Lord Himself. In a word, all speak the same language, all teach the same lesson, all bear the same unequivocal testimony to the solemn truth that at the end of this age, instead of a converted world, prepared for a spiritual millennium, there will be a vine covered and borne down with terrible clusters, fully ripe for the wine-press of the wrath of almighty God.

Oh, may the men and women of christendom, and the teachers thereof, apply their hearts to these solemn realities! May these things sink down into their ears, and into the very depths of their souls, so that they may fling to the winds their fondly cherished delusion, and accept instead the plainly revealed and clearly established truth of God!

But we must draw this section to a close; and ere doing so, we would remind the Christian reader that we are called to exhibit in our daily life the blessed influence of all those great truths presented to us in the three interesting types on which we have been meditating. Christianity is characterized by those three great formative facts—redemption, the presence of the Holy Ghost, and the hope of glory. The Christian is redeemed by the precious blood of Christ, sealed by the Holy Ghost, and he is looking for the Saviour.

Yes, beloved reader, these are solid facts, divine realities, great formative truths. They are not mere principles or opinions, but they are designed to be a living power in our souls, and to shine in our lives. See how thoroughly practical were these solemnities on which we have been dwelling; mark what a tide of praise and thanksgiving and joy and blessing and active benevolence flowed from the assembly of Israel when gathered around Jehovah in the place which He had chosen. Praise and thanksgiving ascended to God, and the blessed streams of a large-hearted benevolence flowed forth to every object of need. "Three times in a year shall all thy males appear before the Lord thy God. . . . . *And they shall not appear before the Lord empty; every man shall give as he is able, according to the blessing of the Lord thy God which He hath given thee.*"

Lovely words! They were not to come empty into the Lord's presence; they were to come with the heart full of praise, and the hands full of the fruits of divine goodness to gladden the hearts of the Lord's workmen and the Lord's poor. All this was perfectly beautiful. Jehovah would gather His people around Himself, to fill them to overflowing with joy and praise, and to make them His channels of blessing to others. They were not to remain under their vine and under their fig-tree, and there congratulate themselves upon the rich and varied mercies which surrounded them. This might be all

right and good in its place, but it would not have
fully met the mind and heart of God. No; three
times in the year they had to arise and betake themselves to the divinely appointed meeting-place, and
there raise their halleluiahs to the Lord their God,
and there, too, to minister liberally of that which
He had bestowed upon them to every form of human
need. God would confer upon His people the rich
privilege of rejoicing the heart of the Levite, the
stranger, the widow, and the fatherless. This is the
work in which He Himself delights—blessed forever
be His name—and He would share His delight with
His people. He would have it to be known, seen,
and felt that the place where He met His people was
a sphere of joy and praise, and a centre from
whence streams of blessing were to flow forth in all
directions.

Has not all this a voice and a lesson for the Church
of God ? Does it not speak home to the writer and
the reader of these lines ? Assuredly it does. May
we listen to it; may it tell upon our hearts. May
the marvelous grace of God so act upon us that our
hearts may be full of praise to Him, and our hands
full of good works. If the mere types and shadows
of our blessings were connected with so much
thanksgiving and active benevolence, how much
more powerful should be the effect of the blessings
themselves !

But ah! the question is, Are we realizing the
blessings ? are we making our own of them ? are we
grasping them in the power of an artless faith ?

Here lies the secret of the whole matter. Where do we find professing Christians in the full and settled enjoyment of what the passover prefigured, namely, full deliverance from judgment and this present evil world? Where do we find them in the full and settled enjoyment of their Pentecost, even the indwelling of the Holy Ghost—the seal, the earnest, the unction, and the witness? Ask the vast majority of professors the plain question, "Have you received the Holy Ghost?" and see what answer you will get. What answer can the reader give? Can he say, Yes, thank God, *I know* I am washed in the precious blood of Christ, and sealed with the Holy Ghost? It is greatly to be feared that comparatively few of the vast multitudes of professors around us know any thing of these precious things, which nevertheless are the chartered privileges of the very simplest member of the body of Christ.

So also as to the feast of tabernacles, how few understand its meaning! True, it has not yet been fulfilled; but the Christian is called to live in the present power of that which it sets forth. "Faith is the substance of things hoped for, the evidence of things not seen." Our life is to be governed and our character formed by the combined influence of the "grace" in which we stand and the "glory" for which we wait.

But if souls are not established in grace—if they do not even know that their sins are forgiven—if they are taught that it is presumption to be sure of salvation, and that it is humility and piety to live in perpetual doubt and fear, and that no one can be sure of their salvation until they stand before the judgment-seat of Christ, how can they possibly take Christian ground, manifest the fruits of Christian life, or cherish proper Christian hope? If an Israelite of old was in doubt as to whether he was a child of Abraham, a member of the congregation of the Lord, and in the land, how could he keep the feast of unleavened bread, Pentecost, or tabernacles? There would have been no sense, meaning, or value in such a thing; indeed, we may safely affirm that no Israelite would have thought for a moment of any thing so utterly absurd.

How is it, then, that professing Christians—many of them, we cannot doubt, real children of God—never seem to be able to enter upon proper Christian ground? They spend their days in doubt and fear, darkness and uncertainty. Their religious exercises and services, instead of being the outcome of life possessed and enjoyed, are entered upon and gone through more as a matter of legal duty, and as a moral preparation for the life to come. Many truly pious souls are kept in this state all their days; and as to "the blessed hope" which grace has set before us, to cheer our hearts and detach us from present things, they do not enter into it or understand it. It is looked upon as a mere speculation, indulged in by a few visionary enthusiasts here and there. They are looking forward to the day of judgment, instead of looking out for "the bright and morning Star;" they are praying for the forgiveness of their sins, and asking God to give them His Holy Spirit, when they ought to be rejoicing in the assured possession of eternal life, divine righteousness, and the Spirit of adoption.

All this is directly opposed to the simplest and clearest teaching of the New Testament; it is utterly foreign to the very genius of Christianity, subversive of the Christian's peace and liberty, and destructive of all true and intelligent Christian worship, service, and testimony. It is plainly impossible that people can appear before the Lord with their hearts full of praise for privileges which they do not enjoy, or their hands full of the blessing which they have never realized.

We call the earnest attention of all the Lord's people, throughout the length and breadth of the professing church, to this weighty subject. We entreat them to search the Scriptures, and see if they afford any warrant for keeping souls in darkness, doubt, and bondage all their days. That there are solemn warnings, searching appeals, weighty admonitions, is most true, and we bless God for them,— we need them, and should diligently apply our hearts to them; but let the reader distinctly understand that it is the sweet privilege of the very babes in Christ to know that their sins are all forgiven, that they are accepted in a risen Christ, sealed by the Holy Ghost, and heirs of eternal glory. Such, through infinite and sovereign grace, are their clearly established and assured blessings—blessings to which the love of God makes them welcome,

17

for which the blood of Christ makes them fit, and as to which the testimony of the Holy Ghost makes them sure.

May the great Shepherd and Bishop of souls lead all His beloved people—the lambs and sheep of His blood-bought flock—to know, by the teaching of His Holy Spirit, the things that are freely given to them of God; and may those who do know them, in measure, know them more fully, and exhibit the precious fruits of them in a life of genuine devotedness to Christ and His service.

It is greatly to be feared that many of us who profess to be acquainted with the very highest truths of the Christian faith are not answering to our profession; we are not acting up to the principle set forth in verse 17 of our beautiful chapter,—"*Every man* shall give *as he is able*, according to the blessing of the Lord thy God which He hath given thee." We seem to forget that although we have nothing to do and nothing to give for salvation, we have much that we can do for the Saviour, and much that we can give to His workmen and to His poor. There is very great danger of pushing the do-nothing and give-nothing principle too far. If in the days of our ignorance and legal bondage we worked and gave upon a false principle and with a false object, we surely ought not to do less and give less now that we profess to know that we are not only saved, but blessed with all spiritual blessings in a risen and glorified Christ. We have need to take care that we are not resting in the mere intellectual perception and verbal profession of these great and glorious truths, while the heart and conscience have never felt their sacred action, nor the conduct and character been brought under their powerful and holy influence.

We venture, in all tenderness and love, just to offer these practical suggestions to the reader for his prayerful consideration. We would not wound, offend, or discourage the very feeblest lamb in all the flock of Christ; and further, we can assure the reader that we are not casting a stone at any one, but simply writing as in the immediate presence of God, and sounding in the ears of the Church a note of warning as to that which we deeply feel to be our common danger. We believe there is an urgent call, on all sides, to consider our ways, to humble ourselves before the Lord on account of our manifold failures, shortcomings, and inconsistencies, and to seek grace from Him to be more real, more thoroughly devoted, more pronounced in our testimony for Him, in this dark and evil day.

CHAPTER XVII.

WE must remember that the division of Scripture into chapters and verses is entirely a human arrangement, often very convenient, no doubt, for reference; but not unfrequently it is quite unwarrantable, and interferes with the connection. Thus we can see at a glance that the closing verses of chapter xvi. are much more connected with what follows than with what goes before.

"Judges and officers shalt thou make thee in all thy gates, which the Lord thy God giveth thee, throughout thy tribes; and they shall judge the people with just judgment. Thou shalt not wrest judgment; thou shalt not respect persons, neither take a gift; for a gift doth blind the eyes of the wise, and pervert the words of the righteous. That which is altogether just shalt thou follow, that thou mayest live and inherit the land which the Lord thy God giveth thee."

These words teach us a twofold lesson; in the first place, they set forth the even-handed justice and perfect truth which ever characterize the government of God. Every case is dealt with according to its own merits and on the ground of its own facts. The judgment is so plain that there is not a shadow of ground for a question; all dissension is absolutely closed; and if any murmur is raised, the murmurer is at once silenced by "Friend, I do thee no wrong." This holds good every where, and at all times, in the holy government of God, and it makes us long for the time when that government shall be established from sea to sea, and from the river to the ends of the earth.

But on the other hand, we learn, from the lines just quoted, what man's judgment is worth if left to himself. It cannot be trusted for a moment. Man is capable of "*wresting* judgment," of "respecting

persons," of "taking a gift," of attaching importance to a person because of his position and wealth.
That he is capable of all this is evident from the fact
of his being told not to do it. We must ever remember this. If God commands man not to steal,
it is plain that man has theft in his nature.

Hence, therefore, human judgment and human
government are liable to the grossest corruption.
Judges and governors, if left to themselves, if not
under the direct sway of divine principle, are capable of perverting justice for filthy lucre's sake—of
favoring a wicked man because he is rich, and of
condemning a righteous man because he is poor—
of giving a judgment in flagrant opposition to the
plainest facts because of some advantage to be
gained, whether in the shape of money or influence
or popularity or power.

To prove this, it is not necessary to point to such
men as Pilate and Herod and Felix and Festus; we
have no need to go beyond the passage just quoted,
in order to see what *man* is, even when clothed in
the robes of official dignity, seated on the throne of
government, or on the bench of justice.

Some, as they read these lines, may feel disposed
to say, in the language of Hazael, "Is thy servant
a dog, that he should do this thing?" But let such
reflect for a moment on the fact that the human
heart is the seed-plot of every sin, and of every vile
and abominable and contemptible wickedness that
ever was committed in this world; and the unanswerable proof of this is found in the enactments,

commandments, and prohibitions which appear on
the sacred page of inspiration.

And herein we have an uncommonly fine reply to
the oft-repeated question, "What have we to do with
many of the laws and institutions set forth in the
Mosaic economy? Why are such things set down
in the Bible? Can they possibly be inspired?"
Yes, they are inspired, and they appear on the page
of inspiration in order that we may see, as reflected
in a divinely perfect mirror, the moral material of
which we ourselves are made—the thoughts we are
capable of thinking, the words we are capable of
speaking, and the deeds we are capable of doing.

Is not this something? Is it not good and wholesome to find, for example, in some of the passages
of this most profound and beautiful book of Deuteronomy, that human nature is capable, and hence *we*
are capable, of doing things that put us morally below the level of a beast? Assuredly it is; and well
would it be for many a one who walks in pharisaic
pride and self-complacency—puffed up with false
notions of his own dignity and high-toned morality,
to learn this deeply humbling lesson.

But how morally lovely, how pure, how refined
and elevated, were the divine enactments for Israel!
They were not to wrest judgment, but allow it to
flow in its own straight and even channel, irrespective altogether of persons. The poor man in vile
raiment was to have the same impartial justice as
the man with a gold ring and gay clothing. The
decision of the judgment-seat was not to be warped

by partiality or prejudice, or the robe of justice to be defiled by the stain of bribery.

Oh, what will it be for this oppressed and groaning earth to be governed by the admirable laws which are recorded in the inspired pages of the Pentateuch, when a king shall reign in righteousness, and princes shall decree justice! "Give the king Thy judgments, O God, and Thy righteousness unto the king's son. He shall judge Thy people with righteousness, and *Thy poor* with judgment"—no wresting, no bribery, no partial judgments then.—"The mountains [or higher dignities] shall bring peace to the people, and the little hills [or lesser dignities], by righteousness. He shall judge [or defend] *the poor* of the people, he shall save the children of *the needy*, and shall break in pieces the oppressor. They shall fear Thee as long as the sun and moon endure, throughout all generations. He shall come down like rain upon the mown grass; as showers that water the earth. In his days shall the righteous flourish, and abundance of peace so long as the moon endureth. He shall have dominion also from sea to sea, and from the river unto the ends of the earth. . . . He shall deliver *the needy* when he crieth, *the poor* also, and *him that hath no helper*. He shall spare *the poor and needy*, and shall save *the souls of the needy*. He shall redeem their souls from deceit and violence, and precious shall their blood be in his sight." (Ps. lxxii.)

Well may the heart long for the time—the bright and blessed time when all this shall be made good,

when the earth shall be full of the knowledge of the
Lord as the waters cover the sea, when the Lord
Jesus shall take to Himself His great power and
reign, when the Church in the heavens shall reflect
the beams of His glory upon the earth, when Israel's
twelve tribes shall repose beneath the vine and fig-
tree in their own promised land, and all the nations
of the earth shall rejoice beneath the peaceful and
beneficent rule of the Son of David. Thanks and
praise be to our God, thus it shall be, ere long, as
sure as His throne is in the heavens. A little while
and all shall be made good, according to the eternal
counsels and immutable promise of God. Till then,
beloved Christian reader, be it ours to live in the
constant, earnest, believing anticipation of this
bright and blessed time, and to pass through this
ungodly scene as thorough strangers and pilgrims,
having no place or portion down here, but ever
breathing forth the prayer, "Come, Lord Jesus!"

In the closing lines of chapter xvi, Israel is warned
against the most distant approach to the religious
customs of the nations around. "Thou shalt not
plant thee a grove of any trees near unto the altar
of the Lord thy God, which thou shalt make thee.
Neither shalt thou set thee up any image which the
Lord thy God hateth." They were carefully to
avoid every thing which might lead them in the
direction of the dark and abominable idolatries of
the heathen nations around. The altar of God was
to stand out in distinct and unmistakable separation
from those groves and shady places where false gods

were worshiped, and things were done which are not to be named.* In a word, every thing was to be most carefully avoided which might in any way draw the heart away from the one living and true God.

Nor this only; it was not enough to maintain a correct outward form; images and groves might be abolished, and the nation might profess the dogma of the unity of the Godhead, and all the while there might be an utter want of heart and genuine devotedness in the worship rendered. Hence we read, "Thou shalt not sacrifice unto the Lord thy God any bullock or sheep wherein is blemish, or any illfavoredness, for that is an abomination unto the Lord."

That which was absolutely perfect could alone suit the altar and answer to the heart of God. To offer a blemished thing to Him was simply to prove the absence of all true sense of what became Him, and of all real heart for Him. To attempt to offer an imperfect sacrifice was tantamount to the horrible

---

*It may interest the reader to know that the Holy Ghost, in speaking of the altar of God in the New Testament, does not apply to it the word used to express a heathen altar, but has a comparatively new word—a word unknown in the world's classics. The heathen altar is βωμόν (Acts xvii. 23.): the altar of God is θυσιαστήριον. The former occurs but once; the latter, twenty-three times. So jealously is the worship of the only true God guarded and preserved from the defiling touch of heathen idolatry. Men may feel disposed to inquire why this should be, or how could the altar of God be affected by a name? We reply, The Holy Ghost is wiser than we are; and although the heathen word was before Him—a short and convenient word, too,—He refuses to apply it to the altar of the one true and living God.

See Trench's "Synonyms of the New Testament," p. 242. New edition revised.

blasphemy of saying that any thing was good enough
for Him.

Let us hearken to the indignant pleadings of the
Spirit of God, by the mouth of the prophet Malachi.
"Ye offer polluted bread upon Mine altar; and ye
say, 'Wherein have we polluted Thee?' In that ye
say, 'The table of the Lord is contemptible.' And
if ye offer the blind for sacrifice, is it not evil? and
if ye offer the lame and sick, is it not evil? offer it
now unto thy governor; will he be pleased with thee,
or accept thy person? saith the Lord of Hosts. And
now, I pray you, beseech God that He will be gracious unto us; this hath been by your means; will
He regard your persons? saith the Lord of Hosts.
Who is there even among you that would shut the
doors for naught? neither do ye kindle fire on Mine
altar for naught. I have no pleasure in you, saith
the Lord of Hosts, neither will I accept an offering
at your hand. For from the rising of the sun unto
the going down of the same, My name shall be great
among the Gentiles; and in every place incense
shall be offered unto My name, and a pure offering;
for My name shall be great among the heathen, saith
the Lord of Hosts. But ye have profaned it, in that
ye say, 'The table of the Lord is polluted, and the
fruit thereof, even His meat is contemptible.' Ye
said also, 'Behold, what a weariness is it!' and ye
have snuffed at it, saith the Lord of Hosts; and ye
brought that which was torn, and the lame, and the
sick; thus ye brought an offering: should I accept
this of your hand? saith the Lord. But cursed be

the deceiver, which hath in his flock a male, and voweth and sacrificeth unto the Lord a corrupt thing; for I am a great King, saith the Lord of Hosts, and My name is dreadful among the heathen. (Mal. i. 7–14.)

Has all this no voice for the professing church? has it no voice for the writer and the reader of these lines? Assuredly it has. Is there not in our private and public worship a deplorable lack of *heart*, of real devotedness, deep-toned earnestness, holy energy, and integrity of purpose? Is there not much that answers to the offering of the lame and the sick, the blemished and the ill-favored? Is there not a deplorable amount of cold formality and dead routine in our seasons of worship, both in the closet and in the assembly? Have we not to judge ourselves for barrenness, distraction, and wandering, even at the very table of our Lord? How often are our bodies at the table while our vagrant hearts and volatile minds are at the ends of the earth! how often do our lips utter words which are not the true expression of our whole moral being! We express far more than we feel; we sing beyond our experience.

And then, when we are favored with the blessed opportunity of dropping our offerings in our Lord's treasury, what heartless formality! what an absence of loving, earnest, hearty devotedness! what little reference to the apostolic rule—"as God hath prospered us"! what detestable niggardliness! how little of the whole-heartedness of the poor widow who having but two mites in the world, and having the option of at least keeping one for her living, willingly cast in both—cast in her all! Pounds may be spent on ourselves, perhaps on superfluities, during the week, but when the claims of the Lord's work, His poor, and His cause in general are brought before us, how meagre is the response!

Christian reader, let us consider these things; let us look at the whole subject of worship and devotedness in the divine presence, and in the presence of the grace that has saved us from everlasting burnings; let us calmly reflect upon the precious and powerful claims of Christ upon us. We are not our own; we are bought with a price. It is not merely our *best*, but our *all*, we owe to that blessed One who gave Himself for us. Do we not fully own it? do not our hearts own it? Then may our lives express it! May we more distinctly declare whose we are and whom we serve. May the heart, the head, the hands, the feet—the whole man be dedicated, in unreserved devotedness, to Him, in the power of the Holy Ghost, and according to the direct teaching of holy Scripture. God grant it may be so, with us and with all His beloved people!

A very weighty and practical subject now claims our attention. We feel it right to adhere as much as possible to the custom of quoting at full length the passages for the reader; we believe it to be profitable to give the very Word of God itself; and moreover, it is convenient to the great majority of readers to be saved the trouble of laying aside the volume and turning to the Bible in order to find the passages for themselves.

"If there be found among you, within any of thy gates which the Lord thy God giveth thee, man or woman that hath wrought wickedness in the sight of the Lord thy God, in transgressing His covenant, and hath gone and served other gods, and worshiped them, either the sun or moon, or any of the hosts of heaven, which I have not commanded ; and it be told thee, and thou hast heard of it, and *inquired diligently*, and, behold, it be *true*, and the thing *certain*, that such abomination is *wrought in Israel ;*"—something affecting the whole nation—"then shalt thou bring forth that man or that woman, which have committed that wicked thing, unto thy gates, even that man or that woman, and shalt stone them with stones till they die. At the mouth of two witnesses, or three witnesses, shall he that is worthy of death be put to death ; but at the mouth of one witness he shall not be put to death. The hands of the witnesses shall be first upon him to put him to death, and afterward the hands of all the people. So thou shalt put the evil away from among you." (Ver. 2–7.)

We have already had occasion to refer to the great principle laid down in the foregoing passage. It is one of immense importance, namely, the absolute necessity of having competent testimony ere forming a judgment in any case. It meets us constantly in Scripture ; indeed, it is the invariable rule in the divine government, and therefore it claims our earnest attention. We may be sure it is a safe and wholesome rule, the neglect of which must always lead us astray. We should never allow ourselves to form, much less to express and act upon, a judgment without the testimony of two or three witnesses. However trustworthy and morally reliable any one witness may be, it is not a sufficient basis for a conclusion. We may feel convinced in our minds that the thing is true because affirmed by one in whom we have confidence; but God is wiser than we. It may be that the one witness is thoroughly upright and truthful, that he would not for worlds tell an untruth or bear false witness against any one, —all this may be true, but we must adhere to the divine rule—"In the mouth of two or three witnesses shall every word be established."

Would that this were more diligently attended to in the Church of God! Its value in all cases of discipline, and in all cases affecting the character or reputation of any one, is simply incalculable. Ere ever an assembly reaches a conclusion or acts on a judgment in any given case, it should insist on adequate evidence. If this be not forthcoming, let all wait on God—wait patiently and confidingly, and He will surely supply what is needed.

For instance, if there be moral evil or doctrinal error in an assembly of Christians, but it is only known to one; that one is perfectly certain—deeply and thoroughly convinced of the fact. What is to be done? Wait on God for further witness. To act without this, is to infringe a divine principle laid down with all possible clearness again and again in the Word of God. Is the one witness to feel himself aggrieved or insulted because his testimony is not acted upon? Assuredly not; indeed he ought not to expect such a thing, yea, he ought not to come forward as a witness until he can corroborate his testimony by the evidence of one or two more. Is the assembly to be deemed indifferent or supine because it refuses to act on the testimony of a solitary witness? Nay, it would be flying in the face of a divine command were it to do so.

And be it remembered that this great practical principle is not confined in its application to cases of discipline, or questions connected with an assembly of the Lord's people; it is of universal application. We should never allow ourselves to form a judgment or come to a conclusion without the divinely appointed measure of evidence; if that be not forthcoming, it is our plain duty to wait, and if it be needful for us to judge in the case, God will, in due time, furnish the needed evidence. We have known a case in which a man was falsely accused because the accuser based his charge upon the evidence of one of his senses; had he taken the trouble of getting the evidence of one or two more of his senses, he would not have made the charge.

Thus the entire subject of evidence claims the serious attention of the reader, let his position be what it may. We are all prone to rush to hasty conclusions, to take up impressions, to give place to baseless surmisings, and allow our minds to be warped and carried away by prejudice. All these have to be most carefully guarded against. We need more calmness, seriousness, and cool deliberation in forming and expressing our judgment about men and things; but especially about men, inasmuch as we may inflict a grievous wrong upon a friend, a brother, or a neighbor by giving utterance to a false impression or a baseless charge. We may allow ourselves to be the vehicle of an utterly groundless accusation, whereby the character of another may be seriously damaged. This is very sinful in the sight of God, and should be most jealously watched against in ourselves, and sternly rebuked in others, whenever it comes before us. Whenever any one brings a charge against another behind his back, we should insist upon his proving or withdrawing his statement. Were this plan adopted, we should be delivered from a vast amount of evil-speaking, which is not only most unprofitable, but positively wicked, and not to be tolerated.

Before turning from the subject of evidence, we may just remark that inspired history supplies us with more than one instance in which a righteous man has been condemned with an appearance of attention to Deuteronomy xvii. 6, 7. Witness the case of Naboth, in 1 Kings xxi; and the case of Stephen, in Acts vi. and vii; and above all, the case of the only perfect Man that every trod this earth. Alas! men can, at times, put on the appearance of wonderful attention to the letter of Scripture when it suits their own ungodly ends; they can quote its sacred words in defense of the most flagrant un-

righteousness and shocking immorality. Two witnesses accused Naboth of blaspheming God and the
king, and that faithful Israelite was deprived of his
inheritance and of his life on the testimony of two
liars, hired by the direction of a godless, cruel
woman. Stephen, a man full of the Holy Ghost,
was stoned to death for blasphemy, on the testimony
of false witnesses received and acted upon by the
great religious leaders of the day, who could doubtless quote Deuteronomy xvii. as their authority.

But all this, while it so sadly and forcibly illustrates what man is, and what mere human religious-
ness without conscience is, leaves wholly untouched
the fine moral rule laid down for our guidance in
the opening lines of our chapter. Religion without
conscience or the fear of God is the most degrading,
demoralizing, hardening thing beneath the canopy
of heaven; and one of its most terrible features is
seen in this, that men under its influence are not
ashamed or afraid to make use of the letter of holy
Scripture as a cloak wherewith to cover the most
horrible wickedness.

But thanks and praise to our God, His Word
stands forth before the vision of our souls in all its
heavenly purity, divine virtue, and holy morality,
and flings back in the face of the enemy his every
attempt to draw from its sacred pages a plea for
aught that is not true, venerable, just, pure, lovely,
and of good report.

We shall now proceed to quote for the reader the
second paragraph of our chapter, in which we shall

18

find instruction of great moral value, and much needed in this day of self-will and independence.

"If there arise a matter too hard for thee in judgment, between blood and blood, between plea and plea, and between stroke and stroke, being matters of controversy within thy gates; then shalt thou arise and get thee up *into the place which the Lord thy God shall choose;* and thou shalt come unto the priests the Levites, and unto the judges that shall be in those days, and inquire; and they shall show thee the sentence of judgment: and thou shalt do according to the sentence which they of *that place which the Lord shall choose* shall show thee; and thou shalt observe to do according to all that they inform thee; according to the sentence of the law which they shall teach thee, and according to the judgment which they shall tell thee, thou shalt do: thou shalt not decline from the sentence which they shall show thee, to the right hand, nor to the left. and the man that will do presumptuously, and will not hearken unto the priest that standeth to minister there before the Lord thy God, or unto the judge, even that man shall die; and thou shalt put away the evil from Israel. And all the people shall *hear* and *fear* and *do no more presumptuously*." (Ver. 8–13.)

Here we have divine provision made for the perfect settlement of all questions which might arise throughout the congregation of Israel. They were to be settled in the divine presence, at the divinely appointed centre, by the divinely appointed authority.

Thus self-will and presumption were effectually guarded against. All matters of controversy were to be definitively settled by the judgment of God as expressed by the priest or the judge appointed by God for the purpose.

In a word, it was absolutely and entirely a matter of divine authority. It was not for one man to set himself up in self-will and presumption against another. This would never do in the assembly of God. Each one had to submit his cause to a divine tribunal, and bow implicitly to its decision. There was to be no appeal, inasmuch as there was no higher court. The divinely appointed priest or judge spoke as the oracle of God, and both plaintiff and defendant had to bow, without a demur, to the decision.

Now, it must be very evident to the reader that no member of the congregation of Israel would ever have thought of bringing his case before a Gentile tribunal for judgment. This, we may feel assured, would have been utterly foreign to the thoughts and feelings of every true Israelite. It would have involved a positive insult to Jehovah Himself, who was in their midst to give judgment in every case which might arise. Surely He was sufficient. He knew the ins and outs, the *pros* and *cons*, the roots and issues, of every controversy, however involved or difficult. All were to look to Him, and to bring their causes to the place which He had chosen, and no where else. The idea of two members of the assembly of God appearing before a tribunal of the uncircumcised for judgment would not have been tolerated for a moment. It would be as much as to say that there was a defect in the divine arrangement for the congregation.

Has this any voice for us ? How are Christians to have their questions and their controversies settled? Are they to betake themselves to the world for judgment ? Is there no provision in the assembly of God for the proper settlement of cases which may arise ? Hear what the inspired apostle says on the point to the assembly at Corinth, and "to all that in every place call on the name of our Lord Jesus Christ, both theirs and ours," and therefore to all true Christians now.

"Dare any of you, having a matter against another, go to law before the unjust, and not before the saints ? Do ye not know that the saints shall judge the world ? and if the world shall be judged by you, are ye unworthy to judge the smallest matters? Know ye not that we shall judge angels? how much more things that pertain to this life ! If then ye have judgments of things pertaining to this life, set them to judge who are least esteemed in the Church. I speak to your shame. Is it so, that there is not a wise man among you? no, not one that shall be able to judge between his brethren ? But brother goeth to law with brother, and that before the unbelievers. Now therefore there is utterly a fault among you, because ye go to law one with another. Why do ye not rather take wrong ? why do ye not rather be defrauded ? Nay, ye do wrong, and defraud, and that your brethren. Know ye not that the unrighteous shall not inherit the kingdom of God ? *Be not deceived.*'' (1 Cor. vi. 1–9.)

Here, then, we have divine instruction for the Church of God in all ages. We must never, for a moment, lose sight of the fact that the Bible is *the* book for every stage of the Church's earthly career. True it is, alas ! the Church is not as it was when the above lines were penned by the inspired apostle ; a vast change has taken place in the Church's practical condition. There was no difficulty in early days in distinguishing between the Church and the world—between ''the saints'' and ''unbelievers''— between ''those within'' and ''those without.'' The line of demarkation was broad, distinct, and unmistakable in those days. Any one who looked at the face of society in a religious point of view would see three things, namely, Paganism, Judaism, and Christianity—the Gentile, the Jew, and the Church of God—the heathen temple, the synagogue, and the assembly of God. There was no confounding these things. The Christian assembly stood out in vivid contrast with all beside. Christianity was strongly and clearly pronounced in those primitive times. It was neither a national, provincial, nor parochial affair, but a personal, practical, living reality. It was not a mere nominal, national, professional creed, but a divinely wrought faith, a living power in the heart flowing out in the life.

But now, things are totally changed. The Church and the world are so mixed up, that the vast majority of professors could hardly understand the real force and proper application of the passage which we have just quoted. Were we to speak to them about "the saints" going to law "before the unbelievers," it would seem like a foreign tongue. Indeed, the term "saint" is hardly heard in the professing church, save when used with a sneer, or as applied to such as have been canonized by a superstitious reverence.

But has any change come over the Word of God, or over the grand truths which that Word unfolds to our souls? Has any change come over the thoughts of God in reference to what His Church is, or what the world is, or as to the proper relation of the one to the other? Does He not know who are "saints" and who are "unbelievers"? Has it ceased to be "a fault" for "brother to go to law with brother, and that before the unbelievers"? In a word, has holy Scripture lost its power, its point, its divine application? Is it no longer our guide, our authority, our one perfect rule and unerring standard? Has the marked change that has come over the Church's moral condition deprived the Word of God of all power of application to *us*—"to all that in every place call on the name of our Lord Jesus Christ"? Has our Father's most precious revelation become, in any one particular, a dead letter—a piece of obsolete writing—a document pertaining to days long gone by? Has our altered condition robbed the Word of God of a single one of its moral glories?

Reader, what answer does your heart return to

these questions? Let us most earnestly entreat of
you to weigh them honestly, humbly, and prayerfully
in the presence of your Lord. We believe your
answer will be a wonderfully correct index of your
real position and moral state. Do you not clearly
see and fully admit that Scripture can never lose its
power? Can the principles of 1 Corinthians vi. ever
cease to be binding on the Church of God? It is
fully admitted—for who can deny that things are
sadly changed?—but "Scripture cannot be broken,"
and therefore what was "a fault" in the first century
cannot be right in the nineteenth; there may be
more difficulty in carrying out divine principles, but
we must never consent to surrender them, or to act
on any lower ground. If once we admit the idea
that because the whole professing church has gone
wrong it is impossible for us to do right, the whole
principle of Christian obedience is surrendered. It
is as wrong for "brother to go to law with brother
before the unbelievers" to-day as when the apostle
wrote his epistle to the assembly at Corinth.* True,

---

* It is well for us to bear in mind that wherever there are "two
or three" gathered to the Name of the Lord Jesus, in ever such
weakness, there will be found, if only they are truly humble and
dependent, spiritual ability to judge in any case that may arise
between brethren. They can count on divine wisdom being supplied for the settlement of any question, plea, or controversy, so
that there need not be any reference to a worldly tribunal.

No doubt worldly men would smile at such an idea; but we must
adhere, with holy decision, to the guidance of Scripture. Brother
must not go to law with brother before the unbelievers. This is
distinct and emphatic. There are resources available for the assembly in Christ, the Head and Lord, for the settlement of every
possible question.

Let the Lord's people seriously apply their hearts to the consid-

the Church's *visible* unity is gone; she is shorn of many gifts, she has departed from her normal condition; but the principles of the Word of God can no more lose their power than the blood of Christ can lose its virtue or His priesthood lose its efficacy.

And further, we must bear in mind that there are resources of wisdom, grace, power, and spiritual gift treasured up for the Church in Christ her Head, ever available for those who have faith to use them. We are not straitened in our blessed and adorable Head. We need never expect to see the body restored to its normal condition on the earth, but for all that, it is our privilege to see what the true

---

eration of this subject. Let them see that they are gathered on the true ground of the Church of God; and then, though ever conscious that things are not as they once were in the Church—though sensible of the greatest weakness, failure, and shortcoming, they will nevertheless find the grace of Christ ever sufficient for them, and the Word of God full of all needed instruction and authority, so that they need never betake themselves to the world for help, counsel, or judgment. "Where two or three are gathered together in My name, there am I in the midst of them."

This surely is enough for every exigence. Is there any question that our Lord Christ cannot settle? Do we want natural cleverness, worldly wisdom, long-headedness, great learning, keen sagacity, if we have Him? Surely not; indeed all such things can only prove like Saul's armor to David. All we want is, simply to use the resources which we have in Christ. We shall assuredly find, "in the place where His name is recorded," priestly wisdom to judge in every case which may arise between brethren.

And further, let the Lord's dear people remember, in all cases of local difficulty which may arise, that there is no need whatever for them to look for extraneous aid, to write to other places to get some wise man to come and help them. No doubt, if the Lord sends any of His beloved servants at the moment, their sympathy, fellowship, counsel, and help will be highly prized. We are not encouraging independence one of the other, but absolute and complete dependence upon Christ, our Head and Lord.

ground of the body is, and it is our duty to occupy that ground and no other.

Now, it is perfectly wonderful the change that takes place in our whole condition—in our view of things, in our thoughts of ourselves and our surroundings—the moment we plant our foot on the true ground of the Church of God. Every thing seems changed; the Bible seems a new book; we see every thing in a new light; portions of Scripture which we have been reading for years without interest or profit now sparkle with divine light, and fill us with wonder, love, and praise. We see everything from a new stand-point; our whole range of vision is changed; we have made our escape from the murky atmosphere which inwraps the whole professing church, and can now look around and see things clearly in the heavenly light of Scripture. In fact, it seems like a new conversion; and we find we can now read Scripture intelligently, because we have the divine key. We see Christ to be the centre and object of all the thoughts, purposes, and counsels of God from everlasting to everlasting, and hence we are conducted into that marvelous sphere of grace and glory which the Holy Ghost delights to unfold in the precious Word of God.

May the reader be led into the thorough understanding of all this, by the direct and powerful ministry of the Holy Spirit. May he be enabled to give himself to the study of Scripture, and to surrender himself, unreservedly, to its teaching and authority. Let him not confer with flesh and blood, but cast Himself, like a little child, on the Lord, and seek to be led on in spiritual intelligence and practical conformity to the mind of Christ.

We must now look for a moment at the closing verses of our chapter, in which we have a remarkable onlook into Israel's future, anticipating the moment in which they should seek to set a king over them.

"When thou art come unto the land which the Lord thy God giveth thee, and shalt possess it, and shalt dwell therein, and shalt say, I will set a king over me, like as all the nations that are about me; thou shalt in any wise set him king over thee whom the Lord thy God shall choose; one from among thy brethren shalt thou set king over thee; thou mayest not set a stranger over thee, which is not thy brother. But he shall not multiply horses to himself, nor cause the people to return to Egypt, to the end that he should multiply horses; forasmuch as the Lord hath said unto you, 'Ye shall henceforth return no more that way.' Neither shall he multiply wives to himself, that his heart turn not away; neither shall he greatly multiply to himself silver and gold."

How very remarkable that the three things which the king was not to do were just *the* very things which were done—and extensively done by the greatest and wisest of Israel's monarchs. "King Solomon made a navy of ships in Ezion-geber, which is beside Eloth, on the shore of the Red Sea, in the land of Edom. And Hiram sent in the navy his servants, shipmen that had knowledge of the sea, with the servants of Solomon. And they came to Ophir, and fetched from thence *gold*, four hundred and twenty talents [over two millions], and brought it to king Solomon." "And Hiram sent to the king sixscore talents of gold." "And the weight of gold that came to Solomon in one year was six hundred threescore and six talents of gold [nearly three and a half millions], beside that he had of the merchantmen, and of the traffic of the spice merchants, and of all the kings of Arabia, and of the governors of the country." Again, we read, "And the king made *silver* to be in Jerusalem as stones. . . . . And Solomon had *horses brought out of Egypt.* . . . . But king Solomon loved many strange women. . . . . And he had seven hundred wives, princesses, and three hundred concubines; and his wives turned away his heart." (1 Kings ix, x, xi.)

What a tale this tells! what a commentary it furnishes upon man in his very best and highest estate! Here was a man endowed with wisdom beyond all others, surrounded by unexampled blessings, dignities, honors, and privileges; his earthly cup was full to the brim; there was nothing lacking which this world could supply to minister to human happiness. And not only so, but his remarkable prayer at the dedication of the temple might well lead us to cherish the brightest hopes respecting him, both personally and officially.

But sad to say, he broke down most deplorably in every one of the particulars as to which the law of his God had spoken so definitely and so clearly.

He was told not to multiply silver and gold, and yet he multiplied them; he was told not to return to Egypt to multiply horses, and yet to Egypt he went for horses; he was told not to multiply wives, and yet he had a thousand of them, and they turned away his heart. Such is man! Oh, how little is he to be counted upon! "All flesh is as grass, and all the glory of man as the flower of grass. The grass withereth, and the flower thereof falleth away." "Cease ye from man whose breath is in his nostrils, for wherein is he to be accounted of?"

But we may ask, How are we to account for Solomon's signal, sorrowful, and humiliating failure? what was the real secret of it? To answer this, we must quote for the reader the closing verses of our chapter.

"And it shall be, when he sitteth upon the throne of his kingdom, that he shall write him a copy of this law in a book out of that which is before the priests the Levites; *and it shall be with him*, and *he shall read therein all the days of his life;* that he may learn to fear the Lord his God, to keep all the words of this law and these statutes, to do them; that his heart be not lifted up above his brethren, and that he turn not aside from the commandment, to the right hand or to the left; to the end that he may prolong his days in his kingdom, he and his children, in the midst of Israel." (Ver. 18–20.)

Had Solomon attended to these most precious and weighty words, his historian would have had a very different task to perform; but he did not. We hear nothing of his having made a copy of the law; and most assuredly, if he did make a copy of it, he did not attend to it—yea, he turned his back upon it, and did the very things which he was told not to do. In a word, the cause of all the wreck and ruin that so rapidly followed the splendor of Solomon's reign, was the neglect of the plain Word of God.

It is this which makes it all so solemn for us, in this our own day, and which leads us to call the earnest attention of the reader to it. We deeply feel the need of seeking to rouse the attention of the whole Church of God to this great subject. Neglect of the Word of God is the source of all the failure, all the sin, all the error, all the mischief and confusion, the heresies, sects, and schisms that have ever been or are now in this world. And we may add, with equal confidence, that the only real, sovereign remedy for our present lamentable condition will be found in returning, *every one for himself and herself*, to the simple but sadly neglected authority of the Word of God. Let each one see his own departure, and that of the whole professing body, from the plain and positive teaching of the New Testament—the commandments of our blessed Lord and Saviour Jesus Christ. Let us humble ourselves under the mighty hand of our God, because of our common sin, and let us turn to Him in true self-judgment, and He will graciously restore and heal and bless us, and lead us in that most blessed path of obedience which lies open before every truly humble soul.

May God the Holy Ghost, in His own resistless power, bring home to the heart and conscience of every member of the body of Christ on the face of the earth, the urgent need of an immediate and unreserved surrender to the authority of the Word of God.

CHAPTER XVIII.

THE opening paragraph of this chapter suggests a deeply interesting and practical line of truth.

"The priests the Levites, and all the tribe of Levi, shall have no part nor inheritance with Israel; they shall eat the offerings of the Lord made by fire, and His inheritance. Therefore shall they have no inheritance among their brethren: the Lord is their inheritance, as He hath said unto them. And this shall be the priest's due from the people, from them that offer a sacrifice, whether it be ox or sheep; and they shall give unto the priest the shoulder, and the two cheeks, and the maw. The first-fruits also of thy corn, of thy wine, and of thine oil, and the first of the fleece of thy sheep shalt thou give him. For the Lord thy God hath chosen him out of all thy tribes, to stand to minister in the name of the Lord, him and his sons forever. And if a Levite come from any of thy gates out of all Israel, where he sojourned, and *come with all the desire of his mind unto the place which the Lord shall choose;* then he shall minister in the name of the Lord his God, as all his brethren the Levites do, which stand there before the Lord. They shall have like portions to eat, beside that which cometh out of the sale of his patrimony." (Ver. 1–8.)

Here, as in every part of the book of Deuteronomy, the priests are classed with the Levites in a very marked way. We have called the reader's attention to this as a special characteristic feature of our book, and shall not dwell upon it now, but merely, in passing, remind the reader of it, as something claiming his attention. Let him weigh the opening words of our chapter, "The priests the Levites," and compare them with the way in which the priests the sons of Aaron are spoken of in Exodus, Leviticus, and Numbers; and if he should be disposed to ask the reason of this distinction, we believe it to be this, that in Deuteronomy the divine object is, to bring the whole assembly of Israel more into prominence, and hence it is that the priests in their official capacity come rarely before us. The grand Deuteronomic idea is, *Israel in immediate relationship with Jehovah.*

Now, in the passage just quoted, we have the priests and the Levites linked together, and presented as the Lord's servants, wholly dependent upon Him, and intimately identified with His altar and His service. This is full of interest, and opens up a very important field of practical truth, to which the Church of God would do well to attend.

In looking through the history of Israel, we observe that when things were in any thing like a

ꞁealthful condition, the altar of God was well at-
ꞇended to, and, as a consequence, the priests and
the Levites were well supplied.   If Jehovah had
His portion, His servants were sure to have theirs;
if He was neglected, so were they.   They were
bound up together.   The people were to bring their
offerings to God, and He shared them with His
servants.   The priests the Levites were not to exact
or demand of the people, but the people were privileged to bring their gifts to the altar of God, and
He permitted His servants to feed upon the fruit
of His people's devotedness to Him.

Such was the true—the divine idea as to the Lord's
servants of old.   They were to live upon the volun-
tary offerings presented to God by the whole congregation.   True it is that in the dark and evil days
of the sons of Eli we find something sadly different
from this lovely moral order.   Then, "the priest's
custom with the people was, that when any one
offered sacrifice, the priest's servant came, while the
flesh was in seething, with a flesh-hook of three
teeth in his hand; and he struck it into the pan, or
kettle, or caldron, or pot; all that the flesh-hook
brought up, the priest took for himself.   So they
did in Shiloh unto all the Israelites that came
thither.   Also before they burnt the fat [God's
special portion], the priest's servant came, and said
to the man that sacrificed, 'Give flesh to roast for
the priest; for he will not have sodden flesh of thee,
but raw.'   And if any man said unto him, Let them
not fail to burn the fat presently, and then take as

much as thy soul desireth; then he would answer him, 'Nay; but thou shalt give it me now; and if not, *I will take it by force.'* Wherefore the sin of the young men was very great before the Lord; for men abhorred the offering of the Lord." (1 Sam. ii. 13–17.)

All this was truly deplorable, and ended in the solemn judgment of God upon the house of Eli. It could not be otherwise. If those who ministered at the altar could be guilty of such terrible iniquity and impiety, judgment must take its course.

But the normal condition of things, as presented in our chapter, was in vivid contrast with all this frightful iniquity. Jehovah would surround Himself with the willing offerings of His people, and from these offerings He would feed His servants who ministered at His altar. Hence, therefore, when the altar of God was diligently, fervently, and devotedly attended to, the priests the Levites had a rich portion—an abundant supply; and on the other hand, when Jehovah and His altar were treated with cold neglect, or merely waited upon in a barren routine or heartless formalism, the Lord's servants were correspondingly neglected. In a word, they stood intimately identified with the worship and service of the God of Israel.

Thus, for example, in the bright days of the good king Hezekiah, when things were fresh and hearts happy and true, we read, "And Hezekiah appointed the courses of the priests and the Levites after their courses, every man according to his service, the

19

priests and Levites for burnt-offerings and for peace-offerings, to minister, and to give thanks, and to praise in the gates of the tents of the Lord. He appointed also the king's portion of his substance for the burnt-offerings, to wit, for the morning and evening burnt-offerings, and the burnt-offerings for the Sabbaths, and for the new moons, and for the set feasts, *as it is written in the law of the Lord*. Moreover, he commanded the people that dwelt in Jerusalem *to give the portion of the priests and the Levites, that they might be encouraged in the law of the Lord.* And as soon as the commandment came abroad, the children of Israel brought *in abundance* the first-fruits of corn, wine, and oil, and honey, and of all the increase of the field; and the tithe of *all things* brought they in *abundantly*. And concerning the children of Israel and Judah, that dwelt in the cities of Judah, they also brought in the tithe of oxen and sheep, and the tithe of holy things which were consecrated unto the Lord their God, *and laid them by heaps.* In the third month they began to lay the foundation of the heaps, and finished them in the seventh month. And when Hezekiah and the princes came and saw the heaps, they blessed the Lord and His people Israel. Then Hezekiah questioned with the priests and the Levites concerning the heaps. And Azariah the chief priest of the house of Zadok answered him, and said, ' *Since the people began to bring the offerings into the house of the Lord, we have had enough to eat, and have left plenty; for the Lord hath blessed His people;*

and that which is left is this great store." (2 Chron.
xxxi. 2-10.)

How truly refreshing is all this! and how encouraging! The deep, full, silvery tide of devotedness flowed around the altar of God, bearing upon its
bosom an ample supply to meet all the need of the
Lord's servants, and "heaps" beside. This, we may
feel assured, was grateful to the heart of the God of
Israel, as it was to the hearts of those who had given
themselves, at His call and by His appointment, to
the service of His altar and His sanctuary.

And let the reader specially note those precious
words, "*As it is written in the law of the Lord.*" Here
was Hezekiah's authority, the solid basis of his whole
line of conduct from first to last. True, the nation's
visible unity was gone; the condition of things when
he began his blessed work was most discouraging;
but the word of the Lord was as true, as real, and as
direct in its application in Hezekiah's day as it was
in the days of David or Joshua. Hezekiah rightly
felt that Deuteronomy xviii. 1-8 applied to his day
and to his conscience, and that he and the people
were responsible to act upon it, according to their
ability. Were the priests and the Levites to starve
because Israel's national unity was gone? Surely
not. They were to stand or fall with the Word, the
worship, and the work of God. Circumstances
might vary, and the Israelite might find himself in a
position in which it would be impossible to carry out
in detail all the ordinances of the Levitical ceremonial, but he never could find himself in circumstances

in which it was not his high privilege to give full expression to his heart's devotedness to the service, the altar, and the law of Jehovah.

Thus, then, we see, throughout the entire history of Israel, that when things were at all bright and healthy, the Lord's worship, His work, and His workmen were blessedly attended to; but on the other hand, when things were low, when hearts were cold, when self and its interests had the uppermost place, then all these great objects were treated with heartless neglect. Look, for example, at Nehemiah xiii. When that beloved and faithful servant returned to Jerusalem, after an absence of certain days, he found, to his deep sorrow, that, even in that short time, various things had gone sadly astray; amongst the rest, the poor Levites had been left without any thing to eat. "And I perceived that the portions of the Levites had not been given them; for the Levites and the singers that did the work were fled every one to his field." There were no "heaps" of first-fruits in those dismal days, and surely it was hard for men to work and sing when they had nothing to eat. This was not according to the law of Jehovah, nor according to His loving heart. It was a sad reproach upon the people that the Lord's servants were obliged, through their gross neglect, to abandon His worship and His work in order to keep themselves from starving.

This, truly, was a deplorable condition of things. Nehemiah felt it keenly, as we read, "Then contended I with the rulers, and said, '*Why is the house of God forsaken?'* And I gathered them together, and set them in their place. Then brought all Judah the tithe of the corn, and the new wine, and the oil, unto the treasuries. And I made treasurers over the treasuries, ... for they were counted faithful ; "—they were entitled to the confidence of their brethren—"and their office was to distribute unto their brethren.'' It needed a number of tried and faithful men to occupy the high position of distributing to their brethren the precious fruit of the people's devotedness ; they could take counsel together, and see that the Lord's treasury was faithfully managed, according to His Word, and the need of His true and *bona-fide* workmen fully met, without prejudice or partiality.

Such was the lovely order of the God of Israel— an order to which every true Israelite such as Nehemiah and Hezekiah would delight to attend. The rich tide of blessing flowed forth from Jehovah to His people, and back from His people to Him, and from that flowing tide His servants were to draw a full supply for all their need. It was a dishonor to Him to have the Levites obliged to return to their fields ; it proved that His house was forsaken, and that there was no sustenance for His servants.

Now, the question may here be asked, What has all this to say to us? what has the Church of God to learn from Deuteronomy xviii. 1–8 ? In order to answer this question, we must turn to 1 Corinthians ix. where the inspired apostle deals with the very important subject of the support of the Christian ministry — a subject so little understood by the great mass of professing Christians. As to *the law of the case*, it is as distinct as possible. "Who goeth a warfare at any time at his own charges? who planteth a vineyard, and eateth not of the fruit thereof? or who feedeth a flock, and eateth not of the milk of the flock? Say I these things as a man? or saith not the law the same also? For it is written in the law of Moses, 'Thou shalt not muzzle the mouth of the ox that treadeth out the corn. Doth God take care for oxen? or saith He it altogether for our sakes? For our sakes, no doubt, this is written; that he that ploweth should plow in hope, and that he that thresheth in hope should be partaker of his hope. If we have sown unto you spiritual things, is it a great thing if we shall reap your carnal things? If others be partakers of this power over you, are not we rather? Nevertheless"—here grace shines out, in all its heavenly lustre—"we have not used this power; but suffer all things lest we should hinder the gospel of Christ. Do ye not know that they which minister about holy things live of the things of the temple? and they which wait at the altar are partakers with the altar? Even so hath the Lord ordained that they which preach the gospel should live of the gospel. But"—here again grace asserts its holy dignity—"I have used none of these things; neither have I written these things that it should be so done unto me; for it were better for me to die than that any man should make my glorying void. For though

I preach the gospel, I have nothing to glory of; for
necessity is laid upon me; yea, woe is unto me if I
preach not the gospel!   For if I do this thing
willingly, I have a reward; but if against my will,
a dispensation of the gospel is committed unto me.
What is my reward, then?   Verily that when I
preach the gospel, I may make the gospel of Christ
without charge, that I abuse not my power in the
gospel." (Ver. 7–18.)

Here we have this interesting and weighty subject
presented in all its bearings.   The inspired apostle
lays down, with all possible decision and clearness,
the divine law on the point.   There is no mistaking
it.   "The Lord hath ordained that they that preach
the gospel should live of the gospel;" that just as
the priests and the Levites of old lived on the offerings presented by the people, so now, those who are
really called of God, gifted by Christ, and fitted by
the Holy Ghost to preach the gospel, and who are
giving themselves constantly and diligently to that
glorious work, are morally entitled to temporal support.   It is not that they should look to those to
whom they preach for a certain stipulated sum.
There is no such idea as this in the New Testament.
The workman must look to his Master, and to Him
alone, for support.   Woe be to him if he looks to the
church, or to men in any way.   The priests and
Levites had their portion in and from Jehovah.   He
was the lot of their inheritance.   True, He expected
the people to minister to Him in the persons of His
servants.   He told them what to give, and blessed

them in giving: it was their high privilege, as well as their bounden duty, to give; had they refused or neglected, it would have brought drought and barrenness upon their fields and vineyards. (Hag. i. 5–11.)

But the priests the Levites had to look *only* to Jehovah. If the people failed in their offerings, the Levites had to fly to their fields and work for their living. They could not go to law with any one for tithes and offerings; their only appeal was to the God of Israel, who had ordained them to the work and given them the work to do.

So also with the Lord's workmen now—they must look *only* to Him. They must be well assured that He has fitted them for the work, and called them to it, ere they attempt to push out (if we may so express it) from the shore of circumstances, and give themselves wholly to the work of preaching. They must take their eyes completely off from men—from all creature-streams and human props, and lean exclusively upon the living God. We have seen the most disastrous consequences resulting from acting under a mistaken impulse in this most solemn matter; men not called of God, or fitted for the work, giving up their occupations, and coming forth, as they said, to live by faith and give themselves to the work. Deplorable shipwreck was the result in every instance. Some, when they began to look the stern realities of the path straight in the face, became so alarmed that they actually lost their mental balance, lost their reason for a time; some lost their peace, and some went right back into the world again.

In short, it is our deep and thorough conviction, after forty years' observation, that the cases are few and far between in which it is morally safe and good for one to abandon his bread-winning calling in order to preach the gospel. It must be so distinct and unquestionable to the man himself, that he has only to say, with Luther, at the Diet of Worms, "Here I am; I can do no otherwise: God help me! Amen." Then he may be perfectly sure that God will sustain him in the work to which He has called him, and meet all his need "according to His riches in glory by Christ Jesus." And as to men and their thoughts respecting him and his course, he has simply to refer them to his Master. He is not responsible to them, nor has he ever asked them for any thing. If they were compelled to support him, reason would that they might complain or raise questions; but as they are not, they must just leave him, remembering that to his own Master he standeth or falleth.

But when we look at the splendid passage just quoted from 1 Corinthians ix, we find that the blessed apostle, after having established, beyond all question, his right to be supported, relinquishes it completely.—"Nevertheless, I have used none of these things." He worked with his hands; he wrought with labor and travail night and day, in order not to be chargeable or burdensome to any. "These hands," he says, "have ministered to my necessities, and those that were with me." He coveted no man's silver or gold or apparel. He traveled, he preached, he visited from house to house, he was the laborious apostle, the earnest evangelist, the diligent pastor, he had the care of all the churches. Was not he entitled to support? Assuredly he was. It ought to have been the joy of the Church of God to minister to his every need. But he never enforced his claim—nay, he surrendered it. He supported himself and his companions by the labor of his hands; and all this as an example, as he says to the elders of Ephesus, "I have showed you all things, how that so laboring ye ought to support the weak, and to remember the words of the Lord Jesus, how He said, 'It is more blessed to give than to receive.'"

Now, it is perfectly wonderful to think of this beloved and revered servant of Christ, with his extensive travels from Jerusalem and round about to Illyricum, his gigantic labors as an evangelist, a pastor, and a teacher, and yet finding time to support himself and others by the work of his hands. Truly he occupied high moral ground. His case is a standing testimony against hirelingism, in every shape and form. The infidel's sneering references to well-paid ministers could have no application whatever to him. He certainly did not preach for hire.

And yet he thankfully received help from those who knew how to give it. Again and again the beloved assembly at Philippi ministered to the necessities of their revered and beloved father in Christ. How well for them that they did so! It will never be forgotten. Millions have read the sweet record of their devotedness, and been refreshed by the odor of their sacrifice; it is recorded in heaven, where nothing of the kind is ever forgotten—yea, it is engraved on the very tablets of the heart of Christ. Hear how the blessed apostle pours out his grateful heart to his much-loved children.—"I rejoiced in the Lord greatly, that now at the last your care of me hath flourished again; wherein ye were also careful, but ye lacked opportunity. Not that I speak in respect of want;"— blessed, self-denying servant!—"for I have learned, in whatsoever state I am, to be content. I know both how to be abased, and I know how to abound; every where and in all things I am instructed both to be full and to be hungry, both to abound and to suffer need. I can do all things through Christ, which strengtheneth me. Notwithstanding, ye have well done that ye did communicate with my affliction. Now ye Philippians know also, that in the beginning of the gospel, when I departed from Macedonia, no church communicated with me as concerning giving and receiving, but ye only. For even in Thessalonica ye sent once and again unto my necessity. Not because I desire a gift; but I desire fruit that may abound to your account. But I have all, and abound; I am full, having received from Epaphroditus the things which were sent from you, an odor of a sweet smell, a sacrifice acceptable, well-pleasing to God. But my God shall supply all your need according to His riches in glory by Christ Jesus." (Phil. iv. 10-19.)

What a rare privilege to be allowed to comfort the heart of such an honored servant of Christ, at the close of his career, and in the solitude of his prison at Rome! How seasonable, how right, how lovely, was their ministry! What joy to receive the apostle's grateful acknowledgments! and then how precious the assurance that their service had gone up, as an odor of sweet smell, to the very throne and heart of God! Who would not rather be a Philippian ministering to the apostle's need, than a Corinthian calling his ministry in question, or a Galatian breaking his heart? How vast the difference! The apostle could not take any thing from the assembly at Corinth; their state did not admit of it. Individuals in that assembly did minister to him, and their service is recorded on the page of inspiration, remembered above, and it will be abundantly rewarded in the kingdom by and by. "I am glad of the coming of Stephanas and Fortunatus and Achaicus; for *that which was lacking on your part they have supplied.* For they have refreshed my spirit and yours, therefore acknowledge ye them that are such." (1 Cor. xvi. 17, 18.)

Thus, then, from all that has passed before us, we learn most distinctly that both under the law and under the gospel it is according to the revealed will, and according to the heart of God, that those who are really called of Him to the work, and who devote themselves earnestly, diligently, and faithfully to it, should have the hearty sympathy and practical help of His people. All who love Christ will count it their deepest joy to minister to Him in the persons of His servants. When He Himself was here upon earth, He graciously accepted help from the hands of those who loved Him, and had reaped the fruit of His most precious ministry—"certain women, which had been healed of evil spirits and infirmities, Mary, called Magdalene, out of whom went seven devils, and Joanna the wife of Chuza, Herod's steward, and Susanna, and many others, which ministered unto Him of their substance." (Luke viii. 2, 3.)

Happy, highly privileged women! What joy to be allowed to minister to the Lord of glory, in the days of His human need and humiliation! There stand their honored names, on the divine page, written down by God the Holy Ghost, to be read by untold millions, to be borne along the stream of time right onward into eternity. How well it was for those women that they did not waste their substance in self-indulgence, or hoard it up to be rust on their souls, or a positive curse, as money must ever be if not used for God!

But on the other hand, we learn the urgent need, on the part of all who take the place of workers, whether in or out of the assembly, of keeping themselves perfectly free from all human influence, all looking to men, in any shape or form. They must have to do with God in the secret of their own souls, or they will assuredly break down, sooner or later. They must look to Him alone for the supply of their need. If the church neglect them, the church will be the serious loser here and hereafter.

If they can support themselves by the labor of
their hands, without curtailing their direct service to
Christ, so much the better; it is unquestionably the
more excellent way. We are as persuaded of this as
of the truth of any proposition that could be submitted to us. There is nothing more spiritually and
morally noble than a truly gifted servant of Christ
supporting himself and his family by the sweat of
his brow or the sweat of his brain, and, at the same
time, giving himself diligently to the Lord's work,
whether as an evangelist, a pastor, or a teacher.
The moral antipodes of this is presented to our view
in the person of a man who, without gift or grace or
spiritual life, enters what is called the ministry, as a
mere profession or means of living. The position
of such a man is morally dangerous and miserable
in the extreme. We shall not dwell upon it, inasmuch as it does not come within the range of the
subject which has been engaging our attention, and
we are only too thankful to leave it and proceed with
our chapter.

"When thou art come into the land which the
Lord thy God giveth thee, thou shalt not learn to do
after the abominations of those nations. There shall
not be found among you any one that maketh his
son or his daughter to pass through the fire, or that
useth divination, or an observer of times, or an
enchanter, or a witch, or a charmer, or a consulter
with familiar spirits, or a wizard, or a necromancer;
for *all that do these things are an abomination unto
the Lord*, and because of these abominations the

Lord thy God doth drive them out from before thee. Thou shalt be perfect with the Lord thy God. For these nations, which thou shalt possess, hearkened unto observers of times, and unto diviners; *but as for thee, the Lord thy God hath not suffered thee so to do.*" (Ver. 9–14.)

Now, it may be that, on reading the foregoing quotation, the reader feels disposed to ask what possible application it can have to professing Christians. We ask, in reply, Are there any professing Christians who are in the habit of going to witness the performances of wizards, magicians, and necromancers? are there any who take part in table-turning, spirit-rapping, mesmerism, or *clairvoyance?* * If so, the passage which we have just quoted bears very pointedly and solemnly upon all such. We most surely believe that all these things which we have named are of the devil. This may sound harsh and severe, but we cannot help that. We are thoroughly persuaded that when people lend themselves to the awful business of bringing up, in any way, the spirits of the departed, they are simply putting themselves into the hands of the devil, to be de-

---

*Some of our readers may object to our classing mesmerism with spirit-rapping and table-turning. It may be they would regard it in the same light, and use it in the same way, as ether or chloroform, in medical practice. We do not attempt to dogmatize on the point. We can only say that we could have nothing whatever to do with it. We consider it a most solemn thing for any one to allow himself to be placed by another in a state of utter unconsciousness, for any purpose whatsoever. And as to the idea of listening to, or being guided by, the ravings of a person in that state, we can only regard it as absolutely absurd, if not positively sinful.

ceived and deluded by his lies. What, we may ask, do those who hold in their hands a perfect revelation from God want of table-turning and spirit-rapping? Surely nothing. And if, not content with that precious Word, they turn to the spirits of departed friends or others, what can they expect but that God will judicially give them over to be blinded and deceived by wicked spirits, who come up and personate the departed, and tell all manner of lies?

We cannot attempt to go fully into this subject here; we have no time, nor space, nor inclination, for any thing of the sort. We merely feel it to be our solemn duty to warn the reader against having any thing whatever to do with consulting departed spirits. We believe it to be *most dangerous* work. We do not enter upon the question as to whether souls can come back to this world; no doubt God could permit them to come if He saw fit, but this we leave. The great point for us to keep ever before our hearts is, the perfect sufficiency of divine revelation. What do we want of departed spirits? The rich man imagined that if Lazarus were to go back to earth and speak to his five brethren, it would have a great effect.—"'I pray thee therefore, father, that thou wouldest send him to my father's house; for I have five brethren; that he may testify unto them, lest they also come into this place of torment.' Abraham saith unto him, 'They have *Moses and the prophets; let them hear them.*' And he said, 'Nay, father Abraham; but if one went unto them from the dead, they will repent.' And he said unto him, 'If they hear not *Moses and the prophets,* neither will they be persuaded though one rose from the dead.'" (Luke xvi. 27–31.)

Here we have a thorough settlement of this question. If people will not hear the Word of God, if they will not believe its clear and solemn statements as to themselves, their present condition, and their future destiny, neither will they be persuaded though a thousand departed souls were to come back and tell them what they saw and heard and felt in heaven above or in hell beneath; it would produce no saving or permanent effect upon them. It might cause great excitement—great sensation, furnish great material for talk, and fill the newspapers far and wide; but there it would end. People would go on all the same with their traffic and gain, their folly and vanity, their pleasure-hunting and self-indulgence. "If they hear not Moses and the prophets, [and, we may add, Christ and His holy apostles,] neither will they be persuaded though one rose from the dead." The heart that will not bow to Scripture will not be convinced by any thing; and as to the true believer, he has in Scripture all he can possibly want, and therefore he has no need to have recourse to table-turning, spirit-rapping, or magic. "And when they shall say unto you, Seek unto them that have familiar spirits, and unto wizards that peep, and that mutter; should not a people seek unto their God? for the living to the dead? *To the law and to the testimony;* if they speak not according to

20

this word, it is because there is no light in them."
(Is. viii. 19, 20.)

Here is the divine resource of the Lord's people,
at all times and in all places; and to this it is that
Moses refers the congregation in the splendid paragraph which closes our chapter. He shows them
very distinctly that they had no need to apply to
familiar spirits, enchanters, wizards, or witches,
which were all an abomination to the Lord. "The
Lord thy God," he says, "will raise up unto thee a
Prophet from the midst of thee, of thy brethren, like
unto me; *unto him ye shall hearken;* according to
all that thou desiredst of the Lord thy God in Horeb
in the day of the assembly, saying, 'Let me not hear
again the voice of the Lord my God, neither let me
see this great fire any more, that I die not.' And
the Lord said unto me, 'They have well spoken
that which they have spoken. I will raise them up
a Prophet from among their brethren, like unto thee,
and will put My words into his mouth; and he shall
speak unto them all that I shall command him.
And it shall come to pass that whosoever will not
hearken unto My words which he shall speak in My
name, I will require it of him. But the prophet
which shall presume to speak a word in My name
which I have not commanded him to speak, or
that shall speak in the name of other gods, even
that prophet shall die. And if thou say in thine
heart, How shall we know the word which the
Lord hath not spoken? When a prophet speaketh
in the name of the Lord, if the thing follow not,

nor come to pass, that is the thing which the Lord hath not spoken, but the prophet hath spoken it presumptuously: thou shalt not be afraid of him." (Ver. 15-22.)

We can be at no loss to know who this Prophet is, namely, our adorable Lord and Saviour Jesus Christ. In the third chapter of Acts, Peter so applies the words of Moses. —"He shall send Jesus Christ, which before was preached unto you; whom the heaven must receive until the times of restitution of all things, which God hath spoken by the mouth of all His holy prophets since the world began. For Moses truly said unto the fathers, 'A Prophet shall the Lord your God raise up unto you of your brethren, like unto me; him shall ye hear in all things whatsoever he shall say unto you. And it shall come to pass that every soul which will not hear that Prophet shall be destroyed from among the people.'" (Ver. 20-23.)

How precious the privilege of hearing the voice of such a Prophet! It is the voice of God speaking through the lips of the Man Christ Jesus—speaking, not in thunder, not with flaming fire, nor the lightning's flash, but in that still small voice of love and mercy which falls in soothing power on the broken heart and contrite spirit, which distills like the gentle dew of heaven upon the thirsty ground. This voice we have in the holy Scriptures—that precious revelation which comes so constantly and so powerfully before us in our studies on this blessed book of Deuteronomy. We must never forget this. The voice of Scripture is the voice of Christ, and the voice of Christ is the voice of God.

We want no more. If any one presumes to come with a fresh revelation, with some new truth not contained in the divine Volume, we must judge him and his communication by the standard of Scripture and reject them utterly. "Thou shalt not be afraid of him." False prophets come with great pretensions, high-sounding words, and sanctimonious bearing. Moreover, they seek to surround themselves with a sort of dignity, weight, and impressiveness which are apt to impose on the ignorant. But they cannot stand the searching power of the Word of God. Some simple clause of holy Scripture will strip them of all their imposing surroundings, and cut up by the roots their wonderful revelations. Those who know the voice of the true Prophet will not listen to any other: those who have heard the voice of the good Shepherd will not listen to the voice of a stranger.

Reader, see that you listen *only* to the voice of Jesus.

CHAPTER XIX.

"WHEN the Lord thy God hath cut off the nations whose land the Lord thy God giveth thee, and thou succeedest them, and dwellest in their cities, and in their houses; thou shalt separate three cities for thee *in the midst of thy land*, which the Lord thy God giveth thee to possess it. *Thou shalt prepare thee a way*, and divide the coasts of thy land, which the Lord thy God giveth thee to inherit, into three parts, *that every slayer may flee thither.*" (Ver. 1–3.)

What a very striking combination of "goodness and severity" we observe in these few lines! We have the "cutting off" of the nations of Canaan because of their consummated wickedness, which had become positively unbearable; and on the other hand, we have a most touching display of divine goodness in the provision made for the poor man-slayer in the day of his deep distress, when flying for his life from the avenger of blood. The government and the goodness of God are, we need hardly say, both divinely perfect. There are cases in which goodness would be nothing but a toleration of sheer wickedness and open rebellion, which is utterly impossible under the government of God. If men imagine that because God is good they may go on and sin with a high hand, they will sooner or later find out their woeful mistake.

"Behold," says the inspired apostle, "the goodness and severity of God!"" * God will most assuredly cut off evil-doers who despise His goodness and long-suffering mercy. He is slow to anger, blessed be His holy name! and of great kindness. For hundreds of years He bore with the seven nations of Canaan, until their wickedness rose up to

---

*The word rendered "severity" is $\dot{\alpha}\pi o \tau o \mu \dot{\iota}\alpha$, which literally means "cutting off."

the very heavens, and the land itself could bear them no longer. He bore with the enormous wickedness of the guilty cities of the plain; and if He had found even ten righteous people in Sodom, He would have spared it for their sakes. But the day of terrible vengeance came, and they were "cut off."

And so will it be ere long with guilty christendom. "Thou also shalt be cut off." The reckoning-time will come, and oh, what a reckoning-time it will be! The heart trembles at the thought of it, while the eye scans and the pen traces the soul-subduing words.

But mark how divine "goodness" shines out in the opening lines of our chapter. See the gracious painstaking of our God to make the city of refuge as available as possible for the slayer. The three cities were to be "*in the midst of thy land.*" It would not do to have them in remote corners, or in places difficult of access. And not only so, but "*thou shalt prepare thee a way;*" and again, "Thou shalt divide the coasts of thy land . . . *into three parts.*" Every thing was to be done to facilitate the slayer's escape. The gracious Lord thought of the feelings of the distressed one "flying for refuge to lay hold on the hope set before him." The city of refuge was to be "brought near," just as "the right-eousness of God" is brought near to the poor broken-hearted helpless sinner—so near, that it is "to him that *worketh not*, but believeth on Him that justifieth the ungodly."

There is peculiar sweetness in the expression, "*Thou shalt prepare thee a way.*" How like our own ever-gracious God—"the God and Father of our Lord Jesus Christ"! and yet it was the same God that cut off the nations of Canaan in righteous judgment who thus made such gracious provision for the man-slayer. "Behold, the goodness and severity of God."

"And this is the case of the slayer, which shall flee thither, *that he may live:* Whoso killeth his neighbor ignorantly, whom he hated not in time past; as when a man goeth into the wood with his neighbor to hew wood, and his hand fetcheth a stroke with the axe to cut down the tree, and the head slippeth from the helve, and lighteth upon his neighbor, that he die; he shall flee unto one of those cities and live; lest the avenger of the blood pursue the slayer, while his heart is hot, and overtake him, *because the way is long,*"—most touching and exquisite grace!—"and slay him; whereas he was not worthy of death, inasmuch as he hated him not in time past. Wherefore I command thee, saying, 'Thou shalt separate three cities for thee.'" (Ver. 4–7.)

Here we have a most minute description of the man for whom the city of refuge was provided. If he did not answer to this, the city was not for him; but if he did, he might feel the most perfect assurance that a gracious God had thought of him, and found a refuge for him, where he might be as safe as the hand of God could make him. Once the slayer found himself within the precincts of the city of refuge, he might breathe freely, and enjoy calm and sweet repose. No avenging sword could reach him there, not a hair of his head could be touched there.

He was safe—yes, perfectly safe; and not only perfectly safe, but perfectly *certain*. He was not hoping to be saved, he was sure of it. He was in the city, and that was enough. Before he got in, he might have many a struggle deep down in his poor terrified heart, many doubts and fears and painful exercises. He was flying for his life, and this was a serious and an all-absorbing matter for him—a matter that would make all beside seem light and trifling. We could not imagine the flying slayer stopping to gather flowers by the roadside. Flowers! he would say, What have I to do with flowers just now? My life is at stake. I am flying for my life. What if the avenger should come and find me gathering flowers? No; the city is my one grand and all-engrossing object; nothing else has the smallest interest or charm for me. I want to be saved; that is my exclusive business now.

But the moment he found himself within the blessed gates, he was safe, *and he knew it.* How did he know it? By his feelings? by his evidences? by experience? Nay; but simply by the Word of God. No doubt he had the feeling, the evidence, and the experience, and most precious they would be to him after his tremendous struggle and conflict to get in; but these things were by no means the ground of his certainty or the basis of his peace. He knew he was safe because God told him so. The *grace* of God had made him *safe*, and the *Word* of God made him *sure*.

We cannot conceive a man-slayer within the walls of the city of refuge expressing himself as many of the Lord's dear people do in reference to the question of safety and certainty. He would not deem it presumption to be sure he was safe. If any one had asked him, Are you sure you are safe? Sure! he would say, How can I be otherwise than sure? Was I not a slayer? have I not fled to this city of refuge? has not Jehovah, our covenant-God, pledged His Word for it? has He not said that "fleeing thither he may live"? Yes, thank God, I am perfectly sure. I had a terrible run for it—a fearful struggle. At times, I almost felt as if the avenger had me in his dreaded grasp. I gave myself up for lost; but then, God, in His infinite mercy, made the way so plain, and made the city so easy of access to me, that, spite of all my doubts and fears, here I am, safe and certain. The struggle is all over, the conflict past and gone. I can breathe freely now, and walk up and down in the perfect security of this blessed place, praising our gracious covenant-God for His great goodness in having provided such a sweet retreat for a poor slayer like me.

Can the reader speak thus as to his safety in Christ? Is he saved, and does he know it? If not, may the Spirit of God apply to his heart the simple illustration of the man-slayer within the walls of the city of refuge. May he know that "strong

consolation" which is the sure, because divinely
appointed, portion of all those who have "fled for
refuge to lay hold on the hope set before them."
(Heb. vi. 18.)

We must now proceed with our chapter; and in
so doing, we shall find that there was more to be
thought of in the cities of refuge than the question
of the slayer's safety. That was provided for
perfectly, as we have seen; but the glory of God,
the purity of His land, and the integrity of His
government had to be duly maintained. If these
things were touched, there could be no safety for
any one. This great principle shines on every page
of the history of God's ways with man. Man's true
blessing and God's glory are indissolubly bound
together, and both the one and the other rest on
the same imperishable foundation, namely, Christ
and His precious work.

"And if the Lord thy God enlarge thy coasts, as
He hath sworn unto thy fathers, and give thee all
the land which He promised to give unto thy
fathers; if thou shalt keep all these commandments
to do them, which I command thee this day, to love
the Lord thy God, and to walk ever in His ways;
then shalt thou add three cities more for thee, beside these three; *that innocent blood be not shed in
thy land*, which the Lord thy God giveth thee for an
inheritance, and so blood be upon thee. But if any
man hate his neighbor, and lie in wait for him, and
rise up against him, and smite him mortally that he
die, and fleeth into one of these cities; then the

elders of his city shall send and fetch him thence, and deliver him into the hand of the avenger of blood, that he may die. Thine eye shall not pity him, *but thou shalt put away the guilt of innocent blood from Israel*, that it may go well with thee." (Ver. 8–13.)

Thus, whether it was *grace* for the slayer, or *judgment* for the murderer, the glory of God and the claims of His government had to be duly maintained. The unwitting man-slayer was met by the provision of mercy; the guilty murderer fell beneath the stern sentence of inflexible justice. We must never forget the solemn reality of divine government. It meets us every where; and if it were more fully recognized, it would effectually deliver us from one-sided views of the divine character. Take such words as these—"Thine eye shall not pity him." Who uttered them? Jehovah. Who penned them? God the Holy Ghost. What do they mean? Solemn judgment upon wickedness. Let men beware how they trifle with these weighty matters. Let the Lord's people beware how they give place to foolish reasonings in reference to things wholly beyond their range. Let them remember that a false sentimentality may constantly be found in league with an audacious infidelity in calling in question the solemn enactments of divine government. This is a very serious consideration. Evil doers must look out for the sure judgment of a sin-hating God. If a willful murderer presumed to avail himself of God's provision for the ignorant man-slayer, the hand of justice laid hold of him and put him to death, without mercy. Such was the government of God in Israel of old, and such will it be in a day that is rapidly approaching. Just now, God is dealing in long-suffering mercy with the world; this is the day of salvation—the acceptable time. The day of vengeance is at hand. Oh that man, instead of reasoning about the justice of God's dealings with evil-doers, would flee for refuge to that precious Saviour who died on the cross to save us from the flames of an everlasting hell ! *

Before quoting for the reader the closing paragraph of our chapter, we would just call his attention to verse 14, in which we have a very beautiful proof of God's tender care for His people, and His most gracious interest in every thing which directly or indirectly concerned them. "Thou shalt not remove thy neighbor's landmark, which they of old time have set in thine inheritance, which thou shalt inherit in the land that the Lord thy God giveth thee to possess it."

This passage, taken in its plain import and primary application, is full of sweetness, as presenting the loving heart of our God, and showing us how marvelously He entered into all the circumstances of His beloved people. The landmarks were not to be meddled with. Each one's portion was to be left intact, according to the boundary-lines set up by those of old time. Jehovah had given the land to

---

* For other points presented in the cities of refuge we must refer the reader to "Notes on the Book of Numbers," chapter xxxv.

Israel, and not only so, but He had assigned to each tribe and to each family their proper portion, marked off with perfect precision, and indicated by land-marks so plain that there could be no confusion, no clashing of interests, no interference one with an-other, no ground for lawsuit or controversy about property. There stood the ancient landmarks, mark-ing off each one's portion in such a manner as to remove all possible ground of dispute. Each one held as a tenant under the God of Israel, who knew all about his little holding, as we say, and every tenant had the comfort of knowing that the eye of the gracious and almighty Landlord was upon his bit of land, and His hand over it to protect it from every intruder. Thus he could abide in peace under his vine and under his fig-tree, enjoying the portion assigned him by the God of Abraham, Isaac, and Jacob.

Thus much as to the obvious sense of this beau-tiful clause of our chapter; but surely it has a deep spiritual meaning also. Are there not spiritual landmarks for the Church of God, and for each individual member thereof, marking off, with divine accuracy, the boundaries of our heavenly inheritance —those landmarks which they of old time, even the apostles of our Lord and Saviour Jesus Christ, have set up. Assuredly there are, and God has His eye upon them, and He will not permit them to be removed with impunity. Woe be to the man that attempts to touch them; he will have to give account to God for so doing. It is a serious thing for any one to interfere, in any way, with the place, portion, and prospect of the Church of God; and it is to be feared that many are doing it without being aware of it.

We do not attempt to go into the question of what these landmarks are; we have sought to do this in our first volume of "Notes on Deuteronomy," as well as in the other four volumes of the series; but we feel it to be our duty to warn, in the most solemn manner, all whom it may concern against doing that which, in the Church of God, answers to the removal of the landmarks in Israel. If any one had come forward in the land of Israel to suggest some new arrangement in the inheritance of the tribes, to adjust the property of each upon some new principle, to set up some new boundary-lines, what would have been the reply of the faithful Israelite? A very simple one, we may be sure. He would have replied in the language of Deuteronomy xix. 14. He would have said, We want no novelties here; we are perfectly content with those sacred and time-honored landmarks which they of old time have set in our inheritance. We are determined, by the grace of God, to keep to them, and to resist, with firm purpose, any modern innovation.

Such, we believe, would have been the prompt reply of every true member of the congregation of Israel; and surely the Christian ought not to be less prompt or less decided in his answer to all those who, under the plea of progress and development, would remove the landmarks of the Church of God

and, instead of the precious teaching of Christ and
His apostles, offer us the so-called light of science
and the resources of philosophy. Thank God, we
want them not. We have Christ and His Word;
what can be added to these? What do we want of
human progress or development, when we have
"that which was *from the beginning*"? What can
science or philosophy do for those who possess "*all
truth*"? No doubt, we want—yea, long to make
progress in the knowledge of Christ; long for a
fuller, clearer development of the life of Christ in
our daily history; but science and philosophy cannot
help us in these; nay, they could only prove a most
serious hindrance.

Christian reader, let us seek to keep close to Christ,
close to His Word. This is our only security in this
dark and evil day. Apart from Him, we are nothing,
have nothing, can do nothing; in Him, we have all.
He is the portion of our cup and the lot of our
inheritance. May we know what it is not only to be
safe *in* Him, but separated *to* Him, and satisfied *with*
Him, till that bright day when we shall see Him as
He is, and be like Him and with Him forever.

We shall now do little more than quote the few
remaining verses of our chapter. They need no
exposition. They set forth wholesome truth, to
which professing Christians, with all their light and
knowledge, may well give attention.

"One witness shall not rise up against a man for
any iniquity, or for any sin, in any sin that he
sinneth; at the mouth of two witnesses, or at the

mouth of three witnesses, shall the matter be established.'' (Ver. 15.)

This subject has already come before us. It cannot be too strongly insisted upon. We may judge of its importance from the fact that not only does Moses again and again press it upon Israel's attention, but our Lord Jesus Christ Himself, and the Holy Ghost in the apostle Paul, in two of his epistles, insists upon the principle of ''two or three witnesses,'' in every case. One witness, be he ever so trustworthy, is not sufficient to decide a case. If this plain fact were more carefully weighed and duly attended to, it would put an end to a vast amount of strife and contention. We, in our fancied wisdom, might imagine that one thoroughly reliable witness ought to be sufficient to settle any question. Let us remember that God is wiser than we are, and that it is ever our truest wisdom, as well as our greatest moral security, to hold fast by His unerring Word.

''If a false witness rise up against any man, to testify against him that which is wrong; then both the men, between whom the controversy is, shall stand before the Lord, before the priests and the judges which shall be in those days; and *the judges shall make diligent inquisition:* and, behold, if the witness be a false witness, and have testified falsely against his brother; then shall ye do unto him as he had thought to have done unto his brother: so shalt thou put the evil away from among you. And those which remain shall hear and fear, and shall henceforth commit no more any such evil among you.

And thine eye shall not pity; but life shall go for life, eye for eye, tooth for tooth, hand for hand, foot for foot." (Ver. 16–21.)

We may here see how God hates false witness; and further, we have to bear in mind that though we are not under law, but under grace, false witness is not less hateful to God; and surely the more fully we enter into the grace in which we stand, the more intensely we shall abhor false witness, slander, and evil-speaking, in every shape and form. The good Lord preserve us from all such.

CHAPTER XX.

"WHEN thou goest out to battle against thine enemies, and seest horses and chariots, and a people more than thou, be not afraid of them; for the Lord thy God is with thee, which brought thee up out of the land of Egypt. And it shall be, when ye are come nigh unto the battle, that the priest shall approach and speak unto the people, and shall say unto them, Hear, O Israel! ye approach this day unto battle against your enemies; let not your hearts faint; fear not, and do not tremble, neither be ye terrified because of them; for the Lord your God is He that goeth with you to fight for you against your enemies, to save you." (Ver. 1–4.)

How wonderful to think of the Lord as a Man of war! Think of His fighting against people! Some

21

find it very hard to take in the idea—hard to understand how a benevolent Being could act in such a
character. But the difficulty arises mainly from not
distinguishing between the different dispensations.
It was just as consistent with the character of the
God of Abraham, Isaac, and Jacob to fight against
His enemies, as it is with the character of the God
and Father of our Lord Jesus Christ to forgive them.
And inasmuch as it is the revealed character of God
that furnishes the model on which His people are to
be formed—the standard by which they are to act,
it was quite as consistent for Israel to cut their
enemies in pieces as it is for us to love them, pray
for them, and do them good.

If this very simple principle were borne in mind,
it would remove a quantity of misunderstanding,
and save a vast amount of unintelligent discussion.
No doubt it is thoroughly wrong for the Church of
God to go to war. No one can read the New Testament with a mind free from bias and not see this.
We are positively commanded to love our enemies,
to do good to them that hate us, and to pray for
them that despitefully use us. "Put up again thy
sword into his place, for all they that take the sword
shall perish with the sword." And again, in another
gospel, "Then said Jesus unto Peter, 'Put up thy
sword into the sheath: the cup which My Father
hath given Me, shall I not drink it?'" Again, our
Lord says to Pilate, "My kingdom is not of this
world: if My kingdom were of this world, *then
would My servants fight*"—it would be perfectly

consistent for them so to do;—"but *now* is **My** kingdom not from hence"—and therefore it would be wholly out of character, utterly inconsistent, thoroughly wrong, for them to fight.

All this is so plain that we need only say, "How readest thou?" Our blessed Lord did not fight; He meekly and patiently submitted to all manner of abuse and ill-treatment, and in so doing, He left us an example, that we should follow His steps. If we only honestly ask ourselves the question, What would Jesus do? it would close all discussion on this point, as well as upon a thousand other points besides. There is really no use in reasoning—no need of it. If the words and ways of our blessed Lord, and the distinct teaching of His Spirit by His holy apostles, be not sufficient for our guidance, all discussion is utterly vain.

And if we be asked, What does the Holy Ghost teach on this great practical point? hear His precious, clear, and pointed words.—"Dearly beloved, avenge not yourselves; but rather give place unto wrath; for it is written, 'Vengeance is Mine; *I will repay*, saith the Lord.' Therefore, if thine enemy hunger, feed him; if he thirst, give him drink; for in so doing, thou shalt heap coals of fire on his head. Be not overcome of evil, but overcome evil with good." (Rom. xii.)

These are the lovely ethics of the Church of God, the principles of that heavenly kingdom to which all true Christians belong. Would they have suited Israel of old? Certainly not. Only conceive Joshua

acting toward the Canaanites on the principles of
Romans xii !   It would have been as flagrant an
inconsistency as for us to act on the principle of
Deuteronomy xx.   How is this ?   Simply because
in Joshua's day God was executing judgment in
righteousness, whereas now He is dealing in unqualified grace.   This makes all the difference.   The
principle of divine action is the grand moral regulator for God's people in all ages.   If this be seen,
all difficulty is removed, all discussion definitively
closed.

But then, if any feel disposed to ask, What about
the world ? how could it get on upon the principle
of grace ?   Could it act on the doctrine of Romans
xii. 20 ?   Not for a moment.   The idea is simply
absurd.   To attempt to amalgamate the principles
of grace with the law of nations, or to infuse the
spirit of the New Testament into the frame-work of
political economy, would instantly plunge civilized
society into hopeless confusion.   And here is just
where many most excellent and well-meaning people
are astray.   They want to press the nations of the
world into the adoption of a principle which would
be destructive of their national existence.   The time
is not come yet for nations to beat their swords into
plowshares, and their spears into pruning-hooks,
and learn war no more.   That blessed time will
come, thank God, when this groaning earth shall be
filled with the knowledge of the Lord as the waters
cover the sea ; but to seek to get nations *now* to act
upon peace principles is simply to ask them to cease

to be—in a word, it is thoroughly hopeless, unintelligent labor. It cannot be. We are not called upon to regulate the world, but to pass through it as pilgrims and strangers. Jesus did not come to set the world right. He came to seek and to save that which was lost; and as to the world, He testified of it that its deeds were evil. He will, ere long, come to set things right; He will take to Himself His great power and reign. The kingdoms of this world shall most assuredly become the kingdoms of our Lord and of His Christ. He will gather out of His kingdom all things that offend, and them that do iniquity. All this is most blessedly true, but we must wait His time. It can be of no possible use for us, by our ignorant efforts, to seek to bring about a condition of things which all Scripture goes to prove can *only* be introduced by the personal presence and rule of our beloved and adorable Lord and Saviour Jesus Christ.

But we must proceed with our chapter.

Israel were called to fight the Lord's battles. The moment they put their foot upon the land of Canaan it was war to the knife with the doomed inhabitants. "Of the cities of these people which the Lord thy God doth give thee for an inheritance, thou shalt save alive nothing that breatheth." This was distinct and emphatic. The seed of Abraham were not only to possess the land of Canaan, but they were to be God's instruments in executing His just judgment upon the guilty inhabitants, whose sins had risen up to heaven, and become absolutely intolerable.

Does any one feel called upon to apologize for the divine actings toward the seven nations of Canaan? If so, let him be well assured of this, that his labor is perfectly gratuitous, entirely uncalled for. What folly for any poor worm of the earth to think of entering upon such work! and what folly, too, for any one to require an apology or an explanation! It was a high honor put upon Israel to exterminate those guilty nations—an honor of which they proved themselves utterly unworthy, inasmuch as they failed to do as they were commanded. They left alive many of those who ought to have been utterly destroyed; they spared them to be the wretched instruments of their own ultimate ruin, by leading them into the self-same sins which had so loudly called for divine judgment.

But let us look for a moment at the qualifications which were necessary for those who would fight the Lord's battles. We shall find the opening paragraph of our chapter full of most precious instruction for ourselves in the spiritual warfare which we are called to wage.

The reader will observe that the people, on approaching to the battle, were to be addressed, first, by the priest, and secondly, by the officers. This order is very beautiful. The priests came forward to unfold to the people their high *privileges;* the officers came to remind them of their holy *responsibilities.* Such is the divine order here. Privilege comes first, and then responsibility. "The priest shall approach and speak unto the people, and shall

say unto them, Hear, O Israel! ye approach this
day unto battle against your enemies; let not your
hearts faint, fear not, and do not tremble, neither
be ye terrified because of them; for the Lord your
God is He that goeth with you, to fight for you
against your enemies, to save you.''

What blessed words are these! how full of comfort and encouragement! how eminently calculated
to banish all fear and depression, and to infuse courage and confidence into the most sinking, fainting
heart! The priest was the very expression of the
grace of God,—his ministry a stream of most
precious consolation flowing from the loving heart
of the God of Israel to each individual warrior.
His loving words were designed and fitted to gird
up the loins of the mind, and nerve the feeblest arm
for fight. He assures them of the divine presence
with them. There is no question, no condition, no
''if,'' no ''but.'' It is an unqualified statement.
Jehovah Elohim was with them. This surely was
enough. It mattered not, in the smallest degree,
how many, how powerful, or how formidable were
their enemies, they would all prove to be as chaff
before the whirlwind in the presence of the Lord
of Hosts, the God of the armies of Israel.

But then the *officer* had to be heard as well as the
priest.—''And the officers shall speak unto the people, saying, What man is there that hath built a new
house and hath not dedicated it? let him go and
return to his house, lest he die in the battle, and
another man dedicate it. And what man is he that

hath planted a vineyard and hath not yet eaten of it? let him also go and return unto his house, lest he die in the battle, and another man eat of it. And what man is there that hath betrothed a wife and hath not taken her? let him go and return unto his house, lest he die in the battle, and another man take her. And the officers shall speak further unto the people, and they shall say, What man is there that is fearful and fainthearted? let him go and return unto his house, lest his brethren's heart faint as well as his heart. And it shall be that when the officers have made an end of speaking unto the people, that they shall make captains of the armies to lead the people." (Ver. 5-9.)

Thus we learn that there were two things absolutely essential to all who would fight the Lord's battles, namely, a heart thoroughly disentangled from the things of nature and of earth, and a bold unclouded confidence in God. "No man that warreth entangleth himself with the affairs of this life, that he may please him who hath chosen him to be a soldier." There is a very material difference between being *engaged* in the affairs of this life and being *entangled* by them. A man might have had a house, a vineyard, and a wife and yet have been fit for the battle. These things were not, in themselves, a hindrance; but it was having them under such conditions as rendered them an entanglement that unfitted a man for the conflict.

It is well to bear this in mind. We, as Christians, are called to carry on a constant spiritual warfare.

We have to fight for every inch of heavenly ground. What the Canaanites were to Israel, the wicked spirits in the heavenlies are to us. We are not called to fight for eternal life; we have gotten that as God's free gift before we begin. We are not called to fight for salvation; we are saved before we enter upon the conflict. It is most needful to know what it is that we have to fight for, and whom we are to fight with. The object for which we fight is, to make good, maintain, and carry out practically our heavenly position and character in the midst of the scenes and circumstances of ordinary human life from day to day. And then as to our spiritual foes, they are wicked spirits, who, during this present time, are permitted to occupy the heavenlies. "We wrestle not against flesh and blood, [as Israel had to do in Canaan,] but against principalities, against powers, against the world-rulers [κοσμοκράτορας] of this darkness, against wicked spirits in the heavenlies."

Now, the question is, what do we want in carrying on such a conflict as this? Must we abandon our lawful earthly callings? must we detach ourselves from those relationships founded on nature and sanctioned of God? Is it needful to become an ascetic, a mystic, or a monk in order to carry on the spiritual warfare to which we are called? By no means; indeed, for a Christian to do any one of these things would, in itself, be a proof that he had completely mistaken his calling, or that he had, at the very outset, fallen in the battle. We are imperatively called upon to work with our hands the thing which is good, that we may have to give to him that needeth. And not only so, but we have the most ample guidance, in the pages of the New Testament, as to how we are to carry ourselves in the varied natural relationships which God Himself has established, and to which He has affixed the seal of His approval. Hence it is perfectly plain that earthly callings and natural relationships are, in themselves, no hindrance to our waging a successful spiritual warfare.

What, then, is needed by the Christian warrior? A heart thoroughly *disentangled* from things earthly and natural, and an unclouded confidence in God. But how are these things to be maintained? Hear the divine reply: "Wherefore take unto you the whole armor of God, that ye may be able to withstand in *the evil day*,"—that is, the whole time from the cross to the coming of Christ,—"and having done all, to stand. Stand, therefore; having your loins girt about with *truth*, and having on the breastplate of *righteousness*, and your feet shod with the preparation of the gospel of *peace;* above all, taking the shield of *faith*, wherewith ye shall be able to quench all the fiery darts of the wicked. And take the helmet of salvation, and the sword of the Spirit, which is the Word of God. Praying always with all prayer and supplication in the Spirit, and watching thereunto with all perseverance and supplication for all saints." (Eph. vi.)

Reader, mark the qualification of a Christian warrior as here set forth by the Holy Ghost. It is not the question of a house, a vineyard, or a wife, but of having the inward man governed by "truth," the outward conduct characterized by real practical "righteousness," the moral habits and ways marked by the sweet "peace" of the gospel, the whole man covered by the impenetrable shield of "faith," the seat of the understanding guarded by the full assurance of "salvation," and the heart continually sustained and strengthened by persevering prayer and supplication, and led forth in earnest intercession for all saints, and specially for the Lord's beloved workmen and their blessed work.   This is the way in which the spiritual Israel of God are to be furnished for the warfare which they are called to wage with wicked spirits in the heavenlies.   May the Lord, in His infinite goodness, make all these things very real in our souls' experience, and in our practical career from day to day.

The close of our chapter contains the principles which were to govern Israel in their warfare.   They were most carefully to discriminate between the cities which were very far off from them and those that pertained to the seven judged nations.   To the former, they were, in the first place, to make overtures of peace ; with the latter, on the contrary, they were to make no terms whatever.   "When thou comest nigh unto a city *to fight against it*, then *proclaim peace* unto it"—a marvelous method of fighting!—"And it shall be, if it make thee answer of peace, and open unto thee, then it shall be that all the people that is found therein shall be tributaries unto thee, and they shall serve thee. And if it will make no peace with thee, but will make war against thee, then thou shalt besiege it; and when the Lord thy God hath delivered it into thine hands, thou shalt smite every male thereof"—as expressing the positive energy of evil—"with the edge of the sword. But the women, and the little ones, and the cattle, and all that is in the city, even all the spoil thereof"—all that was capable of being turned to account in the service of God and of His people —"thou shalt take unto thyself; and thou shalt eat the spoil of thine enemies, which the Lord thy God hath given thee. Thus shalt thou do unto all the cities which are very far off from thee, which are not of the cities of these nations."

Indiscriminate slaughter and wholesale destruction formed no part of Israel's business. If any cities were disposed to accept the proffered terms of peace, they were to have the privilege of becoming tributaries to the people of God; and in reference to those cities which would make no peace, all within their walls which could be made use of was to be reserved.

There are things in nature and things of earth which are capable of being used for God—they are sanctified by the Word of God and prayer. We are told to make to ourselves friends of the mammon of unrighteousness, that when we fail, they may receive us into everlasting habitations; which simply means that if this world's riches come into the Christian's hands, he should diligently and faithfully use them in the service of Christ; he should freely distribute them to the poor, and to all the Lord's needy workmen; in short, he should make them available, in every right and prudent way, for the furtherance of the Lord's work in every department. In this way, the very riches which else might crumble into dust in their hands, or prove to be as rust on their souls, shall produce precious fruit that shall serve to minister an abundant entrance into the everlasting kingdom of our Lord and Saviour Jesus Christ.

Many seem to find considerable difficulty in Luke xvi. 9, but its teaching is as clear and forcible as it is practically important. We find very similar instruction in 1 Timothy vi.—"Charge them that are rich in this world, that they be not high-minded, nor trust in uncertain riches, but in the living God, who giveth us richly all things to enjoy; that they do good, that they be rich in good works, *ready to distribute*, willing to communicate, laying up in store for themselves a good foundation against the time to come, that they may lay hold on eternal life."* There is not a fraction which we spend directly and simply for Christ which will not be before us by and by. The thought of this, though it should not by any means be a motive-spring, may well encourage

---

* It may interest the reader to know that the four leading authorities agree in reading $\acute{o}\nu\tau\omega\varsigma$ instead of $\alpha\iota\omega\nu\acute{\iota}o\upsilon$ in 1 Timothy vi. 19. Thus the passage would be, "That they may lay hold on life in earnest," or in reality. The only real life is, to live for Christ—to live in the light of eternity—to use all we possess for the promotion of God's glory and with an eye to the everlasting mansions. This, and only this, is life in earnest.

us to devote all we have and all we are to the service
of our blessed Lord and Saviour Jesus Christ.

Such is the plain teaching of Luke xvi. and 1
Timothy vi; let us see that we understand it.   The
expression, "That they may receive you into everlasting habitations" simply means that what is spent
for Christ will be rewarded in the day that is coming. Even a cup of cold water given in His precious
name shall have its sure reward in His everlasting
kingdom.   Oh, to spend and be spent for Him!

But we must close this section by quoting the few
last lines of our chapter, in which we have a very
beautiful illustration of the way in which our God
looks after the smallest matters, and His gracious
care that nothing should be lost or injured. "When
thou shalt besiege a city a long time, in making war
against it to take it, thou shalt not destroy the trees
thereof, by forcing an ax against them; for thou
mayest eat of them, and thou shalt not cut them
down (for the tree of the field is man's life) to employ them in the siege; only the trees which thou
knowest that they be not trees for meat, thou shalt
destroy and cut them down; and thou shalt build
bulwarks against the city that maketh war with thee,
until it be subdued." (Ver. 19, 20.)

"Let nothing be lost," is the Master's own word
to us—a word which should ever be kept in remembrance.   "Every creature of God is good, and nothing to be refused."   We should carefully guard
against all reckless waste of aught that can be made
available for human use.   Those who occupy the

place of domestic servants should give their special
attention to this matter. It is painful, at times, to
witness the sinful waste of human food. Many a
thing is flung out as offal which might supply a
welcome meal for a needy family. If a Christian
servant should read these lines, we would earnestly
entreat him or her to weigh this subject in the divine
presence, and never to practice or sanction the waste
of the smallest atom that is capable of being turned
to account for human use. We may depend upon
it that to waste any creature of God is displeasing
in His sight. Let us remember that His eye is upon
us; and may it be our earnest desire to be agreeable to Him in all our ways.

CHAPTER XXI.

"IF one be found slain in the land which the Lord
thy God giveth thee to possess it, lying in the
field, and it be not known who hath slain him; then
thy *elders* and thy *judges*"—the guardians of the
claims of truth and righteousness—"shall come
forth, and they shall measure unto the cities that are
round about him that is slain; and it shall be, that
the city which is next unto the slain man, even the
elders of that city shall take a heifer, which hath
not been wrought with, and hath not drawn in the
yoke; and the elders of that city shall bring down
the heifer unto *a rough valley* which is neither eared

nor sown, and shall strike off the heifer's neck there
in the valley. And *the priests the sons of Levi*"—
exponents of grace and mercy—"shall come near;
for them the Lord thy God hath chosen *to minister*
unto Him, and *to bless* in the name of the Lord, and
by their word shall every controversy and every
stroke be tried;"—blessed, comforting fact!—
"and all the elders of that city that are next unto
the slain man shall wash their hands over the heifer
that is beheaded in the valley; and they shall answer and say, Our hands have not shed this blood,
neither have our eyes seen it. Be merciful, O Lord,
unto Thy people Israel, whom Thou hast redeemed,
and lay not innocent blood to Thy people of Israel's
charge. And the blood shall be forgiven them. So
shalt thou put away the guilt of innocent blood from
among you, when thou shalt do that which is right
in the sight of the Lord." (Ver. 1–9.)

A very suggestive and interesting passage of holy
Scripture now lies open before us, and claims our
attention. A sin is committed—a man is found
slain in the land, but no one knows aught about
it; no one can tell whether it is murder or man-
slaughter, or who committed the deed. It lies entirely beyond the range of human knowledge; and
yet there it is—an undeniable fact. Sin has been
committed, and it lies as a stain on the Lord's land,
and man is wholly incompetent to deal with it.

What, then, is to be done? The glory of God
and the purity of His land must be maintained. He
knows all about it, and He alone can deal with it;

and truly His mode of dealing with it is full of most precious teaching.

First of all, the elders and judges appear on the scene. The claims of truth and righteousness must be duly attended to; justice and judgment must be perfectly maintained. This is a great cardinal truth, running all through the Word of God. *Sin* must be judged ere *sins* can be forgiven or the sinner justified. Ere mercy's heavenly voice can be heard, justice must be perfectly satisfied, the throne of God vindicated, and His name glorified. Grace must reign through righteousness. Blessed be God that it is so! What a glorious truth for all who have taken their true place as sinners! God has been glorified as to the question of sin, and therefore He can, in perfect righteousness, pardon and justify the sinner.

But we must confine ourselves simply to the interpretation of the passage before us, and in so doing, we shall find in it a very wonderful onlook into Israel's future. True, the great foundation-truth of atonement is presented, but it is with special reference to Israel. The death of Christ is here seen in its two grand aspects, namely, as the expression of man's guilt, and the display of God's grace. The former, we have in the man found slain in the field; the latter, in the heifer slain in the rough valley. The elders and the judges find out the city nearest to the slain man, and nothing can avail for that city save the blood of a spotless victim—the blood of the One who was slain at the guilty city of Jerusalem.

22

The reader will note with much interest that the moment the claims of justice were met by the death of the victim, a new element is introduced into the scene. "The priests the sons of Levi shall come near." This is grace acting on the blessed ground of righteousness. The priests are the channels of grace, as the judges are the guardians of righteousness. How perfect, how beautiful, is Scripture, in every page, every paragraph, every sentence! It was not until the blood was shed that the ministers of grace could present themselves. The heifer be-headed in the valley changed the aspect of things completely. "The priests the sons of Levi shall come near; for them the Lord thy God hath chosen to minister unto Him, and to bless in the name of the Lord; and *by their word*"—blessed fact for Israel! blessed fact for every true believer!— "shall *every controversy* and *every stroke be tried*." All is to be settled on the glorious and eternal prin-ciple of grace reigning through righteousness.

Thus it is that God will deal with Israel by and by. We must not attempt to interfere with the primary application of all those striking institutions which come under our notice in this profound and marvel-ous book of Deuteronomy. No doubt there are lessons for us—precious lessons, but we may rest perfectly assured that the true way in which to un-derstand and appreciate those lessons is to see their true and proper bearing. For instance, how pre-cious, how full of consolation, the fact that it is by the word of the minister of grace that every con-

troversy and every stroke is to be tried for repentant
Israel by and by, and for every repentant soul now!
Do we lose aught of the deep blessedness of this by
seeing and owning the proper application of the
scripture? Assuredly not. So far from this, the
true secret of profiting by any special passage of the
Word of God is to understand its true scope and
bearing.

"And all the elders of that city that are next
unto the slain man shall wash their hands over the
heifer that is beheaded in the valley."* "I will
wash my hands in innocency, and so will I compass
Thine altar." The true place to wash the hands is
where the blood of atonement has forever expiated
our guilt. "And they shall answer and say, Our
hands have not shed this blood, neither have our
eyes seen it. Be merciful, O Lord, unto Thy people
Israel, whom Thou hast redeemed, and lay not
innocent blood unto Thy people of Israel's charge.
And the blood shall be forgiven them."

"Father, forgive them, for they know not what

---

*How full of suggestive power is the figure of "the *rough
valley*"! How aptly it sets forth what this world at large, and
the land of Israel in particular, was to our blessed Lord and Saviour! Truly it was a rough place to Him, a place of humiliation,
a dry and thirsty land, a place that had never been eared or sown.
But, all homage to His Name! by His death in this rough valley, He
has procured for this earth and for the land of Israel a rich harvest
of blessing, which shall be reaped throughout the millennial age,
to the full praise of redeeming love. And even now, He, from the
throne of heaven's majesty, and we, in spirit with Him, can look
back to that rough valley as the place where the blessed work was
done which forms the imperishable foundation of God's glory, the
Church's blessing, Israel's full restoration, the joy of countless
nations, and the glorious deliverance of this groaning creation.

they do." "Unto you first, God having raised up His Son Jesus, sent Him to bless you, by turning away every one of you from his iniquities." Thus all Israel shall be saved and blessed by and by, according to the eternal counsels of God, and in pursuance of His promise and oath to Abraham, ratified and eternally established by the precious blood of Christ, to whom be all homage and praise, world without end !

Verses 10–17 bear in a very special way upon Israel's relationship to Jehovah. We shall not dwell upon it here. The reader will find numerous references to this subject throughout the pages of the prophets, in which the Holy Ghost makes the most touching appeals to the conscience of the nation—appeals grounded on the marvelous fact of the relationship into which He had brought them to Himself, but in which they had so signally and grievously failed. Israel has proved an unfaithful wife, and, in consequence thereof, has been set aside; but the time will come when this long-rejected but never-forgotten people shall not only be reinstated, but brought into a condition of blessedness, privilege, and glory beyond any thing ever known in the past.

This must never, for a moment, be lost sight of or interfered with. It runs like a brilliant golden line through the prophetic scriptures, from Isaiah to Malachi, and the lovely theme is resumed and carried on in the New Testament. Take the following glowing passage, which is only one of a hundred :

"For Zion's sake will I not hold my peace, and for Jerusalem's sake I will not rest, until the righteousness thereof go forth as brightness, and the salvation thereof as a lamp that burneth. And the Gentiles shall see thy righteousness, and all kings thy glory; and thou shalt be called by a new name, which the mouth of the Lord shall name. Thou shalt also be a crown of glory in the hand of the Lord, and a royal diadem in the hand of thy God. Thou shalt no more be termed Forsaken, neither shall thy land any more be termed Desolate; but thou shalt be called Hephzi-bah [My delight is in her], and thy land Beulah [married]; for the Lord delighteth in thee, and thy land shall be married. For as a young man marrieth a virgin, so shall thy sons marry thee; and as the bridegroom rejoiceth over the bride, so shall thy God rejoice over thee. I have set watchmen upon thy walls, O Jerusalem, which shall never hold their peace day nor night: ye that make mention of the Lord, keep not silence, and give Him no rest, till He establish, and till He make Jerusalem a praise in the earth. The Lord hath sworn by His right hand, and by the arm of His strength"—let men beware how they meddle with this !—"Surely I will no more give thy corn to be meat for thine enemies; and the sons of the stranger shall not drink thy wine, for the which thou hast labored; but they that have gathered it shall eat it and praise the Lord, and they that have brought it together shall drink it in the courts of My holiness. . . . . Behold, the Lord hath pro-

claimed unto the end of the world, 'Say ye to the
daughter of Zion, Behold, thy salvation cometh; be-
hold, His reward is with Him, and His work before
Him.   And they shall call them, The holy people,
The redeemed of the Lord; and thou shalt be called,
Sought out, A city not forsaken.' '' (Is. lxii.)

To attempt to alienate this sublime and glorious
passage from its proper object, and apply it to the
Christian Church, either on earth or in heaven, is to
do positive violence to the Word of God, and introduce a system of interpretation utterly destructive
of the integrity of holy Scripture.   The passage
which we have just transcribed, with intense spiritual
delight, applies only to the literal Zion, the literal
Jerusalem, the literal land of Israel.   Let the reader
see that he thoroughly seizes and faithfully holds
fast this fact.

As to the Church, her position on earth is that of
an espoused virgin, not of a married wife.   Her
marriage will take place in heaven.   (Rev. xix. 7, 8.)
To apply to her such passages as the above is to
falsify her position entirely, and deny the plainest
statements of Scripture as to her calling, her portion, and her hope, which are purely heavenly.

Verses 18–21 of our chapter record the case of "a
stubborn and rebellious son."   Here again we have
Israel viewed from another stand-point.   It is the
apostate generation, for which there is no forgiveness.   "If a man have a stubborn and rebellious
son, which will not obey the voice of his father, or
the voice of his mother, and that when they have

chastened him will not hearken unto them; then shall his father and his mother lay hold on him and bring him out unto the elders of his city, and unto the gate of his place; and they shall say unto the elders of his city, This our son is stubborn and rebellious; he will not obey our voice; he is a glutton and a drunkard. And all the men of his city shall stone him with stones, that he die; so shalt thou put evil away from among you; and all Israel shall hear and fear."

The reader may with much interest contrast the solemn action of law and government in the case of the rebellious son, with the lovely and familiar parable of the prodigal son in Luke xv. Our space does not admit of our dwelling upon it here, much as we should delight to do so. It is marvelous to think that it is the same God who speaks and acts in Deuteronomy xxi. and in Luke xv; but oh, how different the action! how different the style! Under the law, the father is called upon to lay hold of his son and bring him forth to be stoned; under grace, the father runs to meet the returning son, falls on his neck and kisses him; clothes him in the best robe, puts a ring on his hand, and shoes on his feet, has the fatted calf killed for him, seats him at the table with himself, and makes the house ring with the joy that fills his own heart at getting back the poor wandering spendthrift.

Striking contrast! In Deuteronomy xxi, we see *the hand of God*, in righteous government, executing judgment upon the rebellious; in Luke xv, we see *the heart of God* pouring itself out, in soul-subduing tenderness, upon the poor repentant one, giving him the sweet assurance that it is His own deep joy to get back His lost one. The persistent rebel meets the stone of judgment; the returning penitent meets the kiss of love.

But we must close this section by calling the reader's attention to the last verse of our chapter. It is referred to in a very remarkable way by the inspired apostle in the third chapter of Galatians. "Christ hath redeemed us from the curse of the law, being made a curse for us; for it is written, 'Cursed is every one that hangeth on a tree.'"

This reference is full of interest and value, not only because it presents to us the precious grace of our Lord and Saviour Jesus Christ, in making Himself a curse for us, in order that the blessing of Abraham might come on us poor sinners of the Gentiles, but also because it furnishes a very striking illustration of the way in which the Holy Spirit puts His seal upon the writings of Moses in general, and upon Deuteronomy xxi. in particular. All Scripture hangs together so perfectly that if one part be touched, you mar the integrity of the whole. The same Spirit breathes in the writings of Moses, in the pages of the prophets, in the four evangelists, in the Acts, in the apostolic epistles, general and particular, and in that most profound and precious section which closes the divine volume. We deem it our sacred duty—as it is most assuredly our high privilege—to press this weighty fact upon all with whom we come in contact; and we would very earnestly entreat the reader to give it his earnest attention, to hold it fast, and bear a steady testimony to it, in this day of carnal laxity, cold indifference, and positive hostility.

CHAPTERS XXII.—XXV.

THE portion of our book on which we now enter, though not calling for elaborate exposition, yet teaches us two very important practical lessons. In the first place, many of the institutions and ordinances here set forth prove and illustrate, in a most striking way, the terrible depravity of the human heart. They show us, with unmistakable distinctness, what man is capable of doing if left to himself. We must ever remember, as we read some of the paragraphs of this section of Deuteronomy, that God the Holy Ghost has indited them. We, in our fancied wisdom, may feel disposed to ask why such passages were ever penned. Can it be possible that they are actually inspired by the Holy Ghost? and of what possible value can they be to us? If they were written for our learning, then what are we to learn from them?

Our reply to all these questions is at once simple and direct; and it is this: The very passages which we might least expect to find on the page of inspiration teach us, in their own peculiar way, the moral material of which we are made, and the moral depths into which we are capable of plunging. And is not this of great moment? Is it not well to have a faithful mirror held up before our eyes, in which we may see every moral trait, feature, and lineament perfectly reflected? Unquestionably. We hear a great deal about the dignity of human nature, and very many find it exceedingly hard to admit that they are really capable of committing some of the sins prohibited in the section before us, and in other portions of the divine volume; but we may rest assured that when God commands us not to commit this or that particular sin, we are verily capable of committing it. This is beyond all question. Divine wisdom would never erect a dam if there was not a current to be resisted. There would be no necessity to tell an angel not to steal; but man has theft in his nature, and hence the command applies to him. And just so in reference to every other prohibited thing; the prohibition proves the tendency—proves it beyond all question. We must either admit this or imply the positive blasphemy that God has spoken in vain.

But then, it may be said, and is said by many, that while some very terrible samples of fallen humanity are capable of committing some of the abominable sins prohibited in Scripture, yet all are not so. This is a most thorough mistake. Hear what the Holy Ghost says in the seventeenth chapter of the prophet Jeremiah. "*The heart* is deceitful above all things, and desperately wicked." Whose heart is he speaking of? Is it the heart of some atrocious criminal, or of some untutored savage? Nay; it is the human heart—the heart of the writer and of the reader of these lines.

Hear also what our Lord Jesus Christ says on this subject.—"Out of *the heart* proceed evil thoughts, murders, adulteries, fornications, thefts, false witness, blasphemies." Out of what heart? Is it the heart of some hideously depraved and abominable wretch, wholly unfit to appear in decent society? Nay; it is out of the human heart—the heart of the writer and of the reader of these lines.

Let us never forget this; it is a wholesome truth for every one of us. We all need to bear in mind that if God were to withdraw His sustaining grace for one moment, there is no depth of iniquity into which we are not capable of plunging; indeed, we may add—and we do it with deep thankfulness— it is His own gracious hand that preserves us, each moment, from becoming a complete wreck in every way,—physically, mentally, morally, spiritually, and in our circumstances. May we keep this ever in the remembrance of the thoughts of our hearts, so that we may walk humbly and watchfully, and lean upon that arm which alone can sustain and preserve us.

But we have said there is another valuable lesson furnished by this section of our book which now lies open before us. It teaches us, in a manner peculiar to itself, the marvelous way in which God provided for every thing connected with His people

Nothing escaped His gracious notice; nothing was too trivial for His tender care. No mother could be more careful of the habits and manners of her little child than the almighty Creator and moral Governor of the universe was of the most minute details connected with the daily history of His people. By day and by night, waking and sleeping, at home and abroad, He looked after them. Their clothing, their food, their manners and ways toward one another, how they were to build their houses, how they were to plow and sow their ground, how they were to carry themselves in the deepest privacy of their personal life,—all was attended to and provided for in a manner that fills us with wonder, love, and praise. We may here see, in a most striking way, that there is nothing too small for our God to take notice of when His people are concerned. He takes a loving, tender, fatherly interest in their most minute concerns. We are amazed to find the Most High God, the Creator of the ends of the earth, the Sustainer of the vast universe, condescending to legislate about the matter of a bird's nest; and yet why should we be amazed when we know that it is just the same to Him to provide for a sparrow as to feed a thousand millions of people daily?

But there was one grand fact which was ever to be kept prominently before each member of the congregation of Israel, namely, the divine presence in their midst. This fact was to govern their most private habits, and give character to all their ways.

"The Lord thy God walketh in the midst of thy camp, to deliver thee, and to give up thine enemies before thee; *therefore shall thy camp be holy;* that He see no unclean thing in thee, and turn away from thee." (Chap. xxiii. 14.)

What a precious privilege to have Jehovah walking in their midst! what a motive for purity of conduct, and refined delicacy in their personal and domestic habits! If He was in their midst to secure victory over their enemies, He was also there to demand holiness of life. They were never for one moment to forget the august Person who walked up and down in their midst. Would the thought of this prove irksome to any? Only to such as did not love holiness, purity, and moral order. Every true Israelite would delight in the thought of having One dwelling in their midst who could not endure aught that was unholy, unseemly, or impure.

The Christian reader will be at no loss to seize the moral force and application of this holy principle. It is our privilege to have God the Spirit dwelling in us, individually and collectively. Thus we read, in 1 Corinthians vi. 19, "What! know ye not that *your body* is the temple of the Holy Ghost, which is in you, which ye have of God, and ye are not your own?" This is individual. Each believer is a temple of the Holy Ghost, and this most glorious and precious truth is the ground of the exhortation given in Ephesians iv. 30—"*Grieve* not the holy Spirit of God, whereby ye are sealed unto the day of redemption."

How very important to keep this ever in the remembrance of the thoughts of our hearts! what a mighty moral motive for the diligent cultivation of purity of heart and holiness of life! When tempted to indulge in any wrong current of thought or feeling, any unworthy manner of speech, any unseemly line of conduct, what a powerful corrective would be found in the realization of the blessed fact that the Holy Spirit dwells in our body as in His temple! If only we could keep this ever before us, it would preserve us from many a wandering thought, many an unguarded and foolish utterance, many an unbecoming act.

But not only does the Holy Spirit dwell in each individual believer, He also dwells in the Church collectively. "Know ye not that *ye are the temple of God*, and that the Spirit of God dwelleth *in you?*" (1 Cor. iii. 16.) It is upon this fact that the apostle grounds his exhortation in 1 Thessalonians v. 19— "*Quench* not the Spirit." How divinely perfect is Scripture? how blessedly it hangs together! The Holy Ghost dwells in us individually, hence we are not to *grieve* Him; He dwells in the assembly, hence we are not to *quench* Him, but give Him His right place, and allow full scope for His blessed operations. May these great practical truths find a deep place in our hearts, and exert a more powerful influence over our ways, both in private life and in the public assembly.

We shall now proceed to quote a few passages from the section of our book which now lies open before us strikingly illustrative of the wisdom, goodness, tenderness, holiness, and righteousness which marked all the dealings of God with His people of old. Take, for example, the very opening paragraph. "Thou shalt not see thy brother's ox or his sheep go astray, and *hide thyself from them;* thou shalt in any case bring them again unto thy brother. And if thy brother be not nigh unto thee, or if thou know him not, then thou shalt bring it unto thine own house, and it shall be with thee until thy brother seek after it, and thou shalt restore it to him again. In like manner shalt thou do with his ass; and so shalt thou do with his raiment; and with all lost thing of thy brother's which he hath lost, and thou hast found, shalt thou do likewise; *thou mayest not hide thyself.* Thou shalt not see thy brother's ass or his ox fall down by the way, *and hide thyself from them;* thou shalt surely help him to lift them up again." (Chap. xxii. 1–4.)

Here the two lessons of which we have spoken are very distinctly presented. What a deeply humbling picture of the human heart have we in that one sentence, "Thou mayest not hide thyself"! We are capable of the base and detestable selfishness of hiding ourselves from our brother's claims upon our sympathy and succor—of shirking the holy duty of looking after his interests—of pretending not to see his real need of our aid. Such is man!—such is the writer!

But oh, how blessedly the character of our God shines out in this passage! The brother's ox, or his sheep, or his ass, was not (to use a modern phrase) to be thrust into pound for trespass; it was to be brought home, cared for, and restored, safe and sound, to the owner, without charge for damage. And so with the raiment. How lovely is all this! how it breathes upon us the very air of the divine presence, the fragrant atmosphere of divine goodness, tenderness, and thoughtful love! What a high and holy privilege for any people to have their conduct governed and their character formed by such exquisite statutes and judgments!

Again, take the following passage, so beautifully illustrative of divine thoughtfulness: "When thou buildest a new house, then thou shalt make a battlement for thy roof, that thou bring not blood upon thine house, if any man fall from thence." The Lord would have His people thoughtful and considerate of others; and hence, in building their houses, they were not merely to think of themselves and their convenience, but also of others and their safety.

Cannot Christians learn something from this? How prone we are to think only of ourselves, our own interests, our own comfort and convenience! How rarely it happens that in the building or furnishing of our houses we bestow a thought upon other people! We build and furnish for ourselves. Alas! self is too much our object and motive-spring in all our undertakings; nor can it be otherwise unless the heart be kept under the governing power of those motives and objects which belong to Christianity. We must live in the pure and heavenly atmosphere of the new creation in order to get above and beyond the base selfishness which characterizes fallen humanity. Every unconverted man, woman, and child on the face of the earth is governed simply by self in some shape or another. Self is the centre, the object, the motive-spring, of every action.

True, some are more amiable, more affectionate, more benevolent, more unselfish, more disinterested, more agreeable, than others; but it is utterly impossible that "the natural man" can be governed by spiritual motives, or an earthly man be animated by heavenly objects. Alas! we have to confess, with shame and sorrow, that we who profess to be heavenly and spiritual are so prone to live for ourselves, to seek our own things, to maintain our own interests, to consult our own ease and convenience. We are all alive and on the alert when *self*, in any shape or form, is concerned.

All this is most sad and deeply humbling. It really ought not to be, and it would not be if we were looking more simply and earnestly to Christ as our great Exemplar and model in all things. Earnest and constant occupation of heart with Christ is the true secret of all practical Christianity. It is not rules and regulations that will ever make us Christ-like in our spirit, manner, and ways. We must drink into His spirit, walk in His footsteps, dwell more profoundly upon His moral glories, and then we shall, of blessed necessity, be conformed to His image. "We all with open face beholding as in a glass [or mirroring—κατοπτριζόμενοι] the glory, are

23

changed into the same image, from glory to glory even as by the Spirit of the Lord." (2 Cor. iii.)

We must now ask the reader to turn for a moment to the following very important practical instructions —full of suggestive power for all Christian workers: "Thou shalt not sow thy vineyard with *divers seeds*, lest the fruit of thy seed which thou hast sown and the fruit of thy vineyard be defiled." (Chap. xxii. 9.)

What a weighty principle is here! Do we really understand it? do we see its true spiritual application? It is to be feared there is a terrible amount of "mingled seed" used in the so-called spiritual husbandry of the present day. How much of "philosophy and vain deceit," how much of "science falsely so called," how much of "the rudiments of the world," do we find mixed up in the teaching and preaching throughout the length and breadth of the professing church! How little of the pure, unadulterated seed of the Word of God, the "incorruptible seed" of the precious gospel of Christ, is scattered broad-cast over the field of christendom in this our day! How few, comparatively, are content to confine themselves within the covers of the Bible for the material of their ministry! Those who are, by the grace of God, faithful enough to do so, are looked upon as men of one idea, men of the old school, narrow, and behind the times.

Well, we can only say, with a full and glowing heart, God bless the men of one idea—men of the precious old school of apostolic preaching! Most heartily do we congratulate them on their blessed narrowness, and their being behind these dark and infidel times. We are fully aware of what we expose ourselves to in thus writing, but this does not move us. We are persuaded that every true servant of Christ must be a man of one idea, and that idea is Christ; he must belong to the very oldest school—the school of Christ; he must be as narrow as the truth of God; and he must, with stern decision, refuse to move one hair's breadth in the direction of this infidel age. We cannot shake off the conviction that the effort on the part of the preachers and teachers of christendom to keep abreast of the literature of the day must, to a very large extent, account for the rapid advance of rationalism and infidelity. They have got away from the holy Scriptures, and sought to adorn their ministry by the resources of philosophy, science, and literature. They have catered more for the intellect than for the heart and conscience. The pure and precious doctrines of holy Scripture, the sincere milk of the Word, the gospel of the grace of God and of the glory of Christ, were found insufficient to attract and keep together large congregations. As Israel of old despised the manna, got tired of it, and pronounced it light food, so the professing church grew weary of the pure doctrines of that glorious Christianity unfolded in the pages of the New Testament, and sighed for something to gratify the intellect and feed the imagination. The doctrines of the cross, in which the blessed apostle gloried, have lost their charm for the professing

church, and any who would be faithful enough to
adhere and confine themselves in their ministry
to those doctrines might abandon all thought of
popularity.

But let all the true and faithful ministers of
Christ, all true workers in His vineyard, apply
their hearts to the spiritual principle set forth in
Deuteronomy xxii. 9; let them, with unflinching
decision, refuse to make use of "divers seeds" in
their spiritual husbandry; let them confine themselves, in their ministry, to "the form of sound
words," and ever seek "rightly to divide the word
of truth," that so they may not be ashamed of their
work, but receive a full reward in that day when
every man's work shall be tried of what sort it is.
We may depend upon it, the Word of God—the
pure seed—is the only proper material for the spiritual workman to use. We do not despise learning;
far from it; we consider it most valuable in its right
place. The *facts* of science, too, and the resources
of sound philosophy, may all be turned to profitable
account in unfolding and illustrating the truth of
holy Scripture. We find the blessed Master Himself and His inspired apostles making use of the
facts of history and of nature in their public teaching; and who, in his sober senses, would think of
calling in question the value and importance of a
competent knowledge of the original languages of
Hebrew and Greek in the private study and public
exposition of the Word of God?

But admitting all this, as we most fully do, it

leaves wholly untouched the great practical principle
before us—a principle to which all the Lord's people
and His servants are bound to adhere, namely, that
the Holy Ghost is the only power, and holy Scripture the only material, for all true ministry in the
gospel and the Church of God. If this were more
fully understood and faithfully acted upon, we
should witness a very different condition of things
throughout the length and breadth of the vineyard
of Christ.

Here, however, we must close this section. We
have elsewhere sought to handle the subject of "The
Unequal Yoke," and shall not therefore dwell upon
it here.* The Israelite was not to plow with an
ox and an ass together; neither was he to wear a
garment of divers sorts, as of woolen and linen.
The spiritual application of both these things is as
simple as it is important. The Christian is not to
link himself with an unbeliever for any object whatsoever, be it domestic, religious, philanthrophic, or
commercial; neither must he allow himself to be
governed by mixed principles. His character must
be formed and his conduct ruled by the pure and
lofty principles of the Word of God. Thus may it be
with all who profess and call themselves Christians.

*See a pamphlet entitled "The Unequal Yoke," post-paid, 10 cts.

CHAPTER XXVI

"AND it shall be, *when thou art come* in unto the land which the Lord thy God giveth thee for an inheritance, and *possessest it*, and *dwellest* therein ; that thou shalt take of the first of all the fruit of the earth, which thou shalt bring of thy land that the Lord thy God giveth thee, and shalt put it in a basket, and shalt go unto *the place which the Lord thy God shall choose to place His name there*"—not to a place of their own or others' choosing.—"And thou shalt go unto the priest that shall be in those days, and say unto him, I profess this day unto the Lord thy God that *I am come* unto the country which the Lord sware unto our fathers for to give us. And the priest shall take the basket out of thine hand, and set it down before the altar of the Lord thy God." (Ver. 1–4.)

The chapter on which we now enter contains the lovely ordinance of the basket of first-fruits, in which we shall find some principles of the deepest interest and practical importance. It was when the hand of Jehovah had conducted His people into the land of promise that the fruits of that land could be presented. It was obviously necessary to be in Canaan ere Canaan's fruits could be offered in worship. The worshiper was able to say, "I profess this day unto the Lord thy God that I am come unto the country which the Lord sware unto our fathers for to give us."

Here lay the root of the matter.—"*I am come.*"
He does not say, I am coming, hoping to come, or
longing to come. No; but, "I am come." Thus
it must ever be. We must know ourselves saved
ere we can offer the fruits of a known salvation.
We may be most sincere in our desires after salvation, most earnest in our efforts to obtain it; but
then we cannot but see that efforts to be saved, and
the fruits of a known and enjoyed salvation, are
wholly different. The Israelite did not offer the
basket of first-fruits in order to get into the land,
but because he was actually in it. "I profess this
day . . . that I am come." There is no mistake
about it—no question, no doubt, not even a hope.
I am actually in the land, and here is the fruit of it.

"And thou shalt speak, and say before the Lord
thy God, A Syrian ready to perish was my father;
and he went down into Egypt, and sojourned there
with a few, and became there a nation, great,
mighty, and populous; and the Egyptians evil
entreated us, and afflicted us, and laid upon us
hard bondage; and when we cried unto the Lord
God of our fathers, the Lord heard our voice, and
looked on our affliction and our labor and our
oppression; and the Lord brought us forth out of
Egypt with a mighty hand, and with an outstretched
arm, and with great terribleness, and with signs,
and with wonders; and He hath brought us into
this place, and hath given us this land, even a
land that floweth with milk and honey. And now,
behold. I have brought the first-fruits of the land,

which Thou, O Lord, hast given me. And thou shalt set it before the Lord thy God, and worship before the Lord thy God; and thou shalt rejoice in every good thing which the Lord thy God hath given unto thee, and unto thine house, thou, and the Levite, and the stranger that is among you."

This is a very beautiful illustration of worship. "A Syrian ready to perish." Such was the origin. There is nothing to boast of, so far as nature is concerned. And as to the condition in which grace had found them, what of it? Hard bondage in the land of Egypt; toiling amid the brick-kilns, beneath the cruel lash of Pharaoh's taskmasters. But then, "We cried unto Jehovah." Here was their sure and blessed resource. It was all they could do, but it was enough. That cry of helplessness went directly up to the throne and to the heart of God, and brought Him down into the very midst of the brick-kilns of Egypt. Hear Jehovah's gracious words to Moses—"I have surely seen the affliction of My people which are in Egypt, and have heard their cry, by reason of their taskmasters; for *I know their sorrows;* and I am come down to deliver them out of the hand of the Egyptians, and to bring them up out of that land unto a good land and a large, unto a land flowing with milk and honey. . . . . Now therefore, behold, the cry of the children of Israel is come unto Me; and I have also seen the oppression wherewith the Egyptians oppress them." (Ex. iii. 7-9.)

Such was the immediate response of Jehovah to

the cry of His people. "I am come down to deliver them." Yes, blessed be His name, He came down, in the exercise of His own free and sovereign grace, to deliver His people; and no power of men or devils —earth or hell could hold them for a moment beyond the appointed time. Hence, in our chapter, we have the grand result as set forth in the language of the worshiper and in the contents of his basket. "I am come unto the country which the Lord sware unto our fathers for to give us. . . . . And now, behold, I have brought the first-fruits of the land, which Thou, O Lord, hast given me." The Lord had accomplished all, according to the love of His heart and the faithfulness of His word. Not one jot or tittle had failed.—"I am come" And "I have brought the fruit." The fruit of what? of Egypt? Nay; but "of the land, which Thou, O Lord, hast given me." The worshiper's lips proclaimed the completeness of Jehovah's work; the worshiper's basket contained the fruit of Jehovah's land. Nothing could be simpler, nothing more real. There was no room for a doubt, no ground for a question. He had simply to declare Jehovah's work and show the fruit. It was all of God from first to last. He had brought them out of Egypt, and He had brought them into Canaan. He had filled their baskets with the mellow fruits of His land, and their hearts with His praise.

And now, beloved reader, let us just ask you, do you think it was presumption on the part of the Israelite to speak as he did? Was it right, was it

modest, was it humble, of him to say, "*I am come*"?
Would it have been more becoming in him merely
to give expression to the faint hope that at some
future period he might come? would doubt and
hesitation as to his position and his portion have
been more honoring and gratifying to the God of
Israel? What say you? It may be that, anticipating our argument, you are ready to say, There is
no analogy. Why not? If an Israelite could say,
"I am come unto the country which the Lord sware
unto our fathers for to give us," why cannot the
believer now say, I am come unto Jesus? True,
in the one case, it was sight; in the other, it is
faith. But is the latter less real than the former?
Does not the inspired apostle say to the Hebrews,
"Ye *are come* unto Mount Zion"? and again, "We
receiving a kingdom which cannot be moved, let us
have grace whereby we may serve God with reverence and godly fear." If we are in doubt as to
whether we have "come" or not, and as to whether
we have "received the kingdom" or not, it is impossible to worship in truth or serve with acceptance. It is when we are in intelligent and peaceful
possession of the place and portion in Christ that
true worship can ascend to the throne above, and
effective service be rendered in the vineyard below.

For what, let us ask, is true worship? It is
simply telling out, in the presence of God, what
He is, and what He has done. It is the heart
occupied with and delighting in God and in all
His marvelous actings and ways. Now, if we have

no knowledge of God, and no faith in what He has done, how can we worship Him ? "He that cometh to God must believe that He is, and that He is a rewarder of them that diligently seek Him." But then to know God is eternal life. I cannot worship God if I do not know Him, and I cannot know Him without having eternal life. The Athenians had erected an altar "to the unknown God," and Paul told them that they were worshiping in ignorance, and proceeded to declare unto them the true God as revealed in the Person and work of the Man Christ Jesus.

It is deeply important to be clear as to this. I must know God ere I can worship Him. I may "feel after Him, if haply I may find Him;" but feeling after One whom I have not found, and worshiping and delighting in One whom I have found, are two totally different things. God has revealed Himself, blessed be His name! He has given us the light of the knowledge of His glory in the face of Jesus Christ. He has come near to us in the Person of that blessed One, so that we may know Him, love Him, trust in Him, delight in Him, and use Him, in all our weakness and in all our need. We have no longer to grope for Him amid the darkness of nature, nor yet among the clouds and mists of spurious religion, in its ten thousand forms. No; our God has made Himself known by a revelation so plain that the wayfaring man, though a fool in all beside, may not err therein. The Christian can say, "*I know* whom I have believed." This is the basis of all true worship. There may be a vast amount of fleshly pietism, mechanical religion, and ceremonial routine without a single atom of true spiritual worship. This latter can only flow from the knowledge of God.

But our object is not to write a treatise on worship, but simply to unfold to our readers the instructive and beautiful ordinance of the basket of first-fruits. And having shown that worship was the first thing with an Israelite who found himself in possession of the land—and further, that we now must know our place and privilege in Christ before we can truthfully and intelligently worship the Father—we shall proceed to point out another very important practical result illustrated in our chapter, namely, *active benevolence.*

"When thou hast made an end of tithing all the tithes of thine increase the third year, which is the year of tithing, and hast given it unto the Levite, the stranger, the fatherless, and the widow, that they may eat within thy gates, and be filled; then thou shalt say before the Lord thy God, I have brought away the hallowed things out of mine house, and also have given them unto the Levite, and unto the stranger, to the fatherless, and to the widow, according to all Thy commandments, which Thou hast commanded me; I have not transgressed Thy commandments, neither have I forgotten them." (Ver. 12, 13.)

Nothing can be more beautiful than the moral order of these things. It is precisely similar to

what we have in Hebrews xiii. "By Him therefore
let us offer the sacrifice of praise to God continually, that is, *the fruit* of our lips giving thanks to
His name." Here is the worship. "But to do good
and to communicate forget not; for with such sacrifices God is well pleased." Here is the active benevolence. Putting both together, we have what we
may call the upper and the nether side of the Christian's character—praising God and doing good to
men. Precious characteristics! May we exhibit
them more faithfully. One thing is certain, they
will always go together. Show us a man whose
heart is full of praise to God, and we will show you
one whose heart is open to every form of human
need. He may not be rich in this world's goods;
he may be obliged to say, like one of old who was
not ashamed to say it, "Silver and gold have I
none;" but he will have the tear of sympathy, the
kindly look, the soothing word, and these things tell
far more powerfully upon a sensitive heart than the
opening of the purse-strings, and the jingling of
silver and gold. Our adorable Lord and Master,
our great Exemplar, "went about doing good;" but
we never read of His giving money to any one; indeed, we are warranted in believing that the blessed
One never possessed a penny. When He wanted to
answer the Herodians on the subject of paying tribute to Cæsar, He had to ask them to show Him a
penny; and when asked to pay tribute, He sent
Peter to the sea to get it. He never carried money,
and most assuredly money is not named in the cat-

egory of gifts bestowed by Him upon His servants. Still He went about doing good, and we are to do the same, in our little measure; it is at once our high privilege and our bounden duty to do so.

And let the reader mark the divine order laid down in Hebrews xiii. and illustrated in Deuteronomy xxvi. Worship gets the first, the highest place. Let us never forget this. We, in our wisdom or our sentimentality, might imagine that doing good to men, usefulness, philanthropy, is the highest thing; but it is not so. "Whoso offereth *praise* glorifieth Me." God inhabits the praises of His people. He delights to surround Himself with hearts filled to overflowing with a sense of His goodness, His greatness, and His glory. Hence, we are to offer the sacrifice of praise to God "continually." So also the Psalmist says, "I will bless the Lord at all times; His praise shall continually be in my mouth." It is not merely now and then, or when all is bright and cheery around us, when every thing goes on smoothly and prosperously; no, but "*at all times*"—"*continually.*" The stream of thanksgiving is to flow uninterruptedly. There is no interval for murmuring or complaining, fretfulness or dissatisfaction, gloom or despondency. Praise and thanksgiving are to be our continual occupation. We are ever to cultivate the spirit of worship. Every breath, as it were, ought to be a halleluiah. Thus it shall be by and by. Praise will be our happy and holy service while eternity rolls along its course of golden ages. When we shall have no further call to "communicate," no demand on our resources or our sympathies, when we shall have bid an eternal adieu to this scene of sorrow and need, death and desolation, then shall we praise our God for evermore, without let or interruption, in the sanctuary of His own blessed presence above.

"But to do good and to communicate *forget not*." There is singular interest attaching to the mode in which this is put. He does not say, But to offer the sacrifice of praise forget not. No; but lest, in the full and happy enjoyment of our own place and portion in Christ, we should "forget" that we are passing through a scene of want and misery, trial and pressure, the apostle adds the salutary and much-needed admonition as to doing good and communicating. The spiritual Israelite is not only to rejoice in every good thing which the Lord his God has bestowed upon him, but he is also to remember the Levite, the stranger, the fatherless, and the widow—that is, the one who has no earthly portion, and is thoroughly devoted to the Lord's work, and the one who has no home, the one who has no natural protector, and the one who has no earthly stay. It must ever be thus. The rich tide of grace rolls down from the bosom of God, fills our hearts to overflowing, and in its overflow, refreshes and gladdens our whole sphere of action. If we were only living in the enjoyment of what is ours in God, our every movement, our every act, our every word, yea, our every look, would do good. The Christian, according to the divine idea, is one who stands with one hand lifted up to God in the presentation of the sacrifice of praise, and the other hand filled with the fragrant fruits of genuine benevolence to meet every form of human need.

O beloved reader, let us deeply ponder these things; let us really apply our whole hearts to the earnest consideration of them; let us seek a fuller realization and a truer expression of these two great branches of practical Christianity, and not be satisfied with any thing less.

We shall now briefly glance at the third point in the precious chapter before us. We shall do little more than quote the passage for the reader. The Israelite, having presented his basket and distributed his tithes, was further instructed to say, "I have not eaten thereof in my *mourning*, neither have I taken away aught thereof for any *unclean* use, nor given aught thereof for *the dead;* but I have hearkened to the voice of the Lord my God, and have done according to all that Thou hast commanded me. Look down from Thy holy habitation, from heaven, and bless Thy people Israel, and the land which Thou hast given us, as Thou swarest unto our fathers, a land that floweth with milk and honey. This day the Lord thy God hath commanded thee to do these statutes and judgments; thou shalt therefore *keep* and *do* them, *with all thine heart* and *with all thy soul.* Thou hast avouched the Lord this day to be thy God, and to *walk in His ways*, and to keep His statutes and His commandments and His judgments, and to hearken unto His voice: and the

Lord hath avouched thee this day to be His peculiar people"—that is, a people of His own special possession—"as He hath promised thee, and that thou shouldest keep *all* His commandments; and to make thee high above all nations which He hath made, in praise and in name and in honor; and that thou mayest be *a holy people* unto the Lord thy God, as He hath spoken." (Ver. 14–19.)

Here we have personal holiness, practical sanctification, entire separation from every thing inconsistent with the holy place and relationship into which they had been introduced, in the sovereign grace and mercy of God. There must be no mourning, no uncleanness, no dead works. We have no room, no time, for any such things as these; they do not belong to that blessed sphere in which we are privileged to live and move and have our being. We have just three things to do: We look up to God, and offer the sacrifice of praise; we look around at a needy world, and do good; we look in upon the circle of our own being—our inner life, and seek, by grace, to keep ourselves unspotted. "Pure religion and undefiled before God and the Father is this: To visit the fatherless and widows in their affliction, and to keep himself unspotted from the world." (Jas. i. 27.)

Thus, whether we hearken to Moses in Deuteronomy xxvi, or to Paul in Hebrews xiii, or to James in his most wholesome, needed, practical epistle, it is the same Spirit that speaks to us, and the same grand lessons that are impressed upon us—lessons

24

of unspeakable value and moral importance—lessons loudly called for in this day of easy-going profession, in the which the doctrines of grace are taken up and held in a merely intellectual way, and connected with all sorts of worldliness and self-indulgence.

Truly, there is an urgent need of a more powerful, practical ministry amongst us. There is a deplorable lack of the prophetic and pastoral element in our ministrations. By the prophetic element, we mean that character of ministry that deals with the conscience, and brings it into the immediate presence of God. This is *greatly* needed. There is a good deal of ministry which addresses itself to the intelligence, but sadly too little for the heart and the conscience. The teacher speaks to the understanding; the prophet speaks to the conscience;* the pastor speaks to the heart. We speak, of course, generally. It may so happen that the three elements are found in the ministry of one man; but they are distinct; and we cannot but feel that where the prophetic and pastoral gifts are lacking in any assembly, the teachers should very earnestly wait upon the Lord for spiritual power to deal with the hearts and consciences of His beloved people. Blessed be His name, He has all needed gift, grace, and power

---

* Very many seem to entertain the idea that a prophet is one who foretells future events, but it would be a mistake thus to confine the term. 1 Corinthians xiv. 28–32 lets us into the meaning of the words "prophet" and "prophesying." The teacher and the prophet are closely and beautifully connected. The teacher unfolds truth from the Word of God; the prophet applies it to the conscience; and, we may add, the pastor sees how the ministry of both the one and the other is acting on the heart and in the life.

for His servants. All we need is, to wait on Him in real earnestness and sincerity of heart, and He will most assuredly supply us with all suited grace and moral fitness for whatever service we may be called to render in His Church.

Oh, that all the Lord's servants may be stirred up to a more deep-toned earnestness, in every department of His blessed work! May we be "instant in season, out of season," and in no wise discouraged by the condition of things around us, but rather find in that very condition an urgent reason for more intense devotedness.

CHAPTER XXVII.

"AND Moses, with the elders of Israel, commanded the people, saying, 'Keep all the commandments which I command you this day. And it shall be on the day when ye shall pass over Jordan unto the land which the Lord thy God giveth thee, that thou shalt set thee up great stones, and plaster them with plaster; and thou shalt write upon them all the words of this law, when thou art passed over, that thou mayest go in unto the land which the Lord thy God giveth thee, a land that floweth with milk and honey; as the Lord God of thy fathers hath promised thee. Therefore it shall be when ye be gone over Jordan, that ye shall set up these stones, which I command you this day, in Mount

Ebal, and thou shalt plaster them with plaster. And there shalt thou build an altar unto the Lord thy God, an altar of stones: thou shalt not lift up any iron tool upon them. Thou shalt build the altar of the Lord thy God of whole stones; and thou shalt offer burnt-offerings thereon unto the Lord thy God; and thou shalt offer peace-offerings, and shalt eat there, and rejoice before the Lord thy God. And thou shalt write upon the stones all the words of this law very plainly.' And Moses and the priests the Levites spake unto all Israel, saying, 'Take heed, and hearken, O Israel; *this day thou art become the people of the Lord thy God.* Thou shalt *therefore* obey the voice of the Lord thy God, and do His commandments and His statutes, which I command thee this day.' And Moses charged the people the same day, saying, 'These shall stand upon Mount Gerizim to bless the people, when ye are come over Jordan: Simeon and Levi and Judah and Issachar and Joseph and Benjamin. And these shall stand upon Mount Ebal to curse: Reuben, Gad, and Asher and Zebulun, Dan, and Naphtali.' '' (Ver. 1–13.)

There could not be a more striking contrast than that which is presented in the opening and close of this chapter. In the paragraph which we have just penned, we see Israel entering upon the land of promise—that fair and fruitful land flowing with milk and honey, and there erecting an altar in Mount Ebal, for burnt-offerings and peace-offerings. We read nothing about sin-offerings or trespass-offerings here. The law, in all its fullness, was to be "written very plainly" upon the plastered stones, and the people, in full, recognized, covenant-relationship, were to offer on the altar those special offerings of sweet savor so blessedly expressive of worship and holy communion. The subject here is not the trespasser *in act*, or the sinner *in nature*, approaching the brazen altar with a trespass-offering or a sin-offering; but rather a people fully delivered, accepted, and blessed—a people in the actual enjoyment of their relationship and their inheritance.

True, they were trespassers and sinners, and as such, needed the precious provision of the brazen altar,—this, of course, is obvious, and fully understood and admitted by every one taught of God; but it manifestly is not the subject of Deuteronomy xxvii. 1–13, and the spiritual reader will at once perceive the reason. When we see the Israel of God, in full covenant-relationship, entering into possession of their inheritance, having the revealed will of their covenant-God, Jehovah, plainly and fully written before them, and the milk and honey flowing around them, we must conclude that all question as to trespasses and sins is definitively settled, and that nothing remains for a people so highly privileged and so richly blessed but to surround the altar of their covenant-God and present those sweet-savor offerings which were acceptable to Him and suited to them.

In short, the whole scene unfolded to our view in the first half of our chapter is perfectly beautiful. Israel having avouched Jehovah to be their God, and Jehovah having avouched Israel to be His peculiar people, to make them high above all nations which He had made, in praise and in name and in honor, and a holy people unto the Lord their God, as He had spoken,—Israel thus privileged, blessed, and exalted, in full possession of the goodly land, and having all the precious commandments of God before their eyes, what remained but to present the sacrifices of praise and thanksgiving, in holy worship and happy fellowship?

But in the latter half of our chapter, we find something quite different. Moses appoints six tribes to stand upon Mount Gerizim to bless the people, and six on Mount Ebal to curse; but alas! when we come to the actual history—the positive facts of the case, there is not a single syllable of blessing, nothing but twelve awful curses, each confirmed by a solemn "amen" from the whole congregation.

What a sad change! what a striking contrast! It reminds us of what passed before us in our study of Exodus xix. There could not be a more impressive commentary on the words of the inspired apostle in Galatians iii. 10.—"For as many as are of the works of the law"—as many as are on that ground—"are under the curse; for it is written," —and here he quotes Deuteronomy xxvii.—"Cursed is every one that continueth not in all things which are written in the book of the law to do them."

Here we have the real solution of the question. Israel, as to their actual moral condition, were on the ground of law; and hence, although the opening of our chapter presents a lovely picture of God's thoughts respecting Israel, yet the close of it sets forth the sad and humiliating result of Israel's real state before God. There is not a sound from Mount Gerizim, not one word of benediction; but, instead thereof, curse upon curse falls on the ears of the people.

Nor could it possibly be otherwise. Let people contend for it as they will, nothing but a curse can come upon "as many as are of the works of the law." It does not merely say, As many as fail to keep the law, though that is true; but, as if to set the truth in the very clearest and most forcible manner before us, the Holy Ghost declares that for *all*, no matter who—Jew, Gentile, or nominal Christian —all who are on the ground or principle of works of law, there is and can be nothing but a curse.

Thus, then, the reader will be able intelligently to account for the profound silence that reigned on Mount Gerizim in the day of Deuteronomy xxvii. The simple fact is, if one solitary benediction had been heard, it would have been a contradiction to the entire teaching of holy Scripture on the question of law.

We have so fully gone into the weighty subject of the law in the first volume of these Notes that we do not feel called upon to dwell upon it here. We can only say that the more we study Scripture, and the more we ponder the law question in the light of the New Testament, the more amazed we are at the manner in which some persist in contending for the opinion that Christians are under the law, whether for life, for righteousness, for holiness, or for any object whatsoever. How can such an opinion stand for a moment in the face of that magnificent and conclusive statement in Romans vi.— "YE ARE NOT UNDER LAW, BUT UNDER GRACE"?

CHAPTER XXVIII.

IN approaching the study of this remarkable section of our book, the reader must bear in mind that it is by no means to be confounded with chapter xxvii. Some expositors, in seeking to account for the absence of the blessings in the latter, have sought for them here; but it is a grand mistake— a mistake absolutely fatal to the proper understanding of either chapter. The obvious fact is, the two chapters are wholly distinct, in basis, scope, and practical application. Chapter xxvii. is (to put it as pointedly and briefly as possible) *moral* and *personal;* chapter xxviii. is *dispensational* and *national.* That deals with the great root-principle of man's moral condition as a sinner, utterly ruined and wholly incapable of meeting God on the ground of law; this, on the other hand, takes up the question of Israel as a nation, under the government of God. In short, a careful comparison of the two chapters will enable the reader to see their entire distinctness. For instance, what connection can we trace between the six blessings of our chapter and the twelve curses of chapter xxvii? None whatever. It is not possible to establish the slightest relationship. But a child can see the moral link between the blessings and curses of chapter xxviii.

Let us quote a passage or two in proof. "And it shall come to pass, if thou shalt *hearken diligently unto the voice of the Lord thy God*,"—the grand old Deuteronomic motto, the key-note of the book—"to observe and to do all His commandments which I command thee this day, that the Lord thy God will set thee on high above all nations of the earth; and all these blessings shall come on thee, and overtake thee, *if thou shalt hearken unto the voice of the Lord thy God*"—the only safeguard, the true secret of happiness, security, victory, and strength.—"Blessed shalt thou be in the city, and blessed shalt thou be in the field. Blessed shall be the fruit of thy body, and the fruit of thy ground, and the fruit of thy cattle, the increase of thy kine, and the flocks of thy sheep. Blessed shall be thy basket and thy store. Blessed shalt thou be when thou comest in, and blessed shalt thou be when thou goest out."

Is it not perfectly plain to the reader that these are not the blessings pronounced by the six tribes on Mount Gerizim? What is here presented to us is Israel's national dignity, prosperity, and glory, founded upon their diligent attention to all the commandments set before them in this book. It was the eternal purpose of God that Israel should be pre-eminent on the earth, high above all the nations. This purpose shall assuredly be made good, although Israel, in the past, have shamefully failed to render that perfect obedience which was to form the basis of their national pre-eminence and glory.

We must never forget or surrender this great truth. Some expositors have adopted a system of interpretation by which the covenant-blessings of Israel are spiritualized and made over to the Church of God. This is a most fatal mistake. Indeed, it is hardly possible to set forth in language, or even to conceive, the pernicious effects of such a method of handling the precious Word of God. Nothing is more certain than that it is diametrically opposed to the mind and will of God. He will not and cannot sanction such tampering with His truth, or such an unwarrantable alienation of the blessings and privileges of His people Israel.

True, we read, in Galatians iii, "That the blessing of Abraham might come on the Gentiles through Jesus Christ, that we might receive"—what? Blessings in the city and in the field? blessings in our basket and store? Nay; but "the promise of the Spirit through faith." So also we learn from the same epistle, in chapter iv, that restored Israel will be permitted to reckon amongst her children all those who are born of the Spirit during the Christian period. "But Jerusalem which is above is free, which is the mother of us all. For it is written, 'Rejoice, thou barren, that bearest not; break forth and cry, thou that travailest not; for the desolate hath many more children than she which hath a husband.'"

All this is blessedly true, but it affords no warrant whatever for transferring the promises made to Israel to New-Testament believers. God has pledged Himself by an oath to bless the seed of Abraham His friend—to bless them with all earthly blessings, in the land of Canaan. This promise holds good, and is absolutely inalienable. Woe be to all who attempt to interfere with its literal fulfillment in God's own time. We have referred to this in our studies on the earlier part of this book, and must now rest content with warning the reader most solemnly against every system of interpretation which involves such serious consequences as to the Word and ways of God. We must ever remember that Israel's blessings are earthly; the Church's blessings are heavenly. "Blessed be the God and Father of our Lord Jesus Christ, who hath blessed us with *all spiritual blessings in the heavenlies in Christ.*"

Thus, both the nature and the sphere of the Church's blessings are wholly different from those of Israel, and must never be confounded. But the system of interpretation above referred to does confound them, to the marring of the integrity of holy Scripture, and the serious damage of souls. To attempt to apply the promises made to Israel to the Church of God, either now or hereafter, on earth or in heaven, is to turn things completely upside down, and to produce the most hopeless confusion in the exposition and application of Scripture. We feel

called upon, in simple faithfulness to the Word of
God and to the soul of the reader, to press this
matter upon his earnest attention.   He may rest
assured it is by no means an unimportant question;
so far from this, we are persuaded that it is utterly
impossible for any one who confounds Israel and the
Church—the earthly and the heavenly, to be a sound
or accurate interpreter of the Word of God.

However, we cannot pursue this subject further
here.   We only trust that the Spirit of God will
arouse the heart of the reader to feel its interest and
importance, and give him to see the necessity of
rightly dividing the word of truth.   If this be so,
our object will be fully gained.

With regard to this twenty-eighth of Deuteronomy, if the reader only seizes the fact of its entire
distinctness from its predecessor, he will be able to
read it with spiritual intelligence and real profit.
There is no need whatever for elaborate exposition.
It divides itself naturally and obviously into two
parts.   In the first, we have a full and most blessed
statement of the results of obedience (See verses 1–
15.); in the second, we have a deeply solemn and
affecting statement of the awful consequences of
disobedience. (See verses 16–68.)   And we cannot
but be struck with the fact that the section containing the curses is more than three times the
length of the one containing the blessings.   That
consists of fifteen verses; this, of fifty-three.   The
whole chapter furnishes an impressive commentary
on the government of God, and a most forcible

illustration of the fact that "our God is a consuming fire." All the nations of the earth may learn from Israel's marvelous history that God must punish disobedience, and that, too, first of all, in His own. And if He has not spared His own people, what shall be the end of those who know Him not? "The wicked shall be turned into hell, and all the nations that forget God." "It is a fearful thing to fall into the hands of the living God." It is the very height of extravagant folly for any one to attempt to evade the full force of such passages, or to explain them away. It cannot be done. Let any one read the chapter before us and compare it with the actual history of Israel, and he will see that as sure as there is a God on the throne of the majesty in the heavens, so surely will He punish evildoers, both here and hereafter. It cannot be otherwise. The government that could or would allow evil to go unjudged, uncondemned, unpunished, would not be a perfect government—would not be the government of God. It is vain to found arguments upon one-sided views of the goodness, kindness, and mercy of God. Blessed be His name, He is kind and good and merciful and gracious, long-suffering and full of compassion; but He is holy and just, righteous and true, and "He hath appointed a day, in the which He will judge the world [the habitable earth—οἰκουμένην] in righteousness by that Man whom He hath ordained; whereof He hath given assurance [given proof—πίστιν] unto all, in that He hath raised Him from the dead." (Acts xvii.)

However, we must draw this section to a close, but ere doing so, we feel it to be our duty to call the reader's attention to a very interesting point in connection with verse 13 of our chapter. "The Lord shall make thee the head, and not the tail; and thou shalt be above only, and thou shalt not be beneath; if that thou hearken unto the commandments of the Lord thy God, which I command thee this day, to observe and to do them."

This, no doubt, refers to Israel as a nation. They are destined to be the head of all the nations of the earth. Such is the sure and settled purpose and counsel of God respecting them. Low as they are now sunk, scattered and lost amongst the nations, suffering the terrible consequences of their persistent disobedience, sleeping, as we read in Daniel xii, in the dust of the earth, yet they shall, *as a nation*, arise and shine in far brighter glory than that of Solomon.

All this is blessedly true, and established beyond all question in manifold passages in Moses, the Psalms, the prophets, and the New Testament; but in looking through the history of Israel, we find some very striking instances of individuals who were permitted and enabled, through infinite grace, to make their own of the precious promise contained in verse 13, and that, too, in very dark and depressing periods of the national history, when Israel, as a nation, was the tail and not the head. We shall just give the reader an instance or two, not only to illustrate our point, but also to set before him a principle of immense practical importance and universal application.

Let us turn for a moment to that charming little book of Esther—a book so little understood or appreciated—a book which, we may truly say, fills a niche and teaches a lesson which no other book does. It belongs to a period when most assuredly Israel was not the head, but the tail; but, notwithstanding, it presents to our view the very edifying and encouraging picture of an individual son of Abraham so carrying himself as to reach the very highest position, and gaining a splendid victory over Israel's bitterest foe.

As to Israel's condition in the days of Esther, it was such that God could not publicly own them. Hence it is that His name is not found in this book, from beginning to end. The Gentile was the head and Israel the tail. The relationship between Jehovah and Israel could no longer be publicly owned; but the heart of Jehovah could never forget His people, and, we may add, the heart of a faithful Israelite could never forget Jehovah or His holy law; and these are just the two facts that specially characterize this most interesting little book. God was acting for Israel behind the scenes, and Mordecai was acting for God before the scenes. It is worthy of remark that neither Israel's best Friend nor their worst enemy is once named in the book of Esther, and yet the whole book is full of the actings of both. The finger of God is stamped on every link in the marvelous chain of providence; and on

the other hand, the bitter enmity of Amalek comes
out in the cruel plot of the haughty Agagite.

All this is intensely interesting. Indeed, in rising
from the study of this book, we may well say, "Oh,
scenes surpassing fable and yet true." No romance
could possibly exceed in interest this simple but
most blessed history. But we must not expatiate,
much as we should like to do so. Time and space
forbid. We merely refer to it now in order to point
out to the reader the unspeakable value and importance of individual faithfulness at a moment when
the national glory was faded and gone. Mordecai
stood like a rock for the truth of God. He refused,
with stern decision, to own Amalek. He would save
the life of Ahasuerus, and bow to his authority as
the expression of the power of God; but he would
not bow to Haman. His conduct in this matter was
governed simply by the Word of God. The authority for his course was to be found in this blessed
book of Deuteronomy.—*"Remember* what Amalek
did unto thee by the way, when ye were come forth
out of Egypt; how he met thee by the way, and
smote the hindmost of thee, even all that were feeble
behind thee, when thou wast faint and weary; and
he feared not God"—here was the true secret of the
whole matter—"therefore it shall be, when the Lord
thy God hath given thee rest from all thine enemies
round about, in the land which the Lord thy God
giveth for an inheritance to possess it, that thou
shalt blot out the remembrance of Amalek from under
heaven; *thou shalt not forget it."* (Chap. xxv. 17–19.)

This was distinct enough for every circumcised ear, every obedient heart, every upright conscience. Equally distinct is the language of Exodus xvii.—— "And the Lord said unto Moses, 'Write this for a memorial in a book, and rehearse it in the ears of Joshua; for I will utterly put out the remembrance of Amalek from under heaven.' And Moses built an altar, and called the name of it JEHOVAH-nissi [the Lord my banner]; for he said, 'Because the Lord hath sworn that the Lord will have war with Amalek from generation to generation.'" (Ver. 14–16.)

Here, then, was Mordecai's authority for refusing a single nod of his head to the Agagite. How could a faithful member of the house of Israel bow to a member of a house with which Jehovah was at war? Impossible. He could clothe himself in sackcloth, fast and weep for his people, but he could not, he would not, he dare not, bow to an Amalekite. He might be charged with presumption, blind obstinacy, stupid bigotry, and contemptible narrow-mindedness; but with that he had nothing whatever to do. It might seem the most unaccountable folly to withhold the common mark of respect from the highest noble in the kingdom; but that noble was an Amalekite, and that was enough for Mordecai. The apparent folly was simple obedience.

It is this which makes the case so interesting and important for us. Nothing can ever do away with our responsibility to obey the Word of God. It might be said to Mordecai that the commandment as to Amalek was a by-gone thing, having reference to Israel's palmy days. It was quite right for Joshua to fight with Amalek; Saul, too, ought to have obeyed the word of Jehovah instead of sparing Agag; but now, all was changed; the glory was departed from Israel, and it was perfectly useless to attempt to act on Exodus xvii. or Deuteronomy xxv.

All such arguments, we feel assured, would have no weight whatever with Mordecai. It was enough for him that Jehovah had said, "*Remember* what Amalek did . . . *Thou shalt not forget it.*" How long was this to hold good? "From generation to generation." Jehovah's war with Amalek was never to cease until his very name and remembrance were blotted out from under heaven. And why? Because of his cruel and heartless treatment of Israel. Such was the kindness of God toward His people! How, then, could a faithful Israelite ever bow to an Amalekite? Impossible. Could Joshua bow to Amalek? Nay. Did Samuel? Nay; "he hewed Agag in pieces before the Lord in Gilgal." How, then, could Mordecai bow to him? He could not do it, cost what it might. It mattered not to him that the gallows was erected for him. He could be hanged, but he could never do homage to Amalek.

And what was the result? A magnificent triumph! There stood the proud Amalekite near the throne, basking in the sunshine of royal favor, boasting himself in his riches, his greatness, his glory, and about to crush beneath his foot the seed of Abraham. There, on the other hand, lay poor

Mordecai in sackcloth and ashes and tears. What could he do? He could obey. He had neither sword nor spear; but he had the Word of God, and by simply obeying that Word, he gained a victory over Amalek quite as decisive and splendid in its way as that gained by Joshua in Exodus xvii.—a victory which Saul failed to gain, though surrounded by a host of warriors selected from the twelve tribes of Israel. Amalek sought to get Mordecai hanged; but instead of that, he was obliged to act as his footman, and conduct him, in all but regal pomp and splendor, through the street of the city. "And Haman answered the king, 'For the man whom the king delighteth to honor, let the royal apparel be brought which the king useth to wear, and the horse that the king rideth upon, and the crown royal which is set upon his head; and let this apparel and horse be delivered to the hand of one of the king's most noble princes, that they may array the man withal whom the king delighteth to honor, and bring him on horseback through the street of the city, and proclaim before him, Thus shall it be done to the man whom the king delighteth to honor.' Then the king said to Haman, 'Make haste, and take the apparel and the horse, as thou hast said, and do even so to Mordecai the Jew, that sitteth at the king's gate: let nothing fail of all that thou hast spoken.' Then took Haman the apparel and the horse, and arrayed Mordecai, and brought him on horseback through the street of the city, and proclaimed before him, 'Thus shall it be done unto the man whom the king delighteth to honor.' And Mordecai came again to the king's gate ; but Haman hasted to his house mourning, and having his head covered.''

Here, assuredly, Israel was the head and Amalek the tail—Israel, not nationally, but individually. But this was only the beginning of Amalek's defeat and of Israel's glory. Haman was hanged on the very gallows he had erected for Mordecai, "and Mordecai went out from the presence of the king in royal apparel or blue and white, and with a great crown of gold, and with a garment of fine linen and purple ; and the city of Shushan rejoiced and was glad.''

Nor was this all. The effect of Mordecai's marvelous victory was felt far and wide over the hundred and twenty-seven provinces of the empire. "In every province, and in every city whithersoever the king's commandment and his decree came, the Jews had joy and gladness, a feast and a good day. And many people of the land became Jews, for the fear of the Jews fell upon them.'' And, to crown all, we read that "Mordecai the Jew was next unto king Ahasuerus, and great among the Jews, and accepted of the multitude of his brethren, seeking the wealth of his people, and speaking peace to all his seed.''

Now, reader, does not all this prove to us, in the most striking manner, the immense importance of individual faithfulness ? Is it not eminently calculated to encourage us to stand for the truth of God, cost what it may ? Only see what marvelous results followed from the actings of one man ! Many might have condemned Mordecai's conduct. It might have seemed like unaccountable obstinacy to refuse a simple mark of respect to the highest noble in the empire ; but it was not so. It was simple obedience ; it was decision for God, and it led to a most magnificent victory, the spoils of which were reaped by his brethren at the very ends of the earth.

For further illustration of the subject suggested by Deuteronomy xxviii. 13, we must refer the reader to Daniel iii. and vi. There he will see what morally glorious results can be reached by individual faithfulness to the true God, at a moment when Israel's national glory was gone—their city and temple in ruins. The three worthies refused to worship the golden image. They dared to face the wrath of the king, to withstand the universal voice of the empire, yea, to meet the fiery furnace itself, rather than disobey. They could surrender life, but they could not surrender the truth of God.

And what was the result ? A splendid victory ! They walked through the furnace with the Son of God, and were called forth from the furnace as witnesses and servants of the Most High God. Glorious privilege ! wondrous dignity ! and all the simple result of obedience. Had they gone with the crowd, and bowed the head in worship to the national god, in order to escape the dreadful furnace, see what they would have lost ! But, blessed be God, they were enabled to stand fast in the confession of the

grand foundation-truth of the unity of the Godhead
—that truth which had been trampled underfoot amid
the splendors of Solomon's reign ; and the record of
their faithfulness has been penned for us by the
Holy Spirit in order to encourage us to tread, with
firm step, the path of individual devotedness, in the
face of a God-hating, Christ-rejecting world, and in
the face of a truth-neglecting christendom. It is
impossible to read the narrative and not have our
whole renewed being stirred up and drawn out in
earnest desire for more deep-toned personal devotedness to Christ and His precious cause.

Similar must be the effect produced by the study
of Daniel vi. We cannot allow ourselves to quote or
expatiate ; we can only commend the soul-stirring
record to the attention of the reader. It is uncommonly fine, and it furnishes a splendid lesson for
this day of soft, self-indulgent, easy-going profession, in which it costs people nothing to give a
nominal assent to the truths of Christianity ; but in
which, notwithstanding, there is so little desire or
readiness to follow, with whole-hearted decision, a
rejected Lord, or to yield an unqualified and un-
hesitating obedience to His commandments.

How refreshing, in the face of so much heartless
indifference, to read of the faithfulness of Daniel !
He, with unflinching decision, persisted in his holy
habit of praying three times a day, with his window
open toward Jerusalem, although he knew that the
den of lions was the penalty of his act. He might
have closed his window and drawn his curtains and

retired into the privacy of his chamber to pray, or
he might have waited for the midnight hour, when
no human eye could see or human ear hear him.
But no; this beloved servant of God would not hide
his light under a bed or a bushel. There was a great
principle at stake. It was not merely that he would
pray to the one living and true God, but he would
pray with "*his windows open toward Jerusalem.*"
And why "toward Jerusalem"? Because it was
God's centre. But it was in ruins. True, for the
present, and as looked at from a human stand-point;
but to faith, and from a divine stand-point, Jerusalem was God's centre for His earthly people. It
was, and it shall be, beyond all question. And not
only so, but its dust is precious to Jehovah; and
hence Daniel was in full communion with the mind
of God when he opened his windows toward Jerusalem and prayed. He had Scripture for what he
did, as the reader may see by referring to 2 Chroni-
cles vi. "If they return to thee with all their hea. ;
and with all their soul in the land of their captivity,
whither they have carried them captives, and pray
toward their land, which Thou gavest unto their
fathers, and *toward the city* which Thou hast chosen,
and *toward the house* which I have built for Thy
name."

Here was Daniel's warrant. This was what he did,
utterly regardless of human opinions, and utterly
regardless, too, of pains and penalties. He would
rather be thrown into the den of lions than surrender
the truth of God; he would rather go to heaven

with a good conscience than remain on earth with a bad one.

And what was the result? Another splendid triumph! "Daniel was taken up out of the den, and no manner of hurt was found upon him, BE-CAUSE HE BELIEVED IN HIS GOD."

Blessed servant! noble witness! Assuredly he was the head on this occasion, and his enemies the tail. And how? Simply by obedience to the Word of God. This is what we deem to be of such vast moral importance for this our day. It is to illustrate and enforce this that we refer to those brilliant examples of individual faithfulness at a time when Israel's national glory was in the dust, their unity gone, and their polity broken up. We cannot but regard it as a fact full of interest, full of encourage-ment, full of suggestive power, that in the darkest days of Israel's history as a nation we have the brightest and noblest examples of personal faith and devotedness. We earnestly press this upon the attention of the Christian reader. We consider it eminently calculated to strengthen and cheer up our hearts in standing for the truth of God at a moment like the present, when there is so much to discourage us in the general condition of the professing church. It is not that we are to look for such speedy, strik-ing, and splendid results as were realized in those cases to which we have referred. This is by no means the question. What we have to keep before our hearts is the fact that, no matter what may be the condition of the ostensible people of God at any given time, it is the privilege of the individual man of God to tread the narrow path and reap the precious fruits of simple obedience to the Word of God and the precious commandments of our Lord and Saviour Jesus Christ.

This, we feel persuaded, is a truth for the day. May we all feel its holy power. We are in imminent danger of lowering the standard of personal devotedness because of the general condition. This is a fatal mistake, yea, it is the positive suggestion of the enemy of Christ and His cause. If Mordecai, Shadrach, Meshach, Abednego, and Daniel had acted thus, what would have been the result?

Ah, no, reader; we have ever to bear in mind that our one great business is, to obey, and leave results with God. It may please Him to permit His servants to see striking results, or He may see fit to allow them to wait for that great day that is coming, when there will be no danger of our being puffed up by seeing any little fruit of our testimony. Be this as it may, it is our plain and bounden duty to tread that bright and blessed path indicated for us by the commandments of our precious and adorable Lord and Saviour Jesus Christ. May God enable us, by the grace of His Holy Spirit, so to do. May we cleave to the truth of God with purpose of heart, utterly regardless of the opinions of our fellow-men who may charge us with narrowness, bigotry, intolerance, and such like. *We have just to go on with the Lord!*

CHAPTER XXIX

THIS chapter closes the second grand division of our book. In it we have a most solemn appeal to the conscience of the congregation. It is what we may term the summing up and practical application of all that has gone before in this most profound, practical, and hortatory section of the five books of Moses.

"These are the words of the covenant, which the Lord commanded Moses to make with the children of Israel *in the land of Moab, beside the covenant which He made with them in Horeb.*" Allusion has already been made to this passage as one of the many proofs of the entire distinctness of the book of Deuteronomy from the preceding section of the Pentateuch; but it claims the reader's attention on another ground. It speaks of a special covenant made with the children of Israel in the land of Moab, in virtue of which they were to be brought into the land. This covenant was as distinct from the covenant made at Sinai as it was from the covenant made with Abraham, Isaac, and Jacob. In a word, it was neither pure *law* on the one hand, nor pure *grace* on the other, but *government* exercised in sovereign mercy.

It is perfectly clear that Israel *could* not enter the land on the ground of the Sinai or Horeb-covenant, inasmuch as they had completely failed under it, by making a golden calf. They forfeited all right and title to the land, and were only saved from instant destruction by sovereign mercy exercised toward them through the mediation and earnest intercession of Moses. It is equally plain that they *did* not enter the land on the ground of the Abrahamic covenant of grace, for had they done so, they would not have been turned out of it. Neither the extent nor the duration of their tenure answered to the terms of the covenant made with their fathers. It was by the terms of the Moab-covenant that they entered upon the limited and temporary possession of the land of Canaan; and inasmuch as they have as signally failed under the Moab-covenant as under that of Horeb—failed under government as completely as under law, they are expelled from the land and scattered over the face of the earth, under the governmental dealings of God.

But not forever. Blessed be the God of all grace, the seed of Abraham IIis friend shall yet possess the land of Canaan according to the magnificent terms of the original grant. "The gifts and calling of God are without repentance." Gifts and calling must not be confounded with law and government. Mount Zion can never be classed with Horeb and Moab. The new and everlasting covenant of grace, ratified by the precious blood of the Lamb of God, shall be gloriously fulfilled to the letter, spite of all the powers of earth and hell—men and devils combined. "'Behold, the days come, saith the Lord, when I will make a new covenant with the house of Israel and with the house of Judah; not according to the covenant that I made with their fathers in the day when I took them by the hand to lead them out of the land of Egypt; because they continued not in My covenant, and I regarded them not, saith the Lord. For this is the covenant that I will make with the house of Israel after those days, saith the Lord: I will put My laws into their mind, and write them in their hearts; and I will be to them a God, and they shall be to Me a people; and they shall not teach every man his neighbor, and every man his brother, saying, Know the Lord; for all shall know Me, from the least to the greatest. For I will be merciful to their unrighteousness, and their sins and their iniquities will I remember no more.' In that He saith, 'A new covenant,' He hath made the first old. Now that which decayeth and waxeth old is ready to vanish away.'' (Heb. viii. 8–13.)

Now, the reader must carefully guard against a system of interpretation that would apply this precious and beautiful passage to the Church. It involves a threefold wrong, namely, a wrong to the truth of God, a wrong to the Church, and a wrong to Israel. We have raised a warning note on this subject again and again in the course of our studies on the Pentateuch, because we feel its immense importance. It is our deep and thorough conviction that no one can understand, much less expound, the Word of God who confounds Israel with the Church. The two things are as distinct as heaven and earth; and hence, when God speaks of Israel, Jerusalem, and Zion, if we presume to apply those names to the New-Testament Church, it can only issue in utter confusion. We believe it to be a simple impossibility to set forth the mischievous consequences of such a method of handling the Word of God. It puts an end to all accuracy of interpretation, and to all that holy precision and divine certainty which Scripture is designed and fitted to impart; it mars the integrity of truth, damages the souls of God's people, and hinders their progress in divine life and spiritual intelligence. In short, we cannot too strongly urge upon every one who reads these lines the absolute necessity of guarding against this fatally false system of handling holy Scripture.

We must beware of meddling with the scope of prophecy, or the true application of the promises of God. We have no warrant whatever to interfere with the divinely appointed sphere of the covenants. The inspired apostle tells us distinctly, in the ninth of Romans, that they pertain to Israel; and if we attempt to alienate them from the Old-Testament fathers and transfer them to the Church of God—the body of Christ, we may depend upon it, we are doing what Jehovah-Elohim will never sanction. The Church forms no part of the ways of God with Israel and the earth. Her place, her portion, her privileges, her prospect, are all heavenly. She is called into existence in this time of Christ's rejection, to be associated with Him where He is now hidden in the heavens, and to share His glory in the coming day. If the reader fully grasps this grand and glorious truth, it will go far toward helping him to put things into their right places and leave them there.

We must now turn our attention to the very solemn, practical application of all that has passed before us to the conscience of every member of the congregation.

"And Moses called unto all Israel, and said unto them, 'Ye have seen all that the Lord did before your eyes in the land of Egypt unto Pharaoh, and unto all his servants, and unto all his land; the great temptations which thine eyes have seen, the signs, and those great miracles; yet the Lord hath not given you a heart to perceive, and eyes to see, and ears to hear, unto this day.'"

This is peculiarly solemn. The most astounding miracles and signs may pass before us, and leave *the heart* untouched. These things may produce a transient effect upon the mind and upon the natural feelings, but unless the conscience is brought into the light of the divine presence, and the heart brought under the immediate action of the truth by the power of the Spirit of God, there is no permanent result reached. Nicodemus inferred from the miracles of Christ that He was a teacher come from God; but this was not enough. He had to learn the deep and wondrous meaning of that mighty sentence, "Ye must be born again." A faith founded on miracles may leave people unsaved, unblessed, unconverted—awfully responsible, no doubt, but wholly unconverted. We read, at the close of the second chapter of John's gospel, of many who professed to believe on Christ when they saw His miracles; but He did not commit Himself unto them. There was no divine work, nothing to be trusted. There must be a new life—a new nature, and miracles and signs cannot impart this. We must be born again—born of the Word and Spirit of God. The new life is communicated by the incorruptible seed of the gospel of God, lodged in the heart by the power of the Holy Ghost. It is not a head-belief founded on miracles, but a heart-belief in the Son of God. It is something which could never be known under law or government. "The *gift* of God is eternal life, through Jesus Christ our Lord." Precious gift! glorious source! blessed channel! Universal and everlasting praise to the Eternal Trinity!

"And I have led you forty years in the wilderness; your clothes are not waxen old upon you, and thy shoe is not waxen old upon thy foot."—Wonderful clothes! wonderful shoes! God took care of them and made them last, blessed forever be His great and holy name!—"Ye have not eaten bread, neither have ye drunk wine or strong drink; that ye might know that I am the Lord your God." They were fed and clothed by God's own gracious hand. "Man did eat angels' food." They had no need of wine or strong drink—no need of stimulants. "They drank of that spiritual rock that followed them, and that rock was Christ." That pure stream refreshed them in the dreary desert, and the heavenly manna sustained them day by day. All they wanted was the capacity to enjoy the divine provision.

Here, alas! like ourselves, they failed; they got tired of the heavenly food, and lusted for other things. How sad that we should be so like them! how very humbling that we should so fail to appreciate that precious One whom God has given to be our life, our portion, our object, our all in all! How terrible to find our hearts craving the wretched vanities and follies of this poor passing world—its riches, its honors, its distinctions, its pleasures, which all perish in the using, and which, even if they were lasting, are not for a moment to be compared with "the unsearchable riches of Christ"! May God, in His infinite goodness, "grant us, according to the riches of His glory, to be strengthened with might by His Spirit in the inner man; that Christ may dwell in our hearts by faith; that we, being rooted and grounded in love, may be able to comprehend with all saints what is the breadth and length and depth and height; and *to know the love of Christ*, which passeth knowledge, that we may be filled with *all the fullness of God*." Oh, that this most blessed prayer may be answered in the deep and abiding experience of the reader and the writer!

"And when ye came unto this place, Sihon the king of Heshbon, and Og the king of Bashan"— formidable and much-dreaded foes!—"came out against us unto battle, and we smote them." And had they been ten thousand times as great and as formidable, they would have proved to be as chaff before the presence of the God of the armies of Israel. "And we took their land, and gave it for an inheritance unto the Reubenites, and to the Gadites, and to the half tribe of Manasseh." Will any one dare to compare this with what human history records respecting the invasion of South America by the Spaniards? Woe be to those who do so! they will find themselves terribly mistaken. There is this grand and all-important difference, that Israel had the direct authority of God for what they did to Sihon and Og; the Spaniards could show no such authority for what they did to the poor ignorant savages of South America. This alters the case completely. The introduction of God and His authority is the one perfect answer to every question, the divine solution of every difficulty. May we ever keep this weighty fact in the remembrance of the thoughts of our hearts, as a divine antidote against every infidel suggestion!

"Keep therefore the words of this [the Moab] covenant, and do them, *that ye may prosper in all that ye do.*" Simple obedience to the Word of God ever has been, is now, and ever shall be the deep and real secret of all true prosperity. To the Christian, of course, the prosperity is not in earthly or material things, but in heavenly and spiritual; and we must never forget that it is the very height of folly to think of prospering or making progress in the divine life if we are not yielding an implicit obedience to all the commandments of our blessed

26

and adorable Lord and Saviour Jesus Christ. "If
ye abide in Me, and My words abide in you, ye shall
ask what ye will, and it shall be done unto you.
Herein is My Father glorified, that ye bear much
fruit; so shall ye be My disciples. As the Father
hath loved Me, so have I loved you; continue ye in
My love. *If ye keep My commandments*, ye shall
abide in My love; even as I have kept My Father's
commandments, and abide in His love." Here is
true Christian prosperity. May we earnestly long
after it, and diligently pursue the proper method of
attaining it.

"Ye stand this day, *all of you*, before the Lord
your God; your captains of your tribes, your elders,
and your officers, with all the men of Israel, *your
little ones*"—touching and interesting fact!—"your
wives, and *thy stranger* that is in thy camp." How
exquisite, how deeply affecting, the expression, "*thy*
stranger"! What a powerful appeal to Israel's
heart on behalf of the stranger! "From the hewer
of thy wood unto the drawer of thy water; that
thou shouldest enter into covenant with the Lord
thy God, and into His oath, which the Lord thy God
maketh with thee this day; that He may establish
thee to-day for a people unto Himself, and that He
may be unto thee a God, as He hath said unto
thee, and as He hath sworn unto thy fathers, to
Abraham, to Isaac, and to Jacob. Neither with you
only do I make this covenant and this oath, but with
him that standeth here with us this day before the
Lord our God, and also with him that is not here

with us this day; for ye know how we have dwelt in the land of Egypt, and how we came through the nations which ye passed by; and ye have seen their abominations [that is, the objects of their worship— their false gods] and their idols, wood and stone. silver and gold, which were among them." (Ver. 10–17.)

This earnest appeal is not only general, but also intensely individual. This is very important. We are ever prone to generalize, and thus miss the application of truth to our individual conscience. This is a grave mistake, and a most serious loss to our souls. We are every one of us responsible to yield an implicit obedience to the precious commandments of our Lord. It is thus we enter into the real enjoyment of our relationship, as Moses says to the people, "that He may establish thee for a people unto Himself, and that He may be unto thee a God."

Nothing can be more precious. And then it is so very simple. There is no vagueness, obscurity, or mysticism about it. It is simply having His most precious commandments treasured up in our hearts, acting upon the conscience, and carried out in the life. This is the true secret of habitually realizing our relationship with our Father and with our Lord and Saviour Jesus Christ.

For any one to imagine that he can enjoy the blessed sense of intimate relationship while living in the habitual neglect of our Lord's commandments is a miserable and mischievous delusion. "If ye keep My commandments, ye shall abide in My

love." This is *the* grand point; let us deeply
ponder it. "If ye love Me, keep My commandments." "Not every one that saith unto Me, Lord,
Lord, shall enter into the kingdom of heaven; but
he that doeth the will of My Father which is in
heaven." "For whosoever shall do the will of My
Father which is in heaven, the same is My brother,
and sister, and mother." "Circumcision is nothing,
and uncircumcision is nothing, but the keeping of
the commandments of God."

These are seasonable words for this day of easy-
going, self-indulgent, worldly profession. May they
sink down into our ears and into our hearts. May
they take full possession of our whole moral being,
and bring forth fruit in our individual history. We
feel persuaded of the need of this practical side of
things. We are in imminent danger, while seeking
to keep clear of every thing like legality, of running
into the opposite evil of carnal laxity. The passages
of holy Scripture which we have just quoted—and
they are but a few of many—supply the divine
safeguard against both these pernicious and deadly
errors. It is blessedly true that we are brought into
the holy relationship of children by the sovereign
grace of God, through the power of His Word and
Spirit. This one fact cuts up by the roots the
noxious weed of legality.

But then, surely the relationship has its suited
affections, its duties, and its responsibilities, the
due recognition of which furnishes the true remedy
for the terrible evil of carnal laxity so prevalent on

all hands. If we are delivered from *law-works*—as, thank God, we are, if we are true Christians—it is not that we should be good-for-nothing self-pleasers, but that *life-works* might be produced in us, to the glory of Him whose name we bear, whose we are, and whom we are bound, by every argument, to love obey, and serve.

May we, beloved reader, earnestly seek to apply our hearts to this practical line of things. We are imperatively called upon to do so, and we may fully count upon the abundant grace of our Lord Jesus Christ to enable us to respond to the call, spite of the ten thousand difficulties and hindrances that lie in our way. Oh, for a deeper work of grace in our souls, a closer walk with God, a more pronounced discipleship! Let us give ourselves to the earnest pursuit of these things!

We must now proceed with the lawgiver's solemn appeal. He warns the people to take heed, "lest there should be among you man or woman or family or tribe whose heart turneth away this day from the Lord our God, to go and serve the gods of these nations; lest there should be among you *a root* that beareth gall and wormwood."

These searching words are referred to by the inspired apostle in his epistle to the Hebrews in a very emphatic manner. "*Looking diligently*," he says, "lest any man fail of the grace of God; lest any root of bitterness springing up trouble you, and thereby many be defiled."

What weighty words are these! how full of wholesome admonition and warning! They set forth the solemn responsibility of all Christians. We are all called upon to exercise a holy, jealous, godly care over each other, which, alas! is but little understood or recognized. We are not all called to be pastors or teachers. The passage just quoted does not refer particularly to such; it refers to all Christians, and we are bound to attend to it. We hear great complaints on all sides, of the sad lack of pastoral care. No doubt there is a great lack of true pastors in the Church of God, as there is of every other gift. This is only what we might expect. How could it be otherwise? How could we expect a profusion of spiritual gifts in our present miserable condition? The Spirit is grieved and quenched by our lamentable divisions, our worldliness, our gross unfaithfulness. Need we, then, marvel at our deplorable poverty?

But our blessed Lord is full of deep and tender compassion toward us in the midst of our ruin and spiritual desolation, and if we only humbled ourselves under His mighty hand, He would graciously lift us up, and enable us, in many ways, to meet the deficiency of pastoral gift.amongst us. We might, through His precious grace, look more diligently and lovingly after one another, and seek each other's spiritual progress and prosperity in a thousand ways.

Let not the reader imagine for a moment that we mean to give the smallest countenance to prying officiousness or unwarrantable espionage on the part of Christians.   Far away be the thought ! We look upon such things as perfectly insufferable in the Church of God.   They stand at the very moral antipodes of that loving, holy, tender, diligent pastoral care of which we speak and for which we long.

But does it not strike the reader that, while giving the widest possible berth to these most contemptible evils to which we have just referred, we might cultivate and exercise a loving, prayerful interest in one another, and a holy watchfulness and care, which might prevent many a root of bitterness from springing up ? We cannot doubt it.   It is quite true we are not all called to be pastors, and it is equally true that there is a grievous dearth of pastors in the Church of God.   We mean, of course, true pastors —pastors given by the Head of the Church—men with a pastor's heart, and real pastoral gift and power.   All this is undeniable, and for this very reason it ought to stir the hearts of the Lord's beloved people every where to seek of Him grace to enable them to exercise a tender, loving, brotherly care over one another, which might go a great way toward supplying the need of pastors amongst us. One thing is clear, that in the passage just quoted from Hebrews xii. there is nothing said about pastors.   It is simply a most stirring exhortation to all Christians to exercise a mutual care, and to watch against the springing up of any root of bitterness.

And oh, how needful this is ! How terrible are those roots ! How bitter they are ! How widely

spread are their pernicious tendrils at times!
What irreparable mischief they do! How many
are defiled by them! How many precious links of
friendship are snapped, and how many hearts broken
by them! Yes, reader, and how often we have felt
persuaded that a little judicious pastoral or even
brotherly care, a little loving, godly counsel, might
have nipped the evil in the bud, and thus hindered
an incalculable amount of mischief and sorrow.
May we all lay these things to heart, and earnestly
seek grace to do what we can to prevent roots of
bitterness springing up and spreading abroad their
defiling influence.

But we must hearken to further weighty and
searching words from the beloved and venerable
lawgiver. He draws a most solemn picture of the
end of the one who caused the root of bitterness to
spring up.

"And it come to pass, when he heareth the words
of this curse, *that he bless himself in his heart*, saying, I shall have peace, though I walk in the imagination of mine heart, to add drunkenness to thirst."
Fatal delusion! Crying, Peace, peace! when there
is no peace, but imminent wrath and judgment.
"The Lord will not spare him, but then the anger
of the Lord and His jealousy shall smoke against
that man, and,"—instead of the "peace" which he
vainly promised himself,—"all the curses that are
written in this book shall lie upon him, and the Lord
shall blot out his name from under heaven." Awful
warning to all who act as roots of bitterness in the

midst of the people of God, and to all who countenance them !

"And the Lord shall separate him unto evil out of all the tribes of Israel, according to all the curses of the covenant that are written in this book of the law; so that the generation to come of your children, that shall rise up after you, and the stranger that shall come from a far land, shall say, when they see the plagues of that land, and the sicknesses which the Lord hath laid upon it; and that the whole land thereof is brimstone and salt and burning, that it is not sown, nor beareth, nor any grass groweth therein, like the overthrow of Sodom and Gomorrah, Admah and Zeboim, which the Lord overthrew in His anger and in His wrath;"—Soul-subduing examples of the governmental dealings of the living God, which ought to speak with a voice of thunder in the ears of all those who are turning the grace of our God into lasciviousness, and denying the Lord that bought them!—"even all nations shall say, Wherefore hath the Lord done thus unto this land? What meaneth the heat of this great anger? Then men shall say, Because they have forsaken the covenant of the Lord God of their fathers, which He made with them when He brought them forth out of the land of Egypt; for they went and served other gods, and worshiped them, gods whom they knew not, and whom He had not given unto them; and the anger of the Lord was kindled against this land, to bring upon it all the curses that are written in this book; and the Lord rooted them out of their land in anger, and in wrath, and in great indignation, and cast them into another land, as it is this day." (Ver. 19–28.)

Reader, how peculiarly solemn is all this! What a powerful illustration of the apostle's words, "It is a fearful thing to fall into the hands of the living God"! and again, "Our God is a consuming fire"! How important that the professing church should give heed to such warning notes! Most assuredly, she is called to learn much from the history of God's dealings with His people Israel; Romans xi. is perfectly clear and conclusive as to this. The apostle, in speaking of the divine judgment upon the unbelieving branches of the olive-tree, thus appeals to christendom: "If some of the branches be broken off, and thou, being a wild olive-tree, wert graffed in among them, and with them partakest of the root and fatness of the olive-tree; boast not against the branches. But if thou boast, thou bearest not the root, but the root thee. Thou wilt say then, The branches were broken off that I might be graffed in. Well; because of unbelief they were broken off; and thou standest by faith. BE NOT HIGH-MINDED, BUT FEAR; for if God spared not the natural branches, take heed lest He also spare not thee. Behold therefore the goodness and severity of God; on them which fell, severity; but toward thee, goodness, *if thou continue in His goodness;* otherwise *thou also shalt be cut off.*"

Alas! the professing church has not continued in the goodness of God. It is utterly impossible to

read her history in the light of Scripture and not
see this. She has grievously departed, and there is
nothing before her save the unmingled wrath of
Almighty God. The beloved members of the body
of Christ who, sad to say, are mingled with the
terrible mass of corrupt profession, will be gathered
out of it and taken to the place prepared in the
Father's house in heaven. Then, if not before, they
will see how wrong it was to have remained in connection with what was so flagrantly opposed to
the mind of Christ as revealed, with divine clearness
and simplicity, in the holy Scriptures.

But as to the great thing known as christendom,
it will be "spued out" and "cut off." It will be
given over to strong delusion, to believe a lie, "that
they all might be damned who believed not the truth,
but *had pleasure in unrighteousness.*"

Tremendous words! May they ring in the ears
and sink down into the hearts of thousands who are
going on from day to day, week to week, and year
to year, content with a mere name to live, a form of
godliness, but denying the power, "*lovers of pleasure
rather than lovers of God.*" What an awfully graphic
picture of so-called Christian England! How appalling the condition and the destiny of the pleasure-
hunting thousands who are rushing blindly, heed-
lessly, and madly down the inclined plane that leads
to hopeless and everlasting misery! May God, in
His infinite goodness, by the power of His Spirit
and by the mighty action of His Word, rouse the
hearts of His people every where to a more

profound and influential sense of these things.

We must now, ere closing this section, briefly direct the reader's attention to the last verse of our chapter. It is one of those passages of Scripture sadly misunderstood and misapplied. "The secret things belong unto the Lord our God; but those things which are revealed belong unto us, and to our children forever, that we may do all the words of this law." This verse is constantly used to hinder the progress of souls in the knowledge of "the deep things of God," but its simple meaning is this: The things "revealed" are what we have had before us in the preceding chapter of this book; the things "secret," on the other hand, refer to those resources of grace which God had in store, to be unfolded when the people should have utterly failed to "do all the words of this law." The revealed things are what Israel ought to have done, but did not do; the secret things are what God would do, spite of Israel's sad and shameful failure, and they are most blessedly presented in the following chapters—the counsels of divine grace, the provisions of sovereign mercy to be displayed when Israel shall have thoroughly learnt the lesson of their utter failure under both the Moab and the Horeb-covenants.

Thus this passage, when rightly understood, so far from affording any warrant for the use so constantly made of it, encourages the heart to search into these things which, though "secret" to Israel in the plains of Moab, are fully and clearly "revealed" to us for our profit, comfort, and edification.* The

Holy Spirit came down, on the day of Pentecost, to lead the disciples into *all truth*. The canon of Scripture is complete; all the purposes and counsels of God are fully revealed. The mystery of the Church completes the entire circle of divine truth. The apostle John could say to all God's children, "Ye have an unction from the Holy One, and know *all things*."

Thus the entire New Testament abounds with evidence to prove the mistaken use that is so constantly made of Deuteronomy xxix. 29. We have dwelt upon it because we are aware that the Lord's beloved people are sadly hindered by it in their progress in divine knowledge. The enemy would ever seek to keep them in the dark, when they ought to be walking in the sunlight of divine revelation— to keep them as babes feeding upon milk, when they ought, as those "of full age," to be feeding upon the "strong meat" so freely provided for the Church of

---

*1 Corinthians ii. 9 is another of the misunderstood and misapplied passages. "But, as it is written, 'Eye hath not seen, nor ear heard, neither have entered into the heart of man, the things which God hath prepared for them that love Him.'" Here, people are sure to stop, and hence conclude that we cannot possibly know aught of the precious things which God has in store for us; but the very next verse proves the gross absurdity of any such conclusion. "But God *hath revealed* them unto us by His Spirit; for the Spirit searcheth all things, yea, the deep things of God. For what man knoweth the things of a man, save the spirit of man which is in him? even so the things of God knoweth no man, but the Spirit of God. Now we [that is, all the Lord's people] have received, not the spirit of the world, but the spirit which is of God; *that we might know the things that are freely given to us of God*." Thus this passage, like Deuteronomy xxix. 29, teaches the very opposite of what is so constantly deduced from it. How important to examine and weigh the context of the passages which are quoted'

God.   We have but little idea of how the Spirit of
God is grieved and Christ dishonored by the low
tone of things amongst us.   How few really "know
the things that are freely given to us of God"!
Where are the proper privileges of the Christian
understood, believed, and realized? How meagre is
our apprehension of divine things! How stunted
our growth! How feeble our practical exposition of
the truth of God!   What a blotted epistle of Christ
we present!

Beloved Christian reader, let us seriously ponder
these things in the divine presence. Let us honestly
search out the root of all this lamentable failure,
and have it judged and put away, that so we may
more faithfully and unmistakably declare whose we
are and whom we serve. May it be more thoroughly
manifest that Christ is our one absorbing object.

CHAPTER XXX.

THIS chapter is one of very deep interest and
importance.   It is prophetic, and presents to
us some of "the secret things" referred to at the
close of the preceding chapter.   It unfolds some of
those most precious resources of grace treasured up
in the heart of God, to be unfolded when Israel,
having utterly failed to keep the law, should be
scattered to the ends of the earth.

"And it shall come to pass, when all these things

are come upon thee, the blessing and the curse, which I have set before thee, and *thou shalt call them to mind* among all the nations, whither the Lord thy God hath driven thee, and *shalt return unto the Lord thy God*, and shalt obey His voice according to all that I command thee this day, *thou and thy children, with all thine heart and with all thy soul;* that then the Lord thy God will turn thy captivity, and *have compassion upon thee*, and will return and gather thee from all the nations, whither the Lord thy God hath scattered thee.''

How touching, how perfectly beautiful, is all this! It is no question of law-keeping, but something far deeper, far more precious; it is the turning of the heart—the whole heart—the whole soul to Jehovah, at a time when a literal obedience to the law is utterly impossible. It is a broken and contrite heart turning to God, and God, in deep and tender compassion, meeting that heart. This is true blessedness, at all times and in all places. It is something above and beyond all dispensational dealings and arrangements. It is God Himself, in all the fullness and ineffable blessedness of what He is, meeting a repentant soul; and we may truly say that when these two meet, all is divinely and eternally settled.

It must be perfectly clear to the reader that what we have now before us is something as far removed from law-keeping and human righteousness as heaven is above earth. The first verse of our chapter proves in the clearest possible manner that the people are viewed as in a condition in which the carrying out of the ordinances of the law is a simple impossibility. But blessed be God, there is not a spot on the face of the earth, be it ever so remote, from which the heart cannot turn to God. The *hands* might not be able to present a victim for the altar, the *feet* might not be able to travel to the appointed place of worship, but the *heart* could travel to God. Yes; the poor crushed, broken, contrite heart could go directly to God, and God, in the depth of His compassion and tender mercy, could meet that heart, bind it up, and fill it to overflowing with the rich comfort and consolation of His love, and the full joy of His salvation.

But let us hearken yet further to those "secret things" which "belong to God"—things precious beyond all human thought. "If any of thine be driven out unto *the utmost parts of heaven*"—as far as they could go—"from thence will the Lord thy God *gather thee*, and from thence will He *fetch thee;* and the Lord thy God will bring thee into the land which thy fathers possessed, and thou shalt possess it; and *He will do thee good*, and multiply thee above thy fathers."

How precious is all this ! But there is something far better still. Not only will He gather them, fetch them, and multiply them—not only will He act in power *for* them, but He will do a mighty work of grace *in* them of far more value than any outward prosperity however desirable. "And the Lord thy God will *circumcise thine heart*"—the very centre

of the whole moral being, the source of all those
influences which go to form the character—"and
the heart of thy seed, to love the Lord thy God with
all thine heart"—the grand moral regulator of the
entire life—"and with all thy soul, that thou mayest
live. And the Lord thy God will put all these curses
upon thine enemies, and on them that hate thee,
which persecuted thee"—a solemn word for all
those nations who have ever sought to oppress the
Jews!—"And thou shalt return, and obey the voice
of the Lord, and do all His commandments, which
I command thee this day."

Nothing can be more morally lovely than all this.
The people gathered, fetched, multiplied, blessed,
circumcised in heart, thoroughly devoted to Jehovah, and yielding a whole-hearted, loving obedience
to all His precious commandments! What can exceed this in blessedness for a people on the earth?

"And the Lord thy God will make thee plenteous
ın every work of thine hand, in the fruit of thy
body, and in the fruit of thy cattle, and in the fruit
of thy land, for good; for the Lord will again rejoice over thee for good, as He rejoiced over thy
fathers: if thou shalt hearken unto the voice of the
Lord thy God, to keep His commandments and His
statutes which are written in this book of the law,
and if thou turn unto the Lord thy God, with all
thine heart and with all thy soul. For this commandment which I command thee this day, it is not
hidden from thee, neither is it far off. It is not in
heaven, that thou shouldest say, Who shall go up

for us to heaven, and bring it unto us, that we may hear it and do it? Neither is it beyond the sea, that thou shouldest say, Who shall go over the sea for us, and bring it unto us, that we may hear it and do it? But the Word is *very nigh unto thee*, in thy *mouth*, and in thy *heart*, that thou mayest do it." (Ver. 10–14.)

This is a singularly interesting passage. It furnishes a key to "the secret things" already referred to, and sets forth the great principles of divine righteousness, in vivid and beautiful contrast to legal righteousness in every possible aspect. According to the truth here unfolded, it matters not in the least where a soul may be—here, there, or any where; "the Word is nigh thee." It could not possibly be nigher. What could be nigher than "in thy mouth, and in thy heart"? We need not, as we say, move a muscle to get it. If it were above us or beyond us, reason would that we might complain of our utter inability to reach it; but no, there is no need of either *hands* or *feet* in this most blessed and all-important matter. The *heart* and the *mouth* are here called into exercise.

There is a very beautiful allusion to the above passage in the tenth chapter of the epistle to the Romans, to which the reader may refer with much interest and profit. Indeed, it is so full of evangelic sweetness, that we must quote it.

"Brethren, my heart's desire and prayer to God for Israel is, that they might be saved. For I bear them record, that they have a zeal of God, but not according to knowledge. For they, being *ignorant of God's righteousness*, and *going about* to establish their own righteousness, *have not submitted themselves* unto the righteousness of God. For Christ is the end of the law for righteousness to *every one that believeth*"—not to every one who *says* he believes, as in James ii. 14.—"For Moses describeth the righteousness which is of the law, that the man which doeth those things shall live by them. But the righteousness which is of faith speaketh on this wise: Say not in thine heart, Who shall ascend into heaven? (that is, to bring Christ down;)"—Striking parenthesis! Marvelous instance of the Spirit's use of Old-Testament scripture! It bears the distinct stamp of His master-hand.—"or, Who shall descend into the deep? (that is, to bring up Christ again from the dead.) But what saith it? The Word is nigh thee, even in thy mouth, and in thy heart; that is, *the word of faith, which we preach;*"—How perfectly beautiful the addition! Who but the Spirit could have supplied it?—"that if thou shalt *confess with thy mouth* the Lord Jesus, and shalt *believe in thine heart* that God hath raised Him from the dead, thou shalt be saved. For with the heart man believeth unto righteousness, and with the mouth confession is made unto salvation. Foi the Scripture saith, 'Whosoever believeth on Him shall not be ashamed.'"

Mark this beautiful word—"whosoever." It most assuredly takes in the Jew. It meets him wherever he may be, a poor exile at the very ends of the earth, under circumstances where obedience to the law as such was simply impossible, but where the rich and precious grace of God and His most glorious salvation could meet him in the depth of his need. There, though he could not keep the law, he could confess with his mouth the Lord Jesus, and believe in his heart that God had raised Him from the dead; and this is salvation.

But then, if it be "whosoever," it cannot possibly be confined to the Jew; nay, it cannot be confined at all; and hence the apostle goes on to say, "There *is* no difference between the Jew and the Greek." There *was* the greatest possible difference under the law. There could not be a broader or more distinct line of demarkation than that which the lawgiver had drawn between the Jew and the Greek; but that line is obliterated, for a double reason: first, because "all have sinned and come short of the glory of God" (chap. iii. 23.); and secondly, because "the same Lord over all is rich unto all that call upon Him; for whosoever shall call upon the name of the Lord shall be saved."

How blessedly simple! "Calling"—"believing"—"confessing"! Nothing can exceed the transcendent grace that shines in these words. No doubt it is assumed that the soul is really in earnest—that the *heart* is engaged. God deals in moral realities. It is not a nominal, notional head-belief; but divine faith wrought in the heart by the Holy Ghost—a living faith, which connects the soul, in a divine way and by an everlasting link, to Christ.

And then there is the confessing with the mouth the Lord Jesus. This is of cardinal importance. A man may say, I believe in my heart, but I am not one for parading my religious belief. I am not a talker. I keep my religion to myself. It is entirely a matter between my soul and God ; I do not believe in that perpetual intruding our religious impressions upon other people. Many who talk loudly and largely about their religion in public, make but a sorry figure in private, and I certainly do not want to be identified with such. I utterly abhor all cant. Deeds, not words, for me.

All this sounds very plausible, but it cannot stand for a moment in the light of Romans x. 9. There must be the confession with the mouth. Many would like to be saved by Christ, but they shrink from the reproach of confessing His precious Name. They would like to get to heaven when they die, but they do not want to be identified with a rejected Christ. Now God does not own such. He looks for the full, bold, clear confession of Christ, in the face of a hostile world. Our Lord Christ, too, looks for this confession. He declares that whoso confesses Him before men, He will confess before the angels of God ; but whoso denies Him before men, He will deny before the angels of God. The thief on the cross exhibited the two great branches of true saving faith. He believed with his heart, and confessed with his mouth. Yes, he gave a flat contradiction to the whole world on the most vital question that ever was or ever could be raised, and that question was Christ. He was a thoroughly pronounced disciple of Christ. Oh, that there were more such ! There is a terrible amount of indefiniteness and cold half-heartedness in the professing church, grievous to the Holy Ghost, offensive to Christ, hateful to God. We long for bold decision, out-and-out, unmistakable testimony to the Lord Jesus. May God the Holy Spirit stir up all our hearts, and lead us forth, in more thorough consecration of heart, to that blessed One who freely gave His life to save us from everlasting burnings !

We shall close this section by quoting for the reader the last few verses of our chapter, in which Moses makes a peculiarly solemn appeal to the hearts and consciences of the people. It is a most powerful word of exhortation.

"See, I have set before thee this day *life and good* and *death and evil.*" Thus it is ever in the government of God. The two things are inseparably linked together. Let no man dare to snap the link. God "will render to every man according to his deeds ; to them who, by patient continuance in well-doing, seek for glory and honor and immortality, eternal life ; but unto them that are contentious, and do not obey the truth, but obey unrighteousness, indignation and wrath, tribulation and anguish, upon *every soul of man that doeth evil*, of the Jew first, and also of the Gentile ; but glory, honor, and peace to *every man that worketh good*, to the Jew first, and also to the Gentile : *for there is no respect of persons with God.*" (Rom. ii. 6-11.)

The apostle does not, in this great practical passage, go into the question of power; he simply states the broad fact—a fact applicable at all times and under all dispensations—government, law, and Christianity; it ever holds good that "God will render to every man according to his deeds." This is of the very last possible importance. May we ever bear it in mind. It may perhaps be said, Are not Christians under grace? Yes, thank God; but does this weaken, in the smallest degree, the grand governmental principle stated above? Nay, it strengthens and confirms it immensely.

But again, some may feel disposed to say, Can any unconverted person do good? We reply, This question is not raised in the scripture just quoted. Every one taught of God knows and feels and owns that not one atom of "good" has ever been done in this world but by the grace of God; that man left to himself will do evil only—evil continually. "Every good gift and every perfect gift is from above, and cometh down from the Father of lights." All this is most blessedly true, and thankfully owned by every pious soul, but it leaves wholly untouched the fact set forth in Deuteronomy xxx. and confirmed by Romans ii, that *life and good, death and evil*, are bound together by an inseparable link. May we never forget it. May it ever abide in the remembrance of the thoughts of our hearts.

"See, I have set before thee this day life and good, and death and evil; in that I command thee this day to love the Lord thy God, to walk in His ways, and to keep His commandments and His statutes and His judgments, that thou mayest live and multiply; and the Lord thy God shall bless thee in the land whither thou goest to possess it. But if *thine heart turn away*, so that *thou wilt not hear*, but shalt be drawn away, and worship other gods, and serve them; I denounce unto you this day, that ye shall surely perish, and that ye shall not prolong your days upon the land, whither thou passest over Jordan to go to possess it. I call heaven and earth to record this day against you, that I have set before you life and death, blessing and cursing; therefore choose life, that both thou and thy seed may live; that thou mayest love the Lord thy God, and that thou mayest obey His voice, and that thou mayest *cleave unto Him*"—the all-important, essential thing for each, for all, the very spring and power of all true religion, in every age, in every place;—"*for He is thy life, and the length of thy days;*"—How close! how vital! how real! how very precious!—"that thou mayest dwell in the land which the Lord sware unto thy fathers, to Abraham, to Isaac, and to Jacob, to give them." (Ver. 15–20.)

Nothing can be more solemn than this closing appeal to the congregation; it is in full keeping with the tone and character of the entire book of Deuteronomy—a book marked throughout by the most powerful exhortations that ever fell on mortal ears. We have no such soul-stirring appeals in any of the preceding sections of the Pentateuch. Each book, we need not say, has its own specific niche to fill, its own distinct object and character; but the great burden of Deuteronomy, from beginning to end, is exhortation; its thesis, the Word of God; its object, obedience—whole-hearted, earnest, loving obedience, grounded on a known relationship and enjoyed privileges.

CHAPTER XXXI.

THE heart of Moses still lingers, with deep tenderness and affectionate solicitude, over the congregation. It seems as though he could never weary of pouring into their ears his earnest exhortations. He felt their need, he foresaw their danger, and, like a true and faithful shepherd, he sought, with all the deep and tender affection of His large, loving heart, to prepare them for what was before them. No one can read his closing words without being struck with their peculiarly solemn tone. They remind us of Paul's touching farewell to the elders of Ephesus. Both these beloved and honored servants realized, in a very vivid manner, the seriousness of their own position and that of the persons they were addressing. They felt the uncommon gravity of the interests at stake, and the urgent need of the most faithful dealing with the heart and conscience. This will account for what we may term the awful solemnity of their appeals. All who really enter into the situation and destiny of the people of God in a world like this *must* be serious. The true sense of these things, the apprehension of them in the divine presence, must, of necessity, impart a holy gravity to the character, and a special pungency and power to the testimony.

"And Moses went and spake these words unto all Israel. And he said unto them, 'I am a hundred and twenty years old this day; I can no more go out and come in; also the Lord hath said unto me, Thou shalt not go over this Jordan.'" How very touching this allusion to his great age, and this fresh and final reference to the solemn governmental dealing of God with himself personally! The direct and manifest object of both was, to give effect to his appeal to the hearts and consciences of the people, to strengthen the moral lever by which this beloved and honored servant of God sought to move them in the direction of simple obedience. If he points to his gray hairs, or to the holy discipline exercised toward him, it most assuredly is not for the purpose of bringing himself, his circumstances, or his feelings before them, but simply to touch the deepest springs of their moral being by every possible means.

"The Lord thy God, He will go over before thee, and He will destroy these nations from before thee, and thou shalt possess them; and Joshua, he shall go over before thee, as the Lord hath said. And the Lord shall do unto them as He did to Sihon and to Og, kings of the Amorites, and unto the land of them whom He destroyed. And the Lord shall give them up before your face, that ye may do unto them according unto all the commandments which I have commanded you." Not a word of murmuring or repining as to himself, not the faintest tinge of envy or jealousy in his reference to the one who was to take his place, not the most distant approach to aught of the kind; every selfish consideration is swallowed up in the one grand object of encouraging the hearts of the people to tread, with firm step, the pathway of obedience, which was then, is now, and ever must be the path of victory, the path of blessing, the path of peace.

"Be strong and of a good courage, fear not, nor be afraid of them; for the Lord thy God, He it is that doth go with thee; He will not fail thee nor forsake thee." What precious, soul-sustaining words are these, beloved Christian reader! how eminently calculated to lift the heart above every discouraging influence! The blessed consciousness of the Lord's presence with us, and the remembrance of His gracious ways with us, in days gone by, must ever prove the true secret of strength in moving onward. The same mighty hand which had subdued before them Sihon and Og, could subdue all the kings of Canaan. The Amorites were quite as formidable as the Canaanites; Jehovah was more than a match for all. "We have heard with our ears, O God, our fathers have told us, what work Thou didst in their days, in the times of old. How Thou didst drive out the heathen with Thy hand, and plantedst them; how Thou didst afflict the people, and cast them out."

Only think of God driving out people with His own hand! What an answer to all the arguments and difficulties of a morbid sentimentality! How very shallow and erroneous are the thoughts of some in reference to the governmental ways of God! How miserably one-sided their notions of His character and actings! How perfectly absurd the attempt to measure God by the standard of human judgment and feeling! It is very evident that Moses had not the smallest particle of sympathy with such sentiments when he addressed to the congregation of Israel the magnificent exhortation quoted above. He knew something of the gravity and solemnity of the government of God, something, too, of the blessedness of having Him as a shield in the day of battle, a refuge and a resource in every hour of peril and need.

Let us hearken to his encouraging words addressed to the man who was to succeed him. "And Moses called unto Joshua, and said unto him in the sight of all Israel, '*Be strong and of a good courage;* for thou must go with this people unto the land which the Lord hath sworn unto their fathers to give them; and thou shalt cause them to inherit it. And the Lord, He it is that doth go before thee; He will be with thee; He will not fail thee, neither forsake thee; fear not, neither be dismayed.'"

Joshua needed a special word for himself, as one called to occupy a prominent and very distinguished place in the congregation. But the word to him embodies the same precious truth as that addressed to the whole assembly. He is assured of the divine presence and power with him. This is enough for each, for all; for Joshua as for the most obscure member of the assembly. Yes, reader, and enough for thee, whoever thou art, or whatever be thy sphere of action. It matters not in the least what difficulties or dangers may lie before us, our God is amply sufficient for all. If only we have the sense of the Lord's presence with us, and the authority of His Word for the work in which we are engaged, we may move on with joyful confidence, spite of ten thousand difficulties and hostile influences.

"And Moses wrote this law, and delivered it unto the priests the sons of Levi, which bear the ark of the covenant of the Lord, and unto all the elders of Israel. And Moses commanded them, saying, 'At the end of every seven years, in the solemnity of the year of release, in the feast of tabernacles, when *all Israel* is come to appear before the Lord thy God in the place which He shall choose, thou shalt read this law before all Israel, in their hearing. Gather the people together, *men* and *women* and *children*, and *thy stranger* that is within thy gates, that they may *hear*, and that they may *learn*, and *fear* the Lord your God, and *observe to do all the words* of this law; and that *their children, which have not known any thing, may hear, and learn to fear the Lord your God*, as long as ye live in the land whither ye go over Jordan to possess it." (Ver. 9–35.)

Two things in the foregoing passage claim our special attention; first, the fact that Jehovah at-

tached the most solemn importance to the public
assembly of His people for the purpose of hearing
His Word. "All Israel"—"men, women, and children"—with the stranger who had cast in his lot
amongst them, were commanded to assemble themselves together to hear the reading of the book of
the law of God, that all might learn His holy will
and their duty. Each member of the assembly,
from the eldest to the youngest, was to be brought
into direct personal contact with the revealed will of
Jehovah, that each one might know his solemn responsibility.

And secondly, we have to weigh the fact that the
children were to be gathered before the Lord to
hearken to His Word. Both these facts are full of
weighty instruction for all the members of the
Church of God—instruction urgently called for on
all sides. There is a most deplorable amount of
failure as to these two points. We sadly neglect
the assembling of ourselves together for the simple
reading of the holy Scriptures. There does not
seem to be sufficient attraction in the Word of God
itself to bring us together. There is an unhealthy
craving for other things ; human oratory, music,
religious excitement of some kind or other seems
needful to bring people together,—any thing and
every thing but the precious Word of God.

It will perhaps be said that people have the Word
of God in their houses, that it is quite different now
from what it was with Israel; every one can read
the Scriptures at home, and there is not the same

necessity for the public reading. Such a plea will not stand the test of truth for a moment. We may rest assured, if the Word of God were loved and prized and studied in private and in the family, it would be loved and prized and studied in public. We should delight to gather together around the fountain of holy Scripture, to drink, in happy fellowship, of the living water, for our common refreshment and blessing.

But it is not so. The Word of God is not loved and studied, either privately or publicly. Trashy literature is devoured in private, and music, ritualistic services, and imposing ceremonies are eagerly sought after in public. Thousands will flock to hear music, and pay for admission, but how few care for a meeting to read the holy Scriptures! These are facts, and facts are powerful arguments. We cannot get over them. There is a growing thirst for religious excitement, and a growing distaste for the calm study of holy Scripture and the spiritual exercises of the Christian assembly. It is perfectly useless to deny it. We cannot shut our eyes to it. The evidence of it meets us on every hand.

Thank God, there are a few, here and there, who really love the Word of God, and delight to meet, in holy fellowship, for the study of its precious truths. May the Lord increase the number of such, and bless them abundantly. May our lot be cast with them, "till traveling days are done." They are but an obscure and feeble remnant every where; but they love Christ and cleave to His Word, and their richest enjoyment is, to get together and think and speak and sing of Him. May God bless them and keep them. May He deepen His precious work in their souls, and bind them more closely to Himself and one another, and thus prepare them, in the state of their affections, for the appearing of "the Bright and Morning Star."

We must now turn for a few moments to the closing verses of our chapter, in which Jehovah speaks to His beloved and honored servant, in tones of deep and touching solemnity, as to his own death, and as to Israel's dark and gloomy future.

"And the Lord said unto Moses, 'Behold, thy days approach that thou must die: call Joshua, and present yourselves in the tabernacle of the congregation, that I may give him a charge.' And Moses and Joshua went and presented themselves in the tabernacle of the congregation. And the Lord appeared in the tabernacle in a pillar of a cloud; and the pillar of the cloud stood over the door of the tabernacle. And the Lord said unto Moses, 'Behold, thou shalt sleep with thy fathers; and this people will rise up and go a whoring after the gods of the strangers of the land, whither they go to be among them, and will forsake Me, and break My covenant which I have made with them. Then My anger shall be kindled against them in that day, and I will forsake them, and I will hide My face from them, and they shall be devoured, and many evils and troubles shall befall them; so that they will say in that day, *Are not these evils come upon us because our*

God is not among us? And I will surely hide My face in that day, for all the evils which they shall have wrought, in that they are turned unto other gods.'"

"Their sorrows shall be multiplied that hasten after another god." So says the Spirit of Christ in Psalm xvi. Israel has proved, is proving, and shall yet more fully prove the solemn truth of these words. Their history in the past, their present dispersion and desolation, and, beyond all, that "great tribulation" through which they have yet to pass, at "the time of the end,"—all go to confirm and illustrate the truth that the sure and certain way to multiply our sorrows is, to turn away from the Lord and look to any creature-resource. This is one of the many and varied practical lessons which we have to gather from the marvelous history of the seed of Abraham. May we learn it effectually. May we learn to cleave to the Lord with purpose of heart, and turn away, with holy decision, from every other object. This, we feel persuaded, is the only path of true happiness and peace. May we ever be found in it.

"Now therefore write ye this song for you, and teach it the children of Israel; put it in their mouths, *that this song may be a witness for Me against the children of Israel.* For when I shall have brought them into the land which I sware unto their fathers, that floweth with milk and honey; and they shall have eaten and filled themselves and waxen fat; then will they turn unto other gods, and serve them, and

28

provoke Me, and break My covenant. And it shall come to pass, when many evils and troubles are befallen them, that this song shall testify against them as a witness; for it shall not be forgotten out of the mouths of their seed; for I know their imaginations which they go about, even now, before I have brought them into the land which I sware.''

How deeply affecting, how peculiarly solemn, is all this! Instead of Israel being a witness for Jehovah before all nations, the song of Moses was to be a witness for Jehovah against the children of Israel. They were called to be His witnesses; they were responsible to declare His name and to show forth His praise in that land into which, in His faithfulness and sovereign mercy, He conducted them; but alas! they utterly and shamefully failed, and hence, in view of this sad and most humiliating failure, a song was to be written which, in the first place, as we shall see, sets forth, in most magnificent strains, the glory of God; and secondly, records, in accents of inflexible faithfulness, Israel's deplorable failure, in every stage of their history.

''Moses therefore wrote this song the same day, and taught it the children of Israel. And he gave Joshua the son of Nun a charge, and said, '*Be strong, and of a good courage;* for thou shalt bring the children of Israel into the land which I sware unto them; and *I will be with thee.*'' Joshua was not to be discouraged or faint-hearted because of the predicted unfaithfulness of the people. He was, like his great progenitor, to be strong in faith giving glory to God. He was to move forward with joyful confidence, leaning on the arm and confiding in the word of Jehovah, the covenant-God of Israel, in nothing terrified by his adversaries, but resting in the precious, soul-sustaining assurance that, however the seed of Abraham might fail to obey, and, as a consequence, bring down judgment on themselves, yet the God of Abraham would infallibly maintain and make good His promise, and glorify His name in the final restoration and everlasting blessing of His chosen people.

All this comes out with uncommon vividness and power in the song of Moses, and Joshua was called to serve in the faith of it. He was to fix his eye, not upon Israel's ways, but upon the eternal stability of the divine covenant with Abraham. He was to conduct Israel across the Jordan and plant them in that fair inheritance designed for them in the purpose of God. Had Joshua occupied his mind with Israel, he must have flung down his sword and given up in despair; but no, he had to encourage himself in the Lord his God, and serve in the energy of a faith that endures as seeing Him who is invisible.

Precious, soul-sustaining, God-honoring faith! May the reader, whatever be his line of life or sphere of action, know, in the profoundest depths of his soul, the moral power of this divine principle. May every beloved child of God and every servant of Christ know it. It is the only thing which will enable us to grapple with the difficulties, hindrances, and hostile influences which surround us in the

scene through which we are passing, and to finish
our course with joy.

"And it came to pass when Moses had made an
end of writing the words of this law in a book, until
they were finished, that Moses commanded the Levites, which bare the ark of the covenant of the
Lord, saying, 'Take this book of the law, and put
it in the side of the ark of the covenant of the Lord
your God, *that it may be there for a witness against
thee*. For I know thy rebellion, and thy stiff neck;
behold, while I am yet alive with you this day, ye
have been rebellious against the Lord; and how
much more after my death? Gather unto me all the
elders of your tribes, and your officers, that I may
speak these words in their ears, and call heaven and
earth to record against them. For I know that after
my death ye will utterly corrupt yourselves, and
turn aside from the way which I have commanded
you; and evil will befall you in the latter days; because ye will do evil in the sight of the Lord, to
provoke Him to anger through the work of your
hands.'"

How forcibly we are here reminded of Paul's
farewell address to the elders of Ephesus!—"For I
know this, that after my departing shall grievous
wolves enter in among you, not sparing the flock.
Also from among your own selves shall men arise,
speaking perverse things, to draw away disciples
after them. Therefore *watch, and remember*, that by
the space of three years I ceased not to warn every
one night and day with tears. And now, brethren,

I commend you to God, and to the word of His grace, which is able to build you up, and to give you an inheritance among all them which are sanctified." (Acts xx. 29–32.)

Man is the same always and every where. His history is a blotted one from beginning to end. But oh, it is such a relief and solace to the heart to know and remember that God is ever the same, and His Word abides and is "settled forever in heaven." It was hid in the side of the ark of the covenant and there preserved intact, spite of all the grievous sin and folly of the people. This gives sweet rest to the heart at all times, in the face of human failure, and the wreck and ruin of every thing committed to man's hand. "The Word of our God shall stand forever;" and while it bears a true and solemn testimony against man and his ways, it also conveys home to the heart the most precious and tranquilizing assurance that God is above all man's sin and folly, that His resources are absolutely inexhaustible, and that ere long His glory shall shine out and fill the whole scene. The Lord be praised for the deep consolation of all this!

CHAPTER XXXII.

"AND Moses spake in the ears of all the congregation of Israel the words of this song, until they were ended." It is not too much to say that one of the very grandest and most comprehensive

sections in the divine volume now lies open before
us and claims our prayerful attention. It takes in
the whole range of God's dealings with Israel from
first to last, and presents a most solemn record of
their grievous sin and of divine wrath and judgment.
But, blessed be God, it begins and ends with Him;
and this is full of deepest and richest blessing for
the soul. If it were not so, if we had only the
melancholy story of man's ways, we should be completely overwhelmed; but in this magnificent song,
as indeed in the entire volume, we begin with God
and we end with God. This tranquilizes the spirit
most blessedly, and enables us, in calm and holy
confidence, to pursue the history of man, to see
every thing going to pieces in his hands, and to mark
the actings of the enemy in opposition to the counsels
and purposes of God. We can afford to see the complete failure and ruin of the creature, in every shape
and form, because we know and are assured that God
will be God in spite of every thing. He will have
the upper hand in the end, and then all will be—
must be right. God shall be all in all, and there
shall be neither enemy nor evil occurrent throughout
that vast universe of bliss of which our adorable
Lord Christ shall be the central sun forever.

But we must turn to the song.

"Give ear, O ye heavens, and I will speak; and
hear, O earth, the words of my mouth." Heaven and
earth are summoned to hearken to this magnificent
outpouring. Its range is commensurate with its vast
moral importance. "My doctrine shall drop as the

rain, my speech shall distill as the dew, as the small rain upon the tender herb, and as the showers upon the grass; because I will publish the name of the Lord; ascribe ye greatness unto our God."

Here lies the solid, the imperishable foundation of every thing. Come what may, the name of our God shall stand forever. No power of earth or hell can possibly countervail the divine purpose, or hinder the outshining of the divine glory. What sweet rest this gives the heart in the midst of this dark, sorrowful, sin-stricken world, and in the face of the apparently successful schemes of the enemy! Our refuge, our resource, our sweet relief and solace, are found in the name of the Lord our God, the God and Father of our Lord Jesus Christ. Truly the publication of that blessed name must ever be as the refreshing dew and tender rain falling upon the heart. This is, of a truth, the divine and heavenly doctrine on which the soul can feed, and by which it is sustained, at all times, and under all circumstances.

"He is *the* Rock"—not merely *a* rock. There is, there can be, no other Rock but Himself. Eternal and universal homage to His glorious name!—"His work is perfect;"—not a single flaw in aught that comes from His blessed hand; all bears the stamp of absolute perfection. This will be made manifest to all created intelligences by and by. It is manifest to faith now, and is a spring of divine consolation to all true believers. The very thought of it distills as the dew upon the thirsty soul. "For *all* His ways are judgment; a God of truth, and without iniquity; just and right is He." Infidels may cavil and sneer; they may, in their fancied wisdom, try to pick holes in the divine actings; but their folly shall be manifest to all. "Let God be true, but every man a liar; as it is written, 'That Thou mightest be justified in Thy sayings, and mightest overcome when Thou art judged.'" God must have the upper hand in the end. Let men beware how they presume to call in question the sayings and doings of the only true, the only wise, and the almighty God.

There is something uncommonly fine in the opening notes of this song. It gives the sweetest rest to the heart to know that however man, and even the people of God, may fail and come to ruin, yet we have to do with One who abideth faithful and cannot deny Himself, whose ways are absolutely perfect, and who, when the enemy has done his very utmost, and brought all his malignant designs to a head, shall glorify Himself, and bring in universal and everlasting blessedness.

True, He has to execute judgment upon man's ways. He is constrained to take down the rod of discipline and use it, at times, with terrible severity upon His own people. He is perfectly intolerant of evil in those who bear His holy name. All this comes out, with special solemnity in the song before us. Israel's ways are exposed and dealt with unsparingly; nothing is allowed to pass; all is set forth with holy precision and faithfulness. Thus we read, "They have corrupted themselves; their spot is not the spot of His children; they are a perverse and crooked generation. Do ye thus requite the Lord, O foolish people and unwise? is not He thy Father that hath bought thee? hath He not made thee, and established thee?''

Here we have the first note of reproof in this song, but no sooner has it fallen on the ear than it is followed by a most precious outpouring of testimony to the goodness, loving-kindness, faithfulness, and tender mercy of Jehovah, the Elohim of Israel, and the Most High, or Elion of all the earth. ''Remember the days of old, consider the years of many generations; ask thy father, and he will show thee; thy elders, and they will tell thee; when the Most High [God's millennial title] divided to the nations their inheritance, when He separated the sons of Adam, He set the bounds of the people according to the number of the children of Israel.

What a glorious fact is here unfolded to our view! a fact but little understood or taken account of by the nations of the earth. How little do men consider that, in the original settlement of the great national boundaries, the Most High had direct reference to ''the children of Israel''! Yet thus it was, and the reader should seek to grasp this grand and intensely interesting fact. When we look at geography and history from a divine stand-point, we find that Canaan and the seed of Jacob are God's centre. Yes; Canaan, a little strip of land lying along the eastern coast of the Mediterranean, with an area of eleven thousand square miles, (about a third of the extent of Ireland,) is the centre of God's geography, and the twelve tribes of Israel are the central object of God's history. How little have geographers and historians thought of this! They have described countries, and written the history of nations, which, in geographical extent and political importance, far outstrip Palestine and its people, according to human thinking, but which, in God's account, are as nothing compared with that little strip of land which He deigns to call His own, and which it is His fixed purpose to inherit through the seed of Abraham His friend.*

---

* How true it is that God's thoughts are not man's thoughts, or His ways as man's ways! Man attaches importance to extensive territories, material strength, pecuniary resources, well-disciplined armies, powerful fleets; God, on the contrary, takes no account of such things; they are to Him as the small dust of the balance. "Have ye not known? have ye not heard? hath it not been told you from the beginning? have ye not understood from the foundations of the earth? It is He that sitteth upon the circle of the earth, and the inhabitants thereof are as grasshoppers; that stretcheth out the heavens as a curtain, and spreadeth them out as a tent to dwell in; that bringeth the princes to nothing; He maketh the judges of the earth as vanity." Hence we may see the moral reason why, in selecting a country to be the centre of His earthly plans and counsels, Jehovah did not select one of vast extent, but a very small and insignificant strip of land, of little account in the thoughts of men. But oh, what importance attaches to that little spot! what principles have been unfolded there! what events have taken place there! what deeds have been done there! what plans and purposes are yet to be wrought out there! There is not a spot on the face of the earth so interesting to the heart of God as the land of Canaan and the city of Jerusalem. Scripture teems with evidence as to this: we could fill a small volume with proofs. The time is rapidly approaching when living facts will do what the fullest and clearest testimony of Scripture fails to do, namely, convince men that the land of Israel was, is, and ever shall be God's earthly centre. All other nations owe their importance, their interest, their place in the pages of inspiration, simply to the

We cannot attempt to dwell upon this most important and suggestive fact, but we would ask the reader to give it his serious consideration. He will find it fully developed and strikingly illustrated in the prophetic scriptures of the Old and New Testaments. "The Lord's portion is His people; Jacob is the lot of His inheritance. He found him in a desert land, and in the waste howling wilderness; He led him about, He instructed him, He kept him *as the apple of His eye*"—the most sensitive, delicate part of the human body.—"As an eagle stirreth up her nest, fluttereth over her young, spreadeth abroad her wings, taketh them, beareth them upon her wings;"—to teach them to fly and to keep them from falling—"so the Lord alone did lead him, and there was no strange god with him. He made him ride on the high places of the earth, that he might eat the increase of the fields; and He made him to suck honey out of the rock, and oil out of the flinty rock; butter of kine, and milk of sheep, with fat of lambs, and rams of the breed of Bashan, and goats, with the fat of kidneys of wheat; and thou didst drink the pure blood of the grape."

Need we say that the primary application of all this is to Israel? No doubt the Church may learn from it and profit by it, but to apply it to the Church would involve a double mistake, a mistake of the most serious nature; it would involve nothing less

---

fact of their being, in some way or other, connected with the land and people of Israel. How little do historians know or think of this! But surely every one who loves God ought to know it and ponder it.

than the reducing of the Church from a heavenly to an earthly level, and the most unwarrantable interference with Israel's divinely appointed place and portion. What, we may lawfully inquire, has the Church of God, the body of Christ, to do with the settlement of the nations of the earth? Nothing whatever. The Church, *according to the mind of God*, is a stranger on the earth. Her portion, her hope, her home, her inheritance, her all, is heavenly. It would make no difference in the current of this world's history if the Church had never been heard of. Her calling, her walk, her destiny, her whole character and course, her principles and morals, are or ought to be heavenly. The Church has nothing to do with the politics of this world. Her citizenship is in heaven, from whence she looks for the Saviour. She proves false to her Lord, false to her calling, false to her principles, in so far as she meddles with the affairs of nations. It is her high and holy privilege to be linked and morally identified with a rejected, crucified, risen, and glorified Christ. She has no more to do with the present system of things, or with the current of this world's history, than her glorified Head in the heavens. "They," says our Lord Christ, speaking of His people, "are not of the world, even as I am not of the world."

This is conclusive. It fixes our position and our path in the most precise and definite way possible. "As He is, so are we in this world." This involves a double truth, namely, our perfect acceptance with God and our complete separation from the world.

We are *in* the world, but not *of* it. We have to pass through it as pilgrims and strangers, looking out for the coming of our Lord, the appearing of the Bright and Morning Star. It is no part of our business to interfere with municipal or political matters. We are called and exhorted to obey the powers that be, to pray for all in authority, to pay tribute, and owe no man any thing; "to be blameless and harmless, the sons of God without rebuke in the midst of a crooked and perverse nation," among whom we are to "shine as lights in the world, holding forth the word of life."

From all this we may gather something of the immense practical importance of "rightly dividing the word of truth." We have but little idea of the injury done, both to the truth of God and to the souls of His people, by confounding Israel with the Church—the earthly and the heavenly. It hinders all progress in the knowledge of Scripture, and mars the integrity of Christian walk and testimony. This may seem a strong statement, but we have seen the truth of it painfully illustrated times without number : and we feel that we cannot too urgently call the attention of the reader to the subject. We have more than once referred to it in the progress of our studies on the Pentateuch, and therefore we shall not further pursue it here, but proceed with our chapter.

At verse 15, we reach a very different note in the song of Moses. Up to this point, we have had before us God and His actings, His purposes, His counsels, His thoughts, His loving interest in His people Israel, His tender, gracious dealings with them. All this is full of deepest, richest blessing. There is, there can be, no drawback here. When we have God and His ways before us, there is no hindrance to the heart's enjoyment. All is perfection—absolute, divine perfection, and as we dwell upon it, we are filled with wonder, love, and praise.

But there is the human side, and here, alas! all is failure and disappointment. Thus at the fifteenth verse of our chapter we read, "But Jeshurun waxed fat and kicked"—what a very full and suggestive statement! How vividly it presents, in its brief compass, the moral history of Israel!—"thou art waxen fat, thou art grown thick, thou art covered with fatness; then he forsook God which made him, and lightly esteemed the Rock of his salvation. They provoked Him to jealousy with strange gods, with abominations provoked they Him to anger. They sacrificed unto devils, not to God; to gods whom they knew not, to new gods that came newly up, whom your fathers feared not. Of the Rock that begat thee thou art unmindful, and hast forgotten God that formed thee."

There is a solemn voice in all this for the writer and the reader. We are each of us in danger of treading the moral path indicated by the words just quoted. Surrounded on all hands by the rich and varied mercies of God, we are apt to make use of them to nourish a spirit of self-complacency. We make use of the gifts to shut out the Giver. In a word, we, too, like Israel, wax fat and kick—we

forget God. We lose the sweet and precious sense
of His presence and of His perfect sufficiency, and
turn to other objects, as Israel did to false gods.
How often do we forget the Rock that begat us, the
God that formed us, the Lord that redeemed us!
And all this is so much the more inexcusable in us,
inasmuch as our privileges are so much higher than
theirs. We are brought into a relationship and a
position of which Israel knew absolutely nothing;
our privileges and blessings are of the very highest
order; it is our privilege to have fellowship with the
Father and with His Son Jesus Christ; we are the
objects of that perfect love which stopped not short
of introducing us into a position in which it can be
said of us, "As He [Christ] is, so are we in this
world." Nothing could exceed the blessedness of
this; even divine love itself could go no further
than this. It is not merely that the love of God
has been manifested to us in the gift and the death
of His only begotten and well-beloved Son, and in
giving us His Spirit, but it has been made perfect
with us by placing us in the very same position as
that blessed One on the throne of God.

All this is perfectly marvelous. It passeth knowledge. And yet how prone we are to forget the
blessed One who has so loved us and wrought for
us and blessed us! How often we slip away from
Him in the spirit of our minds and the affections of
our hearts! It is not merely a question of what the
professing church, as a whole, has done, but the very
much deeper, closer, more pointed question of what

our own wretched hearts are constantly prone to do.
We are apt to forget God, and to turn to other
objects, to our serious loss and His dishonor.

Would we know how the heart of God feels as to
all this? would we form any thing like a correct
idea of how He resents it? Let us hearken to the
burning words addressed to His erring people Israel,
the overwhelming strains of the song of Moses.
May we have grace to hear them aright, and deeply
profit by them.

"And when the Lord saw it, He abhorred them,
*because of the provoking of His sons and of His
daughters.* And He said, 'I will hide My face from
them, I will see what their end shall be;'"—alas!
alas! a truly deplorable end—" 'for they are a very
froward generation, children in whom is no faith.
They have moved Me to jealousy with that which
is not God; they have provoked Me to anger with
their vanities; and I will move them to jealousy
with those which are not a people; I will provoke
them to anger with a foolish nation. For a fire is
kindled in Mine anger, and shall burn unto the
lowest hell, and shall consume the earth with her
increase, and shall set on fire the foundations of the
mountains. I will heap mischiefs upon them; I
will spend Mine arrows upon them. They shall be
burnt with hunger, and devoured with burning heat
and with bitter destruction; I will also send the teeth
of beasts upon them, with the poison of serpents
of the dust. The sword without and terror within
shall destroy both the young man and the virgin,

the suckling also with the man of gray hairs.'"
(Ver. 19–26.)

Here we have a most solemn record of God's
governmental dealings with His people — a record
eminently calculated to set forth the awful truth of
Hebrews x. 31—"It is a fearful thing to fall into
the hands of the living God." The history of Israel
in the past, their condition at present, and what
they are yet to pass through in the future—all goes
to prove, in the most impressive manner, that "our
God is a consuming fire." No nation on the face
of the earth has ever been called to pass through
such severe discipline as the nation of Israel. As
the Lord reminds them in those deeply solemn
words, "You only have I known of all the families
of the earth, therefore will I punish you for your
iniquities." No other nation was ever called to
occupy the highly privileged place of actual relationship with Jehovah. This dignity was reserved for
one nation; but the very dignity was the basis of a
most solemn responsibility. If they were called to
be His people, they were responsible to conduct
themselves in a way worthy of such a wondrous
position, or else have to undergo the heaviest chas-
tenings ever endured by any nation under the sun.
Men may reason about all this; they may raise all
manner of questions as to the moral consistency of
a benevolent Being acting according to the terms
set forth in verses 22–25 of our chapter. But all
such questions and reasonings must sooner or later
be discovered to be utter folly. It is perfectly

25

useless for men to argue against the solemn actings of divine government, or the terrible severity of the discipline exercised toward the chosen people of God. How much wiser and better and safer to be warned by the facts of Israel's history to flee from the wrath to come, and lay hold upon eternal life and full salvation revealed in the precious gospel of God!

And then, with regard to the use which Christians should make of the record of His dealings with His earthly people, we are bound to turn it to most profitable account by learning from it the urgent need of walking humbly, watchfully, and faithfully in our high and holy position. True, we are the possessors of eternal life, the privileged subjects of that magnificent grace which reigns through righteousness unto eternal life by Jesus Christ our Lord; we are members of the body of Christ, temples of the Holy Ghost, and heirs of eternal glory; but does all this afford any warrant for neglecting the warning voice which Israel's history utters in our ears? are we, because of our incomparably higher privileges, to walk carelessly and despise the wholesome admonitions which Israel's history supplies? God forbid! Nay, we are bound to give earnest heed to the things which the Holy Ghost has written for our learning. The higher our privileges, the richer our blessings, the nearer our relationship, the more does it become us, the more solemnly are we bound, to be faithful, and to seek in all things to carry ourselves in such a way as to be well-pleasing to Him who has called us into the very highest and most blessed place that even His perfect love could bestow. The Lord, in His great goodness, grant that we may, in true purpose of heart, ponder these things in His holy presence, and earnestly seek to serve Him with reverence and godly fear.

But we must proceed with our chapter.

At verse 26, we have a point of deepest interest in connection with the history of the divine dealings with Israel. "I said I would scatter them into corners, *I would make the remembrance of them to cease from among men.*" And why did He not? The answer to this question presents a truth of infinite value and importance to Israel—a truth which lies at the very foundation of all their future blessing. No doubt, so far as they are concerned, they deserved to have their remembrance blotted out from among men; but God has His own thoughts and counsels and purposes respecting them; and not only so, but He takes account of the thoughts and actings of the nations in reference to His people. This comes out with singular force and beauty at verse 27. He condescends to give us His reasons for not obliterating every trace of the sinful and rebellious people —and oh, what a touching reason it is!—"*Were it not that I feared the wrath of the enemy,* lest their adversaries should behave themselves strangely, and lest they should say, Our hand is high, and the Lord hath not done all this."

Can aught be more affecting than the grace that breathes in these words? God will not permit the nations to behave themselves strangely toward His poor erring people. He will use them as His rod of discipline, but the moment they attempt, in the indulgence of their own bitter animosity, to exceed their appointed limit, He will break the rod in pieces, and make it manifest to all that He Himself is dealing with His beloved though erring people, for their ultimate blessing and His glory.

This is a truth of unspeakable preciousness. It is the fixed purpose of Jehovah to teach all the nations of the earth that Israel has a special place in His heart, and a destined place of pre-eminence on the earth. This is beyond all question. The pages of the prophets furnish a body of evidence perfectly unanswerable on the point. If nations forget or oppose, so much the worse for them. It is utterly vain for them to attempt to countervail the divine purpose, for they may rest assured that the God of Abraham, Isaac, and Jacob will confound every scheme formed against the people of His choice. Men may think, in their pride and folly, that their hand is high, but they will have to learn that God's hand is higher still.

But our space does not admit of our dwelling upon this deeply interesting subject; we must allow the reader to pursue it for himself, in the light of holy Scripture. He will find it a most profitable and refreshing study. Most gladly would we accompany him through the precious pages of the prophetic scriptures, but we must just now confine ourselves to the magnificent song which is in itself a remarkable epitome of the entire teaching on the point—a brief but comprehensive and impressive history of God's ways with Israel and Israel's ways with God, from first to last—a history strikingly illustrative of the great principles of grace, law, government, and glory.

At verse 29, we have a very touching appeal. "O that they were wise, that they understood this, that they would *consider their latter end!* How should one chase a thousand, and two put ten thousand to flight, except their Rock had sold them, and the Lord had shut them up? For their rock is not as our Rock, even our enemies themselves being judges."— There is, there can be, but the one Rock, blessed throughout all ages be His glorious name!—"For their vine is of the vine of Sodom, and of the fields of Gomorrah; their grapes are grapes of gall, their clusters are bitter; their wine is the poison of dragons, and the cruel venom of asps."

Terrible picture of a people's moral condition drawn by a master-hand! Such is the divine estimate of the real state of all those whose rock was not as the Rock of Israel. But a day of vengeance will come. It is delayed in long-suffering mercy, but it *will* come as sure as there is a God on the throne of heaven. A day is coming when all those nations which have dealt proudly with Israel shall have to answer at the bar of the Son of Man for their conduct, hear His solemn sentence, and meet His unsparing wrath.

"Is not this laid up in store with Me, and *sealed*

up among My treasures? To Me belongeth vengeance and recompense; their foot shall slide in due
time; for the day of their calamity is at hand, and
the things that shall come upon them make haste.
For the Lord shall judge [vindicate, defend, or
avenge] His people, and *repent Himself for His
servants*, when He seeth that their power is gone,
and there is none shut up or left." Precious grace
for Israel by and by—for each, for all, *now*, who
feel and own their need˙

"And He shall say, Where are their gods, their
rock in whom they trusted; which did eat the fat
of their sacrifices, and drank the wine of their drink-
offerings? let them rise up and help you and be your
protection. See now that I, even I, am He, and
there is no god with Me; I kill, and I make alive;
I wound, and I heal;"—wound in governmental
wrath, and heal in pardoning grace; all homage to
His great and holy name, throughout the everlasting
ages!—"neither is there any that can deliver out of
My hand. For I lift up My hand to heaven, and
say, 'I live forever.'"—Glory be to God in the highest! Let all created intelligences adore His match-
less name!—"If I whet My glittering sword, and
Mine hand take hold on judgment,"—as it most
assuredly will—"I will render vengeance to Mine
enemies, and will reward them that hate Me"—
whoever and wherever they are. Tremendous sentence for all whom it may concern, for all haters of
God—all lovers of pleasure rather than lovers of
God!—"I will make Mine arrows drunk with blood,

and My sword shall devour flesh; and that with the blood of the slain and of the captives, *from the beginning of revenges upon the enemy.*"

Here we reach the end of the heavy record of judgment, wrath, and vengeance so briefly presented in this song of Moses, but so largely unfolded throughout the prophetic scriptures. The reader can refer, with much interest and profit, to Ezekiel xxxviii. and xxxix, where we have the judgment of Gog and Magog, the great northern foe who is to come up, at the end, against the land of Israel, and there meet his ignominious fall and utter destruction.

He may also turn to Joel iii, which opens with words of balm and consolation for the Israel of the future.—"For behold, in those days, and in that time, when I shall bring again the captivity of Judah and Jerusalem, I will also gather all nations, and will bring them down into the valley of Jehoshaphat, and will plead with them there for My people and for My heritage Israel, whom they have scattered among the nations, and parted My land." Thus he will see how perfectly the voices of the prophets harmonize with the song of Moses, and how fully, how clearly, and how unanswerably, in both the one and the other, does the Holy Ghost set forth and establish the grand truth of Israel's future restoration, supremacy, and glory.

And then, how truly delightful is the closing note of our song! how magnificently it places the topstone upon the whole superstructure! All the hostile nations are judged, under whatever style or title they appear upon the scene, whether it be Gog and Magog, the Assyrian, or the king of the north—all the foes of Israel shall be confounded and consigned to everlasting perdition, and then this sweet note falls upon the ear,—"REJOICE, O YE NATIONS, WITH HIS PEOPLE; FOR HE WILL AVENGE THE BLOOD OF HIS SERVANTS, AND WILL RENDER VENGEANCE TO HIS ADVERSARIES, AND WILL BE MERCIFUL UNTO HIS LAND AND TO HIS PEOPLE."

Here ends this marvelous song, one of the very finest, fullest, and most forcible utterances in the whole volume of God. It begins and ends with God, and takes in, in its comprehensive range, the history of His earthly people Israel—past, present, and future. It shows us the ordering of the nations in direct reference to the divine purpose as to the seed of Abraham. It unfolds the final judgment of all those nations that have acted or shall yet act in opposition to the chosen seed; and then, when Israel is fully restored and blessed, according to the covenant made with their fathers, the saved nations are summoned to rejoice with them.

How glorious is all this! What a splendid circle of truth is presented to the vision of our souls in the thirty-second chapter of Deuteronomy! Well may it be said, "God is *the* Rock, His work is perfect." Here the heart can rest, in holy tranquillity, come what may. Every thing may go to pieces in man's hand, all that is merely human may and must issue in hopeless wreck and ruin, but "the Rock" shall stand forever, and every "work" of the divine Hand

shall shine in everlasting perfection to the glory of
God and the perfect blessing of His people.

Such, then, is the song of Moses; such its scope,
range, and application. The intelligent reader does
not need to be told that the Church of God, the
body of Christ, the mystery of which the blessed
apostle Paul was made the minister, finds no place
in this song. When Moses wrote this song, the
mystery of the Church lay hid in the bosom of God.
If we do not see this, we are wholly incompetent to
interpret, or even to understand, the holy Scriptures.
To a simple mind, taught exclusively by Scripture,
it is as clear as a sunbeam that the song of Moses
has for its thesis the government of God, in connection with Israel and the nations; for its sphere, the
earth; and for its centre, the land of Canaan.

"And Moses came and spake all the words of this
song in the ears of the people, he, and Hoshea the
son of Nun. And Moses made an end of speaking
all these words to all Israel; and he said unto them,
'*Set your hearts unto all the words* which I testify
among you this day, which *ye shall command your
children to observe to do, all the words of this law.*
For it is not a vain thing for you, because *it is your
life;* and through this thing ye shall prolong your
days in the land, whither ye go over Jordan to possess it.'" (Ver. 44-47.)

Thus, from first to last, through every section of
this precious book of Deuteronomy, we find Moses,
that beloved and most honored servant of God,
urging upon the people the solemn duty of implicit,

unqualified, hearty obedience to the Word of God. In this lay the precious secret of life, peace, progress, prosperity—all. They had nothing else to do but *obey*. Blessed business! happy, holy duty! May it be ours, beloved reader, in this day of conflict and confusion, in the which man's will is so fearfully dominant. The world and the so-called church are rushing on together, with appalling rapidity, along the dark pathway of self-will—a pathway which must end in the blackness of darkness forever. Let us bear this in mind, and earnestly seek to tread the narrow path of simple obedience to all the precious commandments of our Lord and Saviour Jesus Christ. Thus shall our hearts be kept in sweet peace; and although we may seem, to the men of this world, and even to professing Christians, to be odd and narrow-minded, let us not be moved the breadth of a hair from the path indicated by the Word of God. May the word of Christ dwell in us richly, and the peace of Christ rule in our hearts, *until the end.*

It is very remarkable, and indeed eminently impressive, to find our chapter closing with another reference to Jehovah's governmental dealing with His beloved servant Moses. "And the Lord spake unto Moses *that self-same day*"—the very day in which he uttered his song in the ears of the people—"saying,'Get thee up into this mountain Abarim, unto Mount Nebo, which is in the land of Moab, that is over against Jericho; and behold the land of Canaan, which I give unto the children of Israel

for a possession; and die in the mount whither thou
goest up, and be gathered unto thy people; as Aaron
thy brother died in Mount Hor, and was gathered
unto his people; because ye trespassed against Me
among the children of Israel at the waters of
Meribah-Kadesh, in the wilderness of Zin, because
ye sanctified Me not in the midst of the children of
Israel. Yet thou shalt see the land before thee; *but
thou shalt not go thither unto the land which I give the
children of Israel.*'" (Ver. 48–52.)

How solemn and soul-subduing is the government
of God! Surely it ought to make the heart tremble
at the very thought of disobedience. If such an
eminent servant as Moses was judged for speaking
unadvisedly with his lips, what will be the end of
those who live from day to day, week to week, month
to month, and year to year in deliberate and habitual
neglect of the plainest commandments of God, and
positive self-willed rejection of His authority?

Oh, for a lowly mind, a broken and contrite
heart! This is what God looks for and delights in;
it is with such He can make His blessed abode.
"To this man will I look, even to him who is poor
and of a contrite spirit, and trembleth at My word."
God, in His infinite goodness, grant much of this
sweet spirit to each of His beloved children, for
Jesus Christ's sake.

CHAPTER XXXIII

"AND this is the blessing wherewith Moses, the man of God, blessed the children of Israel before his death."

It is full of interest and comfort to find that the last words of the lawgiver were words of unmingled blessing. We have dwelt upon his various discourses—those solemn, searching, and deeply affecting homilies addressed to the congregation of Israel; we have meditated upon that marvelous song, with its mingled notes of grace and government: but we are now called to hearken to words of most precious benediction, words of sweetest comfort and consolation, words flowing from the very heart of the God of Israel and giving His own loving thoughts respecting them, and His onlook into their glorious future.

The reader will doubtless notice a marked difference between the last words of Moses as recorded in Deuteronomy xxxiii. and the last words of Jacob as given in Genesis xlix. It is needless to say that both are given by the same pen—both divinely inspired, and hence, although they differ, they do not and cannot clash; there is, there can be, no discrepancy between two sections of the volume of God. This is a cardinal truth, a vital and fundamental principle with every devout Christian, every true believer—a truth to be tenaciously grasped and faithfully confessed, in the face of all the ignorant and insolent assaults of infidelity.

We are not, of course, going to enter upon an elaborate comparison of the two chapters; this would be impossible just now, on various grounds. We are obliged to be as concise and brief as possible. But there is one grand point of difference, which can be seized at a glance. Jacob gives the history of the actings of his sons—some of them, alas! most sad and humiliating : Moses, on the contrary, presents the actings of divine grace, whether in them or toward them. This will at once account for the difference. The evil actings of Reuben, of Simeon, and of Levi are recorded by Jacob, but entirely omitted by Moses. Is this discrepancy ? Nay, but divine harmony. Jacob views his sons in their personal history ; Moses views them in their covenant-relationship with Jehovah. Jacob gives us human failure, infirmity, and sin : Moses gives us divine faithfulness, goodness, and loving-kindness. Jacob gives us human actings, and judgment thereon : Moses gives us divine counsels, and unmingled blessing flowing out of them. Thanks and praise to our God, His counsels and His blessings and His glory are above and beyond all human failure, sin, and folly. He will ultimately have it all His own way, and that forever ; then, Israel and the nations shall be fully blessed, and shall rejoice together in the abundant goodness of God, and celebrate His praise from shore to shore, and from the river to the ends of the earth.

We shall now do little more than quote for the reader the various blessings of the tribes. They are full of most precious instruction, and do not call for much in the way of exposition.

"And he said, 'The Lord came from Sinai, and rose up from Seir unto them; He shined forth from Mount Paran, and He came with ten thousands of saints [holy ones]; from His right hand went a fiery law for them. Yea, *He loved the people;*"—precious, unfailing source of all their future blessing!—"*all His saints are in Thy hand;*"—true secret of their perfect security!—"and they sat down *at Thy feet;*"—the only safe and proper attitude for them, for us, for each, for all!—"every one shall receive of Thy words."—Blessed boon! precious treasure! Every word that proceedeth out of the mouth of the Lord is more precious, by far, than thousands of gold and silver; sweeter also than honey and the honey-comb.—"Moses commanded us a law, even the inheritance of the congregation of Jacob. And he was king in Jeshurun, when the heads of the people and the tribes of Israel were gathered together. Let Reuben live and not die, and let not his men be few.'"

We have nothing here about Reuben's instability, nothing about his sin. Grace is in the ascendant; blessings are flowing in rich abundance from the loving heart of the One who delights to bless and to surround Himself with hearts filled to overflowing with the sense of His goodness.

"And this is the blessing of Judah; and he said,

'Hear, Lord, the voice of Judah, and bring him unto his people; let his hands be sufficient for him; and be Thou a help to him from his enemies.'" Judah is the royal line. "Our Lord sprang out of Judah," thus illustrating, in a truly marvelous manner, how divine grace rises, in its majesty, above human sin, and triumphs gloriously over circumstances which reveal man's utter weakness. "Judas begat Phares and Zara of Thamar"! Who but the Holy Spirit could have penned these words? How plainly they declare that God's thoughts are not as our thoughts! What human hand would have introduced Thamar into the genealogical line of our adorable Lord and Saviour Jesus Christ? Not one. The stamp of divinity is strikingly impressed on Matthew i. 3, as it is upon every clause of the holy volume from beginning to end. The Lord be praised that it is so!

"Judah, thou art he whom thy brethren shall praise; thy hand shall be in the neck of thine enemies; thy father's children shall bow down before thee. Judah is a lion's whelp; from the prey, my son, thou art gone up; he stooped down, he couched as a lion, and as an old lion; who shall rouse him up? The sceptre shall not depart from Judah, nor a lawgiver from between his feet, until Shiloh come; and unto him shall the gathering of the people be. Binding his foal unto the vine, and his ass's colt unto the choice vine; he washed his garments in wine, and his clothes in the blood of grapes; his eyes shall be red with wine, and his teeth white with milk." (Gen. xlix. 8-12.)

"And I saw in the right hand of Him that sat on the throne a book written within and on the backside, sealed with seven seals. And I saw a strong angel proclaiming with a loud voice, 'Who is worthy to open the book, and to loose the seals thereof?' And no man in heaven, nor in earth, neither under the earth, was able to open the book, neither to look thereon. And I wept much, because no man was found worthy to open and to read the book, neither to look thereon. And one of the elders saith unto me, 'Weep not: behold, *the Lion of the tribe of Juda*, the Root of David, hath prevailed to open the book and to loose the seven seals thereof.' And I beheld, and lo, in the midst of the throne and of the four living creatures, and in the midst of the elders, stood *a Lamb*, as it had been *slain*, having seven horns and seven eyes, which are the seven spirits of God sent forth into all the earth."

How highly favored is the tribe of Judah! Surely, to be in the genealogical line from which our Lord sprang is a high honor, and yet we know —for our Lord Himself has told us—that it is far higher, far more blessed, to hear the Word of God and keep it. To do the will of God, to treasure up in our hearts His precious commandments, brings us morally nearer to Christ than even the fact of being of His kindred according to the flesh. (Matt. xii. 46-50.)

"And of Levi he said, 'Let Thy Thummin and Thy Urim [lights and perfections] be with Thy holy one, whom Thou didst prove at Massah, and with whom Thou didst strive at the waters of Meribah; *who said unto his father and to his mother, I have not seen him; neither did he acknowledge his brethren, nor knew* his own children; *for they have observed Thy word and kept Thy covenant.* They shall teach Jacob Thy judgments, and Israel Thy law; they shall put incense before Thee, and whole burnt-sacrifice upon Thine altar. Bless, Lord, his substance, and accept the work of his hands; smite through the loins of them that rise against him, and of them that hate him, that they rise not again.''' (Ver. 8–11.)

The reader will notice the fact that Simeon is left out here, though so intimately associated with Levi in Genesis xlix. "Simeon and Levi are brethren; instruments of cruelty are in their habitations. O my soul, come not thou into their secret; unto their assembly, mine honor, be not thou united; for *in their anger they slew a man,* and *in their self-will* they digged down a wall. Cursed be their anger, for it was fierce; and their wrath, for it was cruel: I will divide them in Jacob, and scatter them in Israel."

Now, when we compare Genesis xlix, with Deuteronomy xxxiii, we observe two things, namely, human responsibility on the one hand, and divine sovereignty on the other. Moreover, we see nature and its actings; grace and its fruits. Jacob looks at Simeon and Levi linked together in nature, and displaying nature's tempers and ways. So far as they were concerned, they both alike deserved the curse; but in Levi, we see the glorious triumphs

30

of sovereign grace. It was grace which enabled Levi, in the days of the golden calf, to gird on the sword and stand for the glory of the God of Israel. "Then Moses stood in the gate of the camp, and said, 'Who is on the Lord's side? let him come unto me.' And all the sons of Levi gathered themselves together unto him. And he said unto them, 'Thus saith the Lord God of Israel, Put every man his sword by his side, and go in and out from gate to gate throughout the camp, and slay every man his brother, and every man his companion, and every man his neighbor.' And the children of Levi did according to the word of Moses; and there fell of the people that day about three thousand men. For Moses had said, 'Consecrate yourselves to-day to the Lord, even every man upon his son, and upon his brother; that he may bestow upon you a blessing this day.'" (Ex. xxxii. 26–29.)

Where was Simeon on this occasion? He was with Levi in the day of nature's self-will, fierce anger, and cruel wrath; why not in the day of bold decision for Jehovah? He was ready to go with his brother to avenge a family insult, why not to vindicate the honor of God, insulted as it was by the idolatrous act of the whole congregation? Will any one say he was not responsible? Let such an one beware how he raises such a question. The call of Moses was addressed to the whole congregation; Levi alone responded, and he got the blessing. He stood for God in a dark and evil day, and for this he was honored with the priesthood—the very highest

dignity that could be conferred upon him. The call
was addressed to Simeon as well as to Levi, but
Simeon did not respond. Is there any difficulty
here? To a mere theologian there may be, but to
a devout Christian there is none. God is sovereign.
He does as He pleases, and gives none account of
any of His matters. If any one feels disposed to
ask, Why is Simeon omitted in Deuteronomy
xxxiii? The simple and conclusive answer is, "O
man, who art thou that repliest against God?" In
Simeon, we see nature's actings judged; in Levi, we
see the fruits of grace rewarded; in both, we see
God's truth vindicated and His name glorified.
Thus it ever has been, thus it is, and thus it shall
be. Man is responsible: God is sovereign. Are we
called upon to reconcile these two propositions?
Nay; we are called to believe them. They are
reconciled already, inasmuch as they appear side by
side on the page of inspiration. This is enough for
every pious mind; and as for cavilers, they will get
their definitive answer by and by.*

"And of Benjamin ["the son of my right hand"]
he said, 'The beloved of the Lord shall dwell in
safety by Him; and the Lord shall cover him
all the day long, and he shall dwell between His
shoulders.'"

---

* For further remarks on the tribe of Levi, the reader is referred
to "Notes on the Book of Exodus," chapter xxxii; "Notes on the
Book of Numbers," chapter iii, iv, and viii; also a pamphlet, first
published in the year 1846, entitled, "The History of the Tribe of
Levi Considered." All these can be had from Loizeaux Brothers.

Blessed place for Benjamin! blessed place for each beloved child of God! How precious is the thought of dwelling in safety in the divine presence, in conscious nearness to the true and faithful Shepherd and Bishop of our souls, day and night abiding under the covert of His sheltering wings!

"How blest are they who still abide,
　Close sheltered by Thy watchful side!
　Who life and strength from Thee receive,
　And with Thee move and in Thee live."

Reader, seek to know more and more the reality and blessedness of Benjamin's place and portion. Be not satisfied with any thing short of the enjoyed presence of Christ, the abiding sense of relationship and nearness to Him. Be assured of it, it is your happy privilege. Let nothing rob you of it. Keep ever near the Shepherd's side, reposing in His love, lying down in the green pastures and beside the still waters. The Lord grant that the writer and the reader may prove the deep blessedness of this, in this day of hollow profession and empty talk. May we know the unspeakable preciousness of deep, personal intimacy with Himself. This is the special need of the day in which our lot is cast—a day of so much intellectual traffic in truth, but of so little heart-knowledge and true appreciation of Christ.

"And of Joseph he said, 'Blessed of the Lord be his land, for the precious things of heaven, for the dew, and for the deep that coucheth beneath, and for the precious fruits brought forth by the sun, and for the precious things put forth by the moon, and for the chief things of the ancient mountains, and for the precious things of the lasting hills, and for the precious things of the earth and fullness thereof, and for the good-will of Him that dwelt in the bush; let the blessing come upon the head of Joseph, and upon the top of the head of him that was separated from his brethren. His glory is like the firstling of his bullock, and his horns are like the horns of unicorns; with them he shall push the people together to the ends of the earth; and they are the ten thousands of Ephraim, and they are the thousands of Manasseh.'"

Joseph is a very remarkable type of Christ. We have dwelt upon his history in our studies on the book of Genesis. The reader will notice the emphatic way in which Moses speaks of the fact of his having been separated from his brethren. He was rejected and cast into the pit. He passed, in figure, through the deep waters of death, and thus reached the place of dignity and glory. He was raised from the dungeon to be ruler over the land of Egypt, and the preserver and sustainer of his brethren. The iron entered into his soul, and he was made to taste the bitterness of the place of death ere he entered the sphere of glory. Striking type of Him who hung upon the cross, lay in the grave, and is now on the throne of the Majesty of heaven.

We cannot but be struck with the fullness of the blessing pronounced upon Joseph both by Moses in Deuteronomy xxxiii. and by Jacob in Genesis xlix. Jacob's utterance is uncommonly fine. "Joseph is a fruitful bough, even a fruitful bough by a well,"—

Exquisitely beautiful figure!—"whose branches run over the wall. The archers have sorely grieved him, and shot at him, and hated him; but his bow abode in strength, and the arms of his hands were made strong by the hands of the mighty God of Jacob; (*from thence is the Shepherd, the Stone of Israel:*) even by the God of thy father, who shall help thee; and by the Almighty, who shall bless thee with blessings of heaven above, blessings of the deep that lieth under, blessings of the breasts and of the womb: the blessings of thy father have prevailed above the blessings of my progenitors unto the utmost bound of the everlasting hills: they shall be on the head of Joseph, and on the crown of the head of him that was separate from his brethren."

Magnificent range of blessing! And all this flowing from and based upon his sufferings. It is needless to say that all these blessings will be made good in the experience of Israel by and by. The sufferings of the true Joseph will form the imperishable foundation of the future blessedness of His brethren in the land of Canaan; and not only so, but the tide of blessing, deep and full, shall flow forth from that highly favored though now desolate land, in refreshing virtue into all the earth. "And it shall be in that day, that living waters shall go out from Jerusalem; half of them toward the former sea, and half of them toward the hinder sea; in summer and in winter shall it be." Bright and blessed prospect for Jerusalem, for the land of Israel, and for the whole earth! What a sad mistake to apply such scriptures to the gospel dispensation or to the Church of God! How contrary to the testimony of holy Scripture, to the heart of God, and to the mind of Christ!

"And of Zebulun he said, 'Rejoice, Zebulun, in thy going out; and, Issachar, in thy tents. They shall call the people unto the mountain; there they shall offer sacrifices of righteousness: for they shall suck of the abundance of the seas, and of the treasures hid in the sand.'"

Zebulun is to rejoice in his going forth, and Issachar in abiding in his tents. It will be joy at home and abroad; and there will be power to act on others also—calling the people unto the mountain to offer the sacrifices of righteousness. All this grounded upon the fact that they themselves shall suck of the abundance of the seas and of hidden treasures. Thus it is always, in principle. It is our privilege to rejoice in the Lord, come what may, and to draw from those eternal springs and hidden treasures that are to be found in Himself. Then shall we be in a condition of soul to call others to taste and see that the Lord is good; and not only so, but to present to God those sacrifices of righteousness so acceptable to Him.

"And of Gad he said, 'Blessed be he that enlargeth Gad: he dwelleth as a lion, and teareth the arm with the crown of the head. And he provided the first part for himself, because there, in a portion of the lawgiver, was he seated; and he came with the heads of the people, he executed the justice of the Lord, and His judgments with Israel.' And of Dan he said, 'Dan is a lion's whelp; he shall leap from Bashan.' And of Naphtali he said, 'O Naphtali, satisfied with favor, and full with the blessing of the Lord: possess thou the west and the south.' And of Asher he said, 'Let Asher be blessed with children; let him be acceptable to his brethren, and let him dip his foot in oil. Thy shoes shall be iron and brass; and as thy days thy strength. There is none like unto the God of Jeshurun, who rideth upon the heaven in thy help, and in His excellency on the sky. The eternal God is thy refuge, and underneath are the everlasting arms: and He shall thrust out the enemy from before thee; and shall say, Destroy them. Israel then shall dwell in safety alone: the fountain of Jacob shall be upon a land of corn and wine; also his heavens shall drop down dew. Happy art thou, O Israel: who is like unto thee, O people saved by the Lord, the shield of thy help, and who is the sword of thy excellency! and thine enemies shall be found liars unto thee; and thou shalt tread upon their high places.'" (Ver. 20–29.)

Truly we may say human comment is uncalled for here. Nothing can exceed the preciousness of the grace that breathes in the closing lines of our book. The blessings of this chapter, like the song of chapter xxxii, begin and end with God and His marvelous ways with Israel. It is refreshing and comforting beyond expression, at the close of all the appeals, all the exhortations, all the solemn warnings, all the faithful declarations, all the pro-

phetic records as to failure and sin, judgment and
governmental wrath—after all these, to listen to
such accents as those which we have just penned.
It is indeed a most magnificent termination to this
blessed book of Deuteronomy. Grace and glory
shine out with uncommon lustre. God will yet
be glorified in Israel, and Israel fully and forever
blessed in God. Nothing can hinder this. The
gifts and calling of God are without repentance.
He will make good every jot and tittle of His precious Word to Israel. The last words of the lawgiver bear the clearest and fullest testimony to all
this. Had we nothing but the last four verses of
the precious chapter on which we have been dwelling, they would be amply sufficient to prove, beyond
all question, the future restoration, blessing, pre-
eminence, and glory of the twelve tribes of Israel
in their own land.

True it is—blessedly true—that the Lord's people
now can draw instruction, comfort, and refreshment
from the blessings pronounced upon Israel. Blessed
be God, we can know what it is to be "satisfied with
favor, and full of the blessing of the Lord;" we
may take comfort from the assurance that "as our
days shall be our strength ; " we too can say, "The
eternal God is our refuge, and underneath are the
everlasting arms"—we can say all this, and much
more. We can say what Israel never could and
never can say. The Church's blessings and privileges are all heavenly and spiritual, but that does
not hinder our taking comfort from the promises

made to Israel. The grand mistake of professing
Christians is in applying to the Church exclusively
what most manifestly applies to God's earthly
people. We must once more earnestly entreat the
Christian reader to watch against this serious error.
He need not be in the least afraid of losing aught
of his own special blessing by leaving to the seed of
Abraham the place and the portion assigned them
by the counsels and promises of God ; on the contrary, it is only when these are clearly understood
and fully acknowledged that we can make an intelligent use of the entire canon of Old-Testament
scripture. We may lay it down as a great root-
principle that no one can possibly understand or
interpret Scripture who does not clearly recognize
the grand distinction between Israel and the Church
of God.

CHAPTER XXXIV.

THIS brief chapter forms an inspired postscript to
the book of Deuteronomy. We are not told
who was employed as the instrument in the hand of
the inspiring Spirit, but this is a matter of no moment to the devout student of holy Scripture. We
are fully persuaded that the postscript is as truly inspired as the book, and the book as the Pentateuch.
and the Pentateuch as the whole volume of God.

"And Moses went up from the plains of Moab
unto the mountain of Nebo, to the top of Pisgah,

that is over against Jericho. And the Lord showed him all the land of Gilead, unto Dan, and all Naphtali, and the land of Ephraim and Manasseh, and all the land of Judah, unto the utmost sea, and the south, and the plain of the valley of Jericho, the city of palm-trees, unto Zoar. And the Lord said unto him, 'This is the land which I sware unto Abraham, unto Isaac, and unto Jacob, saying, I will give it unto thy seed; I have caused thee to see it with thine eyes, but thou shalt not go over thither.' So Moses the servant of the Lord died there in the land of Moab, according to the word of the Lord. And He buried him in a valley in the land of Moab, over against Beth-peor; but no man knoweth of his sepulchre unto this day."

In our studies on the books of Numbers and Deuteronomy, we have had occasion to dwell upon the very solemn and, we may truly add, soul-subduing fact recorded in the above quotation. It will not therefore be needful to add many words in this our closing section. We would merely remind the reader that if he would have a full understanding of the whole subject, he must look at Moses in a twofold aspect, namely, officially and personally.

Now, looking at this beloved and honored man in his official capacity, it is very plain that it lay not in his province to conduct the congregation of Israel into the promised land. The wilderness was his sphere of action; it pertained not to him to lead the people across the river of death into their destined inheritance. His ministry was connected with man's responsibility under law and the government of God, and hence it never could lead the people into the enjoyment of the promise: it was reserved for his successor to do this. Joshua, a type of the risen Saviour, was God's appointed instrument to lead His people across the Jordan, and plant them in their divinely given inheritance.

All this is plain, and deeply interesting; but we must look at Moses personally, as well as officially; and here too we must view him in a twofold aspect— as the subject of government, and the object of grace. We must never lose sight of this most important distinction: it runs all through Scripture, and is strikingly illustrated in the history of many of the Lord's beloved people and of His most eminent servants. The subject of grace and government demands the reader's most profound attention. We have dwelt upon it again and again in the course of our studies, but no words of ours could adequately set forth its moral importance and immense practical value. We consider it one of the weightiest and most seasonable subjects that could possibly engage the attention of the Lord's people at the present moment.

It was the government of God which, with stern decision, forbad the entrance of Moses into the promised land, much as he longed to do so. He spoke unadvisedly with his lips—he failed to glorify God in the eyes of the congregation at the waters of Meribah, and for this he was forbidden to cross the Jordan and plant his foot on the promised land.

Let us deeply ponder this, beloved Christian reader. Let us see that we fully apprehend its moral force and practical application. It is surely with the greatest tenderness and delicacy that we would refer to the failure of one of the most beloved and illustrious of the Lord's servants, but it has been recorded for our learning and solemn admonition, and therefore we are bound to give earnest heed to it. We should ever remember that we too, though under grace, are also the subjects of divine government. We are here on this earth, in the place of solemn responsibility, under a government which cannot be trifled with. True, we are children of the Father, loved with an infinite and everlasting love—loved even as Jesus is loved; we are members of the body of Christ, loved, cherished, and nourished according to all the perfect love of His heart. There is no question of responsibility here, no possibility of failure; all is divinely settled, divinely sure: but we are the subjects of divine government also. Let us never for a moment lose sight of this. Let us beware of one-sided and pernicious notions of grace. The very fact of our being objects of divine favor and love, children of God, members of Christ, should lead us to yield all the more reverent attention to the divine government.

To use an illustration drawn from human affairs, her majesty's children should, above all others, just because they are her children, respect her government; and were they in any way to transgress her laws, the dignity of government would be strikingly illustrated by their being made to pay the penalty. If they, because of being the queen's children, were to be allowed to transgress with impunity the enactments of her majesty's government, it would be simply exposing the government to public contempt, and affording a warrant to all her subjects to do the same. And if it be thus in the case of a human government, how much more in the government of God! "You only have I known of all the families of the earth, *therefore* will I punish you for your iniquities." "The time is come that judgment must *begin at the house of God;* and if it first begin at us, what shall the end be of them that obey not the gospel of God? And if the righteous scarcely be saved, where shall the ungodly and the sinner appear?" Solemn fact! solemn inquiry! May we ponder them deeply.

But, as we have said, Moses was the subject of grace, as well as of government; and truly that grace shines with special lustre on the top of Pisgah. There the venerable servant of God was permitted to stand in his Master's presence, and, with undimmed eye, survey the land of promise, in all its fair proportions. He was permitted to see it from a divine stand-point—see it, not merely as possessed by Israel, but as given by God.

And what then ? He fell asleep and was gathered to his people. He died, not as a withered and feeble old man, but in all the freshness and vigor of matured manhood. "And Moses was a hundred and twenty years old when he died: his eye was not dim, nor his natural force abated." Striking testimony! Rare fact in the annals of our fallen race! The life of Moses was divided into three important and strongly marked periods of forty years each. He spent forty years in the house of Pharaoh, forty years "at the backside of the desert," and forty years in the wilderness. Marvelous life! eventful history! How instructive! how suggestive! how rich in its lessons from first to last! How profoundly interesting the study of such a life!—to trace him from the river's brink, where he lay a helpless babe, up to the top of Pisgah, where he stood, in company with his Lord, to gaze with undimmed vision upon the fair inheritance of the Israel of God; and to see him again on the Mount of Transfiguration, in company with his honored fellow-servant Elias, "talking with Jesus" on the grandest theme that could possibly engage the attention of men or angels. Highly favored man! blessed servant! marvelous vessel!

And then let us hearken to the divine testimony to this most beloved man of God. "And there arose not a prophet since in Israel like unto Moses, whom the Lord knew face to face, in all the signs and the wonders which the Lord sent him to do in the land of Egypt to Pharaoh, and to all his servants, and to all his land, and in all that mighty hand, and in all the great terror which Moses showed in the sight of all Israel."

May the Lord, in His infinite goodness, bless our study of the book of Deuteronomy. May its precious lessons be engraved upon the tablets of our hearts with the eternal pen of the Holy Ghost, and produce their proper result in forming our character, governing our conduct, and shaping our way through this world. May we earnestly seek to tread, with a humble spirit and firm step, the narrow path of obedience, till traveling days are done.

C. H. M.